A

. . .

BOOK

The Philip E. Lilienthal imprint
honors special books
in commemoration of a man whose work
at the University of California Press from 1954 to 1979
was marked by dedication to young authors
and to high standards in the field of Asian Studies.
Friends, family, authors, and foundations have together
endowed the Lilienthal Fund, which enables the Press
to publish under this imprint selected books
in a way that reflects the taste and judgment
of a great and beloved editor.

The publisher gratefully acknowledges the generous
contribution to this book provided by the Philip E.
Lilienthal Asian Studies Endowment of the University
of California Press Associates, which is supported by
a major gift from Sally Lilienthal.

Seeing through Zen

Seeing through Zen

Encounter, Transformation, and
Genealogy in Chinese Chan Buddhism

John R. McRae

UNIVERSITY OF CALIFORNIA PRESS

Berkeley / Los Angeles / London

University of California Press
Berkeley and Los Angeles, California

University of California Press, Ltd.
London, England

© 2003 by the Regents of the University of California

Library of Congress Cataloging-in-Publication Data

McRae, John R., 1947–
    Seeing through Zen : encounter, transformation, and genealogy
in Chinese Chan Buddhism / John R. McRae.
        p.   cm.
    Includes bibliographical references and index.
    ISBN 0-520-23797-8 (alk. paper)—ISBN 0-520-23798-6 (pbk. :
alk. paper)
        1. Zen Buddhism—China—History.   I. Title.

BQ9262.5 .M367   2004
294.3'927'0951—dc21   2003011741

Manufactured in the United States of America
13   12   11   10   09   08   07   06   05   04
10   9   8   7   6   5   4   3   2   1

Dedicated to YANAGIDA *Seizan,*
with inexpressible gratitude

Contents

Illustrations

Figures

Maps

Preface

This book is intended for those who wish to engage actively in the critical imagination of medieval Chinese Chan, or Zen, Buddhism. The interpretations presented in the following pages represent my best and most cherished insights into this important religious tradition, and I look forward to their critical appraisal and use by general readers, students, and colleagues. More important than the specific content presented here, though, are the styles of analysis undertaken and the types of human processes described. In other words, the primary goal of this book is not to present any single master narrative of Chinese Chan, but to change how we all think about the subject.

I expect the readership of this book to include Zen and other Buddhist practitioners; students and scholars of Chinese religions, Buddhist studies, and related fields; and a general audience interested in Asian religions and human culture. General readers will find here sufficient basis for a far-reaching critique of how Zen is perceived in contemporary international culture. In addition, my analysis of Chinese Chan religious practice as fundamentally genealogical should provide a new point of comparison for the analysis of modern and contemporary developments in Zen, particularly those occurring in North America and Europe. That is, if Chan practice was originally genealogical—by which I mean patriarchal, generational, and relational—in ways that fit so well with medieval Chinese society, how will it be (or, how is it being) transformed as it spreads throughout the globe in the twenty-first century (and as it did in the twentieth)? In other words, how is Zen changing, and how will it change, as it grows and spreads within the context of globalization and Westernization?

Scholars, students, and general readers constitute a natural audience for this book. Why should religious practitioners read it? If Buddhist spiritual practice aims at seeing things as they are, then getting past the foolish over-simplifications and confusing obfuscations that surround most interpretations of Zen should be an important part of the process. That is the short answer. A more specific answer requires a bit of explanation.

The first time I lectured on Chinese Chan to a community of practitioners was in 1987 for the Summer Seminar on the Sutras, held in Jemez Springs, New Mexico, at Bodhi Mandala, which functions within the teaching organization of the Rinzai master Joshu Sasaki Roshi. Among those attending was an elderly American Zen monk, who objected strenuously to my instruction, asking repeatedly, "What good is any of this for my practice?" The organizers of the week-long workshop were somewhat embarrassed by his aggressive attitude, pointing out that, as a former lightweight boxer, he may have taken more than one punch too many. For my own part, I enjoyed the challenge, which forced me to confront the question head-on in a way that never would have happened in university lecturing. Subsequently, I have honed my response (you are welcome to consider it a defensive reaction, if you wish!) in seminars and workshops at Dai Bosatsu in upstate New York, under the direction of another Rinzai teacher, Eido Shimano Roshi; the Zen Center of Los Angeles, a Soto Zen institution founded by the late Taizan Maezumi Roshi; Zen Mountain Monastery at Mt. Tremper, New York, led by John Daido Loori Roshi, a student of Maezumi's; the San Francisco Zen Center, which was founded by Shunryu Suzuki Roshi; the Mount Equity Zen Center, directed by Dai-En Bennage Sensei; Zen Mountain Center, directed by Tenshin Fletcher Sensei, a successor to Maezumi; and Dharma Rain and the Zen Community of Oregon in Portland, directed by Kyogen and Gyokuko Carlson and Chozen and Hogen Bays, respectively. In addition to these American Zen centers, on two separate occasions, I have also taught a two-week intensive class at Foguang Shan in Kaohsiung, Taiwan; on the first occasion (in 1992) the participants were mostly young Taiwanese Buddhist nuns, while on the second (in 2002) the class was composed of Southeast Asian Chinese nuns and monks from Africa, India (a native of Nālandā!), and the United States. These chapters were first prepared for presentation at Templo Zen Luz Serena in Valencia, Spain, under the direction of Dokushō Villalba Sensei. This book has benefited in profound ways from interaction with the participants in all these different practice settings, and I am deeply grateful for their attention, questions, and suggestions.

There is nothing in this book that will aid one's religious practice directly. I am not a Zen master, nor even a meditation instructor, and this is not a do-it-yourself manual. To use a cooking analogy, I am not a Julia Child teaching you how to concoct your life in Zen. Instead, I am more the art critic who evaluates her teaching methods and dramatic performance, or even the chemist who analyzes the dynamic evolution of her recipes as they make their pilgrimage from pan to plate. Art critics are not necessarily good performers themselves, and chemists are not necessarily gourmet cooks. Although I am indeed a Buddhist (in autobiographical blurbs I usually include a line about being "a practitioner of long standing but short attention span"), and even though my religious identity as a youthful convert to Buddhism allows for a certain empathy with my subject matter, I am a scholar and not a guru. As a professor in aggressively secular state universities over the years, I have learned to keep anything resembling preaching out of my classroom presentations, and the same holds true here. I am not aiming to convert you, unless by that is meant an intellectual transformation that may penetrate to the very core of your being.

This volume is resolutely about Zen, not about how to practice Zen. It thus differs from the vast majority of books on Zen in English in that it does not assume the reader to be a potential Zen practitioner. Indeed, even the most dedicated practitioners will benefit by stepping outside their chosen tradition for the endeavor of its reading. I believe our roles as scholars and readers involve the active and critical imagination of the medieval evolution of Chinese Chan Buddhism. By active, I mean that we should constantly work to envision how Chan emerged in the medieval Chinese social and intellectual context; by critical, I mean that we should also work to consider all the available evidence from all possible angles, testing hypotheses and evaluating objections.

In many ways, my training in this process began with my graduate studies under Professor Stanley Weinstein, to whom I am dedicating my second research volume on eighth-century Chan Buddhism, provisionally entitled *Zen Evangelist: Shenhui (684–758), Sudden Enlightenment, and the Southern School of Chinese Chan Buddhism* (forthcoming from the University of Hawai'i Press, under the auspices of the Kuroda Institute). The debt I owe Professor Weinstein, who has dedicated his career to the training of the finest cohort of scholars in American Buddhist studies, is incalculable.

The present volume is in effect my attempt to emulate the creative work of YANAGIDA Seizan 柳田聖山, with whom I had the privilege to study while writing my dissertation. As the greatest scholar of Chinese Chan Buddhism of the twentieth century, Professor Yanagida has brought to his writings both magisterial knowledge and profound sensitivity. Although my tutelage under Professor Yanagida came many years before this book was conceived, I have fond memories of sitting with him in his study, accepting bowls of delicious *matcha* tea, and discussing the contents of Chinese Chan texts. Even when I groped for ordinary Japanese vocabulary in our conversations, and even when I butchered the rules of classical Chinese grammar in our readings, his sympathetic patience was inexhaustible. (I will admit, however, that for the weekly seminars on Chinese Chan texts at Hanazono College, a Rinzai Zen institution, it would have been copacetic had the college marching band not chosen the very same time to practice its John Philip Sousa renditions!)

As the vanguard of a new wave of Japanese scholarship that revolutionized our understanding of Chan through analysis of handwritten manuscripts from the Dunhuang cave in Chinese Central Asia, Professor Yanagida has consistently demonstrated an interpretive brilliance that has energized an entire generation of Western students. If I have inherited even a small part of his legacy, I hope that the playful humanism of his example shines through these pages. I dedicate this book to Professor Yanagida with a depth of gratitude I can only hint at in words.

Thanks are due to many others as well, of course. As mentioned above, these chapters were first prepared for presentation in Spanish translation at Templo Zen Luz Serena, directed by Dokushō Villalba Sensei, in Valencia, Spain, June 19–21, 1999. The invitation was sponsored by the Japanese Sōtō Zen School, and the initial translations were prepared by Ms. Lucía Huélamo and Rev. Aigo Castro, who also served as cotranslators for the oral presentations. My profound thanks are due Villalba Sensei, Rev. Castro, and Ms. Huélamo, as well as all the members of Luz Serena, who made my visit there so enjoyable and productive. Subsequently, the first chapter was presented in Chinese at the Chung-Hwa Institute of Buddhist Studies. The Chinese translation, which was prepared by KUAN Tse-fu [Guan Zefu] 關則富, was published in Chinese as "Shenshi chuancheng—chenshu Chanzong di ling yizhong fangshi" 審視傳承—陳述禪宗的另1種方式. I would like to express my deep gratitude to Ven. Sheng-yen 張聖嚴, as well as to Professor LI Chih-fu 李志夫, director of the Institute, and Secretary CHEN Hsiu-lan 陳秀蘭 and the Institute staff for their kind assistance during my research stay in Taiwan from December 1998 to August 1999. Also, part of chapter 4 has already appeared in print as "The Antecedents of Encounter Dialogue in Chinese Ch'an Buddhism," in Steven Heine and Dale S. Wright, eds., *The Kōan: Texts and Contexts in Zen Buddhism*.

Jan Nattier has gone over the entire manuscript, covering my precious words with a liberal coating of editorial ink. I am immensely grateful, even if only for the occasion to divert her attention temporarily from third-century Chinese Buddhist translations. William Bodiford, Stephen Bokenkamp, Robert Buswell, Robert Campany, and David Eckel have also reviewed the text, and all of them provided suggestions both meaningful and helpful. Even given this assistance, copy editor Nick Murray has found many ways to improve the text. I offer my sincere gratitude to these, my friends and colleagues.

Special thanks are due Reed Malcolm, the editor who appreciated the value of this book and shepherded it through production at the University of California Press. Reed deserves credit for the title, *Seeing through Zen*, which to my ears is wonderfully multivalent. In addition to the workshops and seminars at practice centers mentioned above, over the years I have inflicted these interpretations of Chinese Chan upon classes of undergraduate and graduate students at Harvard, Cornell, Indiana, and Hawai'i Universities, as well as academic audiences at Stanford, Indiana, and Yale. To the participating faculty and students, whose probing questions did so much to push me into different perspectives on familiar material, I offer my thanks. Were there observations gone unheard or errors left uncorrected in spite of all this assistance, the cause is nothing other than my own limited understanding.

Ama ga kobako
Honolulu, Hawai'i
June 2002

Conventions

The goal of this book is to facilitate the different learning needs of a variety of readers. Hence the main text is for all readers, including beginners and nonspecialists, while the notes, character glossary, and bibliography are intended for use by students and scholars. The specific conventions adopted are as follows.

1. I have included frequent cross-references within the text, so that readers can easily keep the different elements of the discussion fresh in their minds. Active reading requires a certain flapping of pages.

2. When I provide two sets of transliterations, unless otherwise noted the first will be Chinese (in Pinyin spelling) and the second Japanese.

3. Chinese book titles are referred to by (sometimes abbreviated) English translations throughout, with the Pinyin spelling given only on first occurrence. Please consult the character glossary for the original Chinese titles.

4. Names of individuals functioning in an East Asian context are given in traditional order, surname (in small caps) followed by given name. This is in contrast to the treatment of authors writing in English and the American Zen teachers of Japanese extraction mentioned in the preface, who are named according to English conventions.

5. Whenever possible I have translated the names of temples and locations. There are exceptions in cases where the Chinese name is already commonly known, as for Shaolin Temple (Shaolinsi).

6. All geographical locations mentioned are identified with modern

Chinese province names and indicated one or both of the maps in chapter 1 (pp. 16 and 20).

7. With only a very few exceptions, Chinese characters have been restricted to the notes, character glossary (which includes only characters for terms and titles used in the main text), and the bibliography.

8. The maps, notes, and character glossary are the only places where I use Pinyin with tone indications, which are based on OGAWA Tamaki et al., *Kadokawa shinjigen, kaitei ban;* OZAKI Yūjirō et al., *Kadokawa daijigen;* and John DeFrancis, ed., *ABC Chinese Dictionary.*

9. For the Pinyin transliteration of Chinese terms, I have followed the orthography rules given in DeFrancis, appendix 1, 835–45.

10. Works cited after the abbreviation "T" are from the standard edition of the East Asian Buddhist canon, TAKAKUSU Junjirō and WATANABE Kaigyoku, eds., *Taishō shinshū daizōkyō.* Works cited with "X" are from the Taiwan reprint of the extended canon, *Xù zàng jīng,* published by Xin wenfeng chubanshe.

11. Unless otherwise noted, all translations are by the author. Material in square brackets in translated passages is interpolated to generate readable English; with one exception (on p. 80), material in parentheses has been added by the author.

McRae's Rules of Zen Studies

1. *It's not true, and therefore it's more important.*
   The contents of Zen texts should not be evaluated using a simple-minded criterion of journalistic accuracy, that is, "Did it really happen?" For any event or saying to have occurred would be a trivial reality involving a mere handful of people at one imagined point in time, which would be overwhelmed by the thousands of people over the centuries who were involved in the creation of Zen legends. The mythopoeic creation of Zen literature implies the religious imagination of the Chinese people, a phenomenon of vast scale and deep significance.

2. *Lineage assertions are as wrong as they are strong.*
   Statements of lineage identity and "history" were polemical tools of self-assertion, not critical evaluations of chronological fact according to some modern concept of historical accuracy. To the extent that any lineage assertion is significant, it is also a misrepresentation; lineage assertions that can be shown to be historically accurate are also inevitably inconsequential as statements of religious identity.

3. *Precision implies inaccuracy.*
   Numbers, dates, and other details lend an air of verisimilitude to a story, but the more they accumulate, the more we should recognize them as literary tropes. Especially in Zen studies, greater detail is an artifact of temporal distance, and the vagueness of earlier accounts should be comforting in its integrity. While we should avoid joining a misguided quest for origins, we should also be quick to distinguish between "good data" and ornamental fluff. Even as we ponder the vectors of medieval polemics.

4. *Romanticism breeds cynicism.*

Storytellers inevitably create heroes and villains, and the depiction of Zen's early patriarchs and icons cripples our understanding of both the Tang "golden age" and the supposedly stagnant formalism of the Song dynasty. If one side is romanticized, the other must be vilified, and both subjects pass incognito. The collusion between Zen romanticists and the apologists for Confucian triumphalism—which has Song Neo-Confucianism climbing to glory on the back of a defeated Buddhism—is an obstacle to the understanding of both Chan and the Chinese civil tradition. The corollary is this: Cold realism eliminates dismissive misapprehension.

CHAPTER I

Looking at Lineage

A Fresh Perspective on Chan Buddhism

How should we begin this discussion of Chan Buddhism? One device would be to begin with a story, some striking anecdote to arouse the reader's curiosity. There are certainly many good possibilities within the annals of Chan. One is the account of an earnest Chinese supplicant—the eventual second patriarch, Huike—cutting off his arm in order to hear the teachings from the enigmatic Indian sage, Bodhidharma. How many times this story must have been told in meditation halls in China and throughout the world, in order to inspire trainees to greater effort! Or we could find something a bit less gruesome—perhaps the tale about Layman Pang sinking all his possessions to the bottom of a river because he had learned the futility of chasing after worldly riches. Surely this example of unencumbered freedom is meant to teach us a deep spiritual message? The stock of legendary accounts that might be used, each with slightly different import, is endless. And there are other possible beginnings, as well. Many authors have their own favored ways of characterizing the most essential features of Chan, presenting some short list of features to sum up the entire tradition. Or we could avoid such bland generalization and simply celebrate the incredible creativity of the Chan tradition over the centuries, its vibrancy as a religious phenomenon.

The approach adopted here—already taken by posing these very deliberations—is to begin by asking questions, to arouse in the reader not merely a raw curiosity but the faculties of critical interrogation as well. Specifically, let us begin by directly considering the question of how we should look at Chan Buddhism: What approaches should we adopt, and which should we avoid? What forms of analysis will be fruitful, and which would merely repeat commonly accepted stereotypes?

The question of how we should look at Chan Buddhism is one we should not attempt to avoid; to simply ignore the issue and begin a recitation of facts and concepts would be to make an unspoken decision, to answer the question by adopting a policy of denial. But neither would it be appropriate for me to dictate the answer in flat and simple terms: as I compose these lines on the outskirts of Taipei at the very end of the twentieth century, and edit them in Honolulu at the beginning of the twenty-first, I am conscious of the incredible multivalence of cultural identity implicit in this process of exposition, both in my own person and those of my intended audiences. That is, in various ways and at different times I have been a scholar and practitioner, student and teacher, lover and hermit, and what I am about to present here I have learned through a series of extended educational encounters in America, Japan, and Taiwan. This text is intended for use by listeners and readers not only in China, but in Europe, the United States, and Japan as well—so how could I possibly presume to argue that there should be *one* way to look at Chan Buddhism? A multiplicity of perspectives and a certain fluidity of analytical typologies are givens in this postmodern world.

Deconstructing the Chan Lineage Diagram

For convenience, let me begin by defining a perspective on Chan that I wish to deconstruct and thereby avoid. I should confess that I mean only to caricature this perspective, so that we can use the observations made now to form a lever with which to push ourselves into a certain type of understanding (to paraphrase the positivist philosopher John Dewey and his student Hu Shih, who spoke of studying the past to create a lever with which to push China into a certain sort of future). The perspective to which I refer is the traditionalist approach depicted graphically in the lineage diagram presented in figure 1. Diagrams such as this are included in virtually every book on Chan that has ever been written, where they are used as a framework for presenting a historical narrative. Instead of plunging directly into that narrative and building upon the content of the diagram per se, though, we should first consider its semiotic impact as a medium of interpretation and communication. If the medium is the message (according to the saying popularized by Marshall McLuhan), what message is conveyed by the structure of the diagram itself? It is often noted that Chan claims to "not posit words" *(bu li wenzi, furyū monji)* and that it represents a "separate transmission outside the teachings" *(jiaowai bie-*

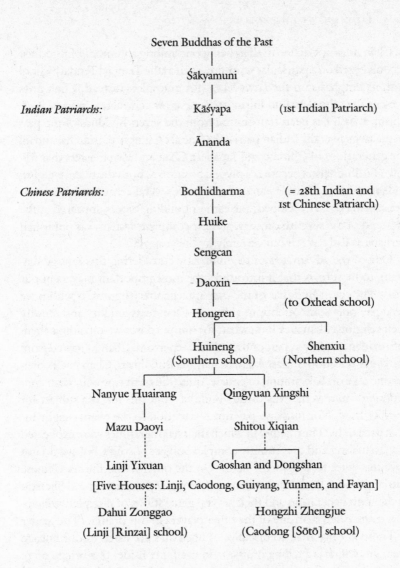

Seven Buddhas of the Past
|
Śākyamuni
|
Indian Patriarchs: Kāśyapa   (1st Indian Patriarch)
|
Ānanda
⋮
Chinese Patriarchs: Bodhidharma   (= 28th Indian and
| 1st Chinese Patriarch)
Huike
|
Sengcan
|
Daoxin ─────────────────────
| (to Oxhead school)
Hongren

Huineng   Shenxiu
(Southern school)   (Northern school)

Nanyue Huairang   Qingyuan Xingshi
| |
Mazu Daoyi   Shitou Xiqian
⋮   ⋮
Linji Yixuan   Caoshan and Dongshan
[Five Houses: Linji, Caodong, Guiyang, Yunmen, and Fayan]
⋮   ⋮
Dahui Zonggao   Hongzhi Zhengjue
(Linji [Rinzai] school)   (Caodong [Sōtō] school)

FIGURE 1. Lineage diagram of Chinese Chan Buddhism.

zhuan, kyōge betsuden). Almost always—as I am about to do right now—these phrases are introduced with the ironic observation that Chan certainly does use a lot of words in describing its own teachings. We will come back to the Chan use of language and its not "positing" of words later, but here we can observe that the lineage diagram provides the basic model for how Chan appreciates its own historical background. That is, Chan does not define itself as being one among a number of Buddhist schools based on a particular scripture (such as the Tiantai [Tendai] school with its emphasis on the *Lotus Sūtra*, for example). Instead, Chan texts present the school as Buddhism itself, or as *the* central teaching of Buddhism, which has been transmitted from the seven Buddhas of the past to the twenty-eight Indian patriarchs, the six Chinese patriarchs, and all the generations of Chinese and Japanese Chan and Zen masters that follow. (Bodhidharma occupies a pivotal position as both the twenty-eighth Indian and first Chinese patriarch.) It took several centuries for this entire schema to be developed; the earliest building blocks appeared at the very end of the seventh century, and the complete system was published perhaps as early as 801 but certainly by the year 952.

One of the advantages of beginning by considering this lineage diagram, to be sure, is that it introduces the most important players in our story. The seven Buddhas of the past are legendary figures to whom we need pay only scant attention; although Chan texts amplify and modify their religious identities somewhat, for our purposes we can admit them into evidence solely as part of the cultural repertoire Chan inherited from the larger tradition of East Asian Mahāyāna Buddhism. Chan has its own mythic take on Śākyamuni, of course, quite different from our own conception of him as the "historical" Buddha—but this too is a subject for another time. Nor must we pay much attention to the twenty-eight Indian patriarchs. The manner in which their hagiographies were explicated is a fascinating and exceedingly complex subject of study, but we do not have the space to consider it here.[1] On the other hand, the six Chinese patriarchs from Bodhidharma onward, along with Huineng and Shenxiu in the sixth generation and their several generations of disciples, will appear more often than any of the other players in this drama. (The reader will note at once that no disciples of Shenxiu's are listed in our lineage diagram, which is a telling omission in itself. I consider this briefly on p. 14 below.) The figures remembered as icons of the Linji (Rinzai) and Caodong (Sōtō) schools, whose names adorn the balance of the diagram, are among the most important in the history of the tradition.

We can draw some important basic inferences from this transmission diagram. First, a note on historical origins: the Chan lineage scheme is a combined product of Indian and Chinese culture. Often authors describe Chan as the "most Chinese" of all the Chinese Buddhist schools, and part of what they are referring to is the Chan genealogical model. (I am particularly allergic to this rhetoric, since such expressions are generally little more than unexplicated tautologies generated through a sense of cultural chauvinism rather than real analytical insight. And the fact that D. T. Suzuki and others say virtually the same thing with regard to Japanese Zen, that it represents somehow the essence of *Japanese* culture, should alert us to both the essential vacuity and the strategic intentions of such sentiments.)[2] Actually, the origins of this lineage-based transmission scheme are to be found in Indian Buddhism and the fourth- and fifth-century Buddhist meditation tradition of Kashmir. There are a number of parallels between the Chan transmission scheme and Chinese family genealogies of the eighth century and later, but we should remember that Indian Buddhists had parents and teachers, family genealogies and initiation lineages, just as the Chinese did.[3] As an amalgamation of Indian and Chinese elements, though, the Chinese Chan transmission schema developed within the Chinese Buddhist context and was particularly well adapted to that milieu. Just as DENG Xiaoping talked about "socialism with Chinese characteristics," we could refer to the Chinese Chan transmission model as a "Buddhist genealogical theory with Chinese characteristics."

Second, by using the lineage diagram to define Chan as a "separate transmission outside the teachings," the advocates of Chan were declaring their school to be profoundly different from, and fundamentally better than, all other Buddhist schools: where the other schools represented only interpretations of Buddhism, Chan constitutes the real thing, Buddhism itself. This is a polemical move, meant to establish the superiority of Chan over all other schools. Other East Asian Buddhist schools reacted in part by devising their own lineage transmission schemes, and in part by saying that Chan emphasized only one of the "three learnings" of morality, meditation, and wisdom. Whether we view medieval Chinese Buddhists as concerned solely with the highest forms of wisdom or as working to obtain imperial patronage and other this-worldly benefits, or engaged in both endeavors simultaneously, at the very least they were competing with their contemporaries for intellectual and cultural hegemony. We should thus not overlook the polemical quality of the lineage theory. Incidentally, to describe Chan Buddhism in terms of polemics and contestation is not to exercise any value judgment, let alone to denigrate the tradition, but merely to recognize historical fact.

Third, what counts in the Chan transmission scheme are not the "facts" of what happened in the lives of Śākyamuni, Bodhidharma, Huineng, and others, but rather how these figures were perceived in terms of Chan mythology. This point will come up repeatedly here, and I will argue a rather complex position: In case after case, what the texts say happened almost certainly did *not* occur, in terms of a straightforward but simple-minded criterion of journalistic accuracy. But rather than being fixated on notions of fact and fabrication, we should notice the very dynamism of the mythopoeic processes involved. Whether or not any anecdote actually represents the words spoken and events that occurred "accurately" is only a historical accident, and in any case the supposedly "original" events would have involved only a very small number of people, at most the members of a single local community. What is of far greater consequence is the process by which that anecdote was generated and circulated, edited and improved, and thus transmitted throughout an entire population of Chan practitioners and devotees, until it became part of the fluid body of legendary lore by which Chan masters came to be identified throughout Chinese culture. This is McRae's first law of Zen studies: "It's not true, and therefore it's more important." This is to say that fiction—actually, a different sort of truth—is more important than the simplistic criterion of the question "Did it really happen?"[4]

Fourth, based on the rhetoric of *śūnyatā*, or emptiness,[5] nothing is actually transmitted in this transmission scheme. What occurs between each teacher and his successor is merely an approval or authorization *(yinke; inka)* of the successor's attainment of complete enlightenment.[6] This is first of all a doctrinal principle of Chan Buddhism itself, but we should recognize that the most important parts of the diagram are not the separate names of individual patriarchs, but the spaces between them, the lines that join them. That is, what is being represented is not only a series of human figures but the encounters between each figure and his immediate predecessor and successor. As is frequently stressed in the texts of Chan, there is no "thing"—such as enlightenment, the Buddha-mind, or whatever—that is actually passed from one patriarch to the next. The existence of such an entity would violate a fundamental Buddhist doctrinal theme, the denial of unchanging, substantive, and individual identity to the things and beings of this world. With regard to persons, this doctrinal theme is called "no-self" *(anātman)*; with regard to all the various component elements of existence, including persons, this is called "emptiness" *(śūnyatā)*. This is not a merely philosophical consideration, but rather an existential posture with profound genealogical impact: the focus is not on "what" is being transmitted, but on the relationship of encounter between the Buddhas and Patriarchs. The act of transmission thus involves not the bestowing of some "thing" from one master to the next, but the recognition of shared spiritual maturity. It is a cosmic dance involving a special set of partners, a relationship of encounter, a meeting at the deepest spiritual level.

Fifth, since the enlightenment of each Buddha and Patriarch is complete, there is no differentiation between the religious status of the Indian Buddhas and Patriarchs and their Chinese counterparts. This was perhaps the most important reason why this lineage-based exposition was attractive to medieval Chinese Buddhists, since it raised the authority of native Chinese figures to equal those of their Indian predecessors. This is very important in terms of the sinification of Buddhism, that is, the adaptation of Buddhism within Chinese culture, a subject that is vitally relevant to a wide range of subjects in Chinese religions and Chinese studies in general. At the moment, though, what I want to emphasize is the most striking and most frequently overlooked characteristic of this diagram: the homologizing impact of its very simple lines of succession.

By representing Chan Buddhism in terms of a straight-line succession from the seven Buddhas of the past through the six Chinese Patriarchs, diagrams such as this are used to simplify fantastically complicated sets of cultural and religious phenomena. Every time a straight-line relationship between two masters is posited in a lineage diagram, an entire world of complexity, an intricate universe of human relationships and experiences, is effectively eliminated from view. Could any religious figure's identity possibly be adequately summarized by selecting only one out of a whole lifetime of relationships? Even a quick look at the biographies of Chinese Chan masters shows the extent of the distortion involved: where the sources are adequate, we sometimes see multiple awakening experiences[7] catalyzed by different teachers and events, yet in the lineage diagrams these are all reduced to single lines of transmission. The use of lineage diagrams to represent the Chan tradition, then—and their use is as old as the tradition itself, since it was by explicating genealogical specifics that Chan generated its own identity as a specific religious movement— is a hegemonic trope, the willful extension of one way of perceiving the world to the exclusion of all other viewpoints. (I briefly discuss the various branches and divisions of the diagram beginning on p. 9 below.)

Sixth, the "genealogical model" is important not only for the historical self-understanding of the Chan school in its transmission from Śākyamuni Buddha through Bodhidharma and onward, but also for the manner in which it defines how Chan spiritual practice itself is carried out. That is, in contrast to a basically Indian conception of meditation practice as an individual yogic endeavor of self-purification and progressive advancement toward buddhahood, the Chan genealogical model implies that the most important aspect of spiritual cultivation takes place in the *encounter* between teacher and student. Chan trainees still spent long hours in the meditation hall—we can be sure of that, even though the texts often do not bother confirming the fact—but the focus of Chan rhetoric and literature is on the dialogues and exchanges between each master and his students, or between each student destined to be a master and his various teachers. It is thus not only the Chan school's self-understanding of its own religious history, but the religious practice of Chan itself that is fundamentally genealogical. By saying that Chan practice is fundamentally *genealogical,* I mean that it is derived from a genealogically understood encounter experience that is *relational* (involving interaction between individuals rather than being based solely on individual effort), *generational* (in that it is organized according to parent-child, or rather teacher-student, generations), and *reiterative* (i.e., intended for emulation and repetition in the lives of present and future teachers and students). No matter what the comparison or relationship between Chinese Chan and earlier forms of Indian Buddhist meditation practice, this particular complex of qualities is not found in other schools or forms of Buddhist training.[8]

In the most basic historical terms, though, we should recognize that the homologizing impact of the Chan lineage diagram represents a profound distortion of the subject matter. This is McRae's second rule of Zen studies: "Lineage assertions are as wrong as they are strong." In more formal language, this means that lineage assertions are problematic in direct proportion to their significance. That is, every time we read that the masters of such-and-such a group are related to each other in a lineal succession, the statement is probably inaccurate in some sense, and the more important it is to the religious identity of the individuals involved, the less accurate it will be. If nothing much is made of the relationship, the lineage assertion is more likely to be correct than if a great deal rides on it. Almost always, of course, the figure at the end of the list, or even that individual's students, has the most at stake in making such assertions. And if his religious identity must be defined on the basis of a lineal succession, if his historical status depends on being the recipient of the cumulative charisma of one particular set of predecessors, then it always seems that some significant distortion of the facts has taken place. Of course, my use of the word *facts* should remind you of the first rule, which remains relevant here: The presentation of reality in lineage schema represents a certain type of myth-making, and what is not "true" per se is inevitably more important!

Seventh, I referred above to "each teacher and *his* successor" (see p. 6), and the gender-specific terminology is appropriate. The Chan tradition is overwhelmingly male-dominated, and the strong implications of the term *patriarchal* in English (referring both to Chan figureheads and a male-centered ideology) is entirely suitable here. Nancy Jay has analyzed how genealogical systems tend to create justifications for removing women from the nexus of power and fecundity,[9] and in a later chapter, we will consider the manner in which Chan represented a way of organizing power within the Chinese Buddhist monastic establishment. There is also, of course, a broader, gender-related issue concerning Chan as a patriarchal ideology: to put it bluntly, Was Chan a weapon used to oppress women within Chinese society? Alas, I cannot deliberate on this issue in these pages, but when the subject comes up, scholars should certainly not shrink from it. This awareness, however, is helpful here in a different and perhaps even larger sense. I do find it germane to deal with the following variant of the question: Was Chan a weapon in the oppression of Chinese religious practitioners in general, or did it serve to suppress certain groups of them? This is a shocking question, to be sure, but it seems to me that any means by which knowledge is structured—and the lineage format is certainly that—both *allows* and *suppresses* different types of perspectives. I am by no means unsympathetic to the Chan tradition, nor to the realm of Buddhist meditation and spiritual cultivation in general, but a consideration of how the Chan school's dominance in Chinese Buddhism may have militated against alternative viewpoints seems an obvious aspect of our intellectual responsibility.

At this point, you may be surprised that we have derived so many inferences from one simple diagram, but we could certainly coax numerous additional insights from it if space were not an issue. Let us leave further comment on the Chan lineage diagram and the genealogical identity of the Chan tradition until later, though, and turn instead to the reason we began this discussion in the first place.

Avoiding the "String of Pearls" Fallacy

The preceding observations regarding the lineage diagram are to some extent preventive medicine, prophylaxis against a type of interpretation to be avoided. Simply put, the message is this: To represent Chan Buddhism in terms that are congruent with the lineage paradigm is to run the risk of mere repetition, without saying anything fundamentally insightful. Rather than performing legitimate analytical investigations, to do so would be merely to recapitulate an inherited symbolic system, and in this context one's most cherished intellectual nuances would be nothing more than trivial variations on the genealogical model. Here it is useful to make a clear insider/outsider distinction: What is both expected and natural for a religious practitioner operating *within* the Chan episteme, what is necessary in order to achieve membership within the patriarchal lineage, becomes intellectually debilitating for those standing, even if only temporarily, *outside* the realm of Chan as its observers and analysts. What from the standpoint of Chan religious practice may be absolutely essential becomes, from the standpoint of intellectual analysis, the passive submission to a hegemony, the unwitting contraction of an intellectual pathology.

So what is it that we should not be doing? Or, to put it another way, how can we recognize when we are falling, or in danger of falling, into patterns that inhibit our ability to see the history of Chan in all its rich complexity?

Seen from this perspective, the issue is really quite simple: Whenever we pretend to explain Chan in terms of lineal successions from one great master to another, we run the risk of committing the "string of pearls" fallacy, in which the evolution of Chan Buddhism is described in terms of a sequence of individual masters like pearls on a string. This is a variant of the "great man" fallacy of historical writing, in which one explains the inevitably messy details of past realities in terms of the willful endeavors of a limited number of heroic men. (Once again, the gender-specific terminology is warranted.) To be more logically precise, it is also an example of the fallacy of archetypes, which "consists in conceptualizing change in terms of the re-enactment of primordial archetypes which exist outside of time."[10]

In terms of Zen studies, this tendency is starkly apparent in the way Dunhuang manuscripts have been used to supplement rather than radically transform the appreciation of Chan in many writings. A trove of cultural treasures similar to the Dead Sea scrolls, the Dunhuang manuscripts were discovered in a walled-up cave in Chinese Central Asia at the turn of the twentieth century and then dispersed to various libraries throughout the world. They provided a cross-section of Chan documents from the eighth to the tenth centuries, just before the great editorial homogenization of the Song dynasty took place.[11] Access to these manuscripts has allowed scholars to explore the early phases of Chinese Chan Buddhism in ways that would simply not have been possible in their absence, and the analysis of this magnificent trove has occupied the attentions of scholars (not only in Chan, but in other fields of Buddhist and Daoist studies, and various realms of historical and sociological research as well) for the entire twentieth century. However, in Chan studies, evidence from the Dunhuang manuscripts has most often been used merely to paint better features onto the same old traditional picture, merely to add attractive detail to the genealogical model described above. Thus, scholars have used Dunhuang manuscripts in conjunction with other evidence to devise more vivid portraits of Bodhidharma, Huineng, and others as *individual* figures, without changing the framework in which these individuals are presented in any substantial manner, and certainly without trying to work out the cultural and religious dynamics that led to their inclusion in the genealogical paradigm in the first place. There are exceptions, of course, but they are comparatively few and far between.

I am not suggesting that we never include descriptions of lineage successions in our writing on Chan—far from it—but only that, when we do so, we should be conscious of the reasons for their use and remain aware of the risks involved. Not only would it be impossible to talk about Chan without ever using concepts related to lineage—to the extent it can be described as a continuous set of processes, Chan is at its most profound level a *genealogical* set of phenomena—but we will gain the greatest benefit from shifting our focus and perspective repeatedly as we move through the evidence. To commit the "string of pearls" fallacy is to remain fixed and unaware in a single posture. Rather than simply move to a different static position, however, we should work to illuminate our subject from a number of angles, to encounter it with different aspects of our interpretive capacities.

A Provisional Device: The Phases of Chan

Figure 2 (p. 13) is a simple chart describing Chan in a manner quite different from that of the lineage diagram (fig. 1) discussed above. Where the traditional Chan diagram lists names of individual human beings, this chart lists named phases or trends in the evolution of Chan.[12] The names of these phases or trends are not universally accepted in writings about Chan, and the boundaries between them are subject to debate. I preserve these ambiguities by not adopting this terminology and periodization without question throughout these chapters; on the contrary, we should pay close attention to the intrinsic fuzziness of the borders between the phases named so uniquely and unambiguously here. It is in large part through considering the failure of any margins to tightly capture these arbitrary entities that we will be able to see the utility of this periodization.

Each of the named phases refers not to a specific set of individuals per se (although some of the most representative figures are listed), but to a style or configuration of religious activity that is known through a variety of sources. One of the primary models by which each phase is characterized is, of course, a list of teachers, known as patriarchs in the traditional lineage scheme, who function as figureheads for a certain type of religious identity. These men (and very occasionally women) serve as exemplars of enlightened behavior, whose stories are told and retold in order to pattern the behavior of subsequent generations of students.[13] (Even as Chan involves the transcendence of patterned behavior in enlightened spontaneity, this abandoning of patterning must itself be patterned in order to be understood, modeled before it can be imitated, deconstructed, and refigured.) Information about these figureheads, as well as doctrinal explanations and other types of information, was circulated both orally and through written texts. Hence each phase of Chan can be described in terms of multiple dimensions: its exemplary human representatives, the geography and timing of their activities, the texts that describe their activities and convey their teachings, and so forth. Figure 2 provides information of this sort briefly in the summary for each phase.

Hence, the basic difference between the lineage diagram and the chart in figure 2 is that, where the diagram tends to homologize all the individuals represented as identically enlightened representatives of a single confraternity—to enable (and simultaneously limit) the understanding of them according to a meaningful yet unitary religious mode—the chart seeks to distinguish qualitative differences along a chronological axis, to facilitate multiple perspectives and modes of understanding. The goal of the chart is the generation of meaningful distinctions, not the assertion of an unbroken continuity of patriarchal authority.

You will note that the lineage diagram is not monolithically unilinear, that there are divisions into double lines at a number of points, and that five different "houses" of Chan are specified. How can we account for these differentiations, while at the same time acknowledging the "homologizing" impact of the lineage diagram and its underlying religious assumptions? We will consider most of these examples in detail later, but they are to a certain extent exceptions that prove the rule. It has long been recognized that Huineng and Shenxiu, the figureheads of the so-called Southern and Northern schools, function within traditional Chan ideology not as two isolated individuals, but as an inextricably related

FIGURE 2. Simplified chart of the phases of Chinese Chan.

PROTO-CHAN ca. 500–600	Bodhidharma (d. ca. 530) Huike (ca. 485 to ca. 555 or after 574) *Treatise on the Two Entrances and Four Practices* SUMMARY: Multiple locations in north China; practice based on Buddha-nature; no known lineage theory. Known through traditional texts and a few Dunhuang documents.
EARLY CHAN ca. 600–900	Hongren (601–74) Shenxiu (606?–706), Huineng (638–713) Shenhui (684–758) Northern, Southern, Oxhead factions *Platform Sūtra of the Sixth Patriarch* SUMMARY: Various loosely defined factions/groups, with different approaches to "contemplation of the mind"; relationship between this and proto-Chan unclear; lineage theories appear from 689 on as a unifying ideology; known through numerous Dunhuang documents and traditional sources.
MIDDLE CHAN ca. 750–1000	Mazu (709–88), Shitou (710–90) Linji (d. 867), Xuefeng Yicun (822–908) Hongzhou and Hubei factions, antecedents of the Five Houses *Anthology of the Patriarchal Hall* SUMMARY: Emergence of "encounter dialogue" as primary mode of practice and discourse, recorded in colloquial form and massive quantity in 952, and implying a genealogical model of religious cultivation; not present in Dunhuang documents but known through Song dynasty texts and idealized as a golden age during Song.
SONG-DYNASTY CHAN ca. 950–1300	Dahui (1089–1163), Hongzhi (1091–1157) Five Houses, Linji and Caodong schools *Blue Cliff Record* SUMMARY: Greatest flourishing of Chan, which as an administrative ideology dominated the Chinese monastic establishment; the image of Tang-dynasty masters operating in enlightened spontaneity was inscribed in highly ritualized Song-dynasty settings; snippets of encounter dialogue were collected, edited to serve as precedents of enlightened activity, and used as topics of meditative inquiry.

NOTE: In order to cover Chan from the end of the Song dynasty up to the present, this chart should include at least a postclassical phase or perhaps multiple later phases. However, since the developments of these later periods are not treated in this book, I will not attempt a periodization here.

pair simultaneously linked in collaborative and competitive relationship. Together they constitute a single literary and religious polarity expressed as a relationship between two human exemplars. A convenient shorthand for this complex bimodality is the French word *duel,* which carries the meanings of both "duel" and "dual" in English.[14] Thus the doctrine of sudden enlightenment associated with the Southern school cannot be explained without reference to a gradualist doctrine attributed to the Northern school. (This simplistic explanation of sudden versus gradual is woefully inadequate in the face of historical reality, but it must have been very effective in disabusing trainees of their simplistic notions of meditative "achievement.") Note that these two schools, along with Oxhead Chan, are included together in the "early Chan" phase of the eighth century— and this is an intentional grouping, meant to indicate that these three factions were more alike than different, or at least that their religious identities were so intimately intertwined that they must be represented together. The fact that none of Shenxiu's disciples are included in the Chan lineage diagram (already noticed on p. 4 above) is due to their exclusion from consideration in traditionalistic accounts of Chan; here their meaningful absence serves to highlight the unilinearity of the "orthodox" line traced from the legendary (i.e., fictional, but therefore more important) Huineng. In chapter 6 (see p. 138) we consider whether the distinction between the Linji/Rinzai and Caodong/Sōtō schools implies a similar polarity, that is, two groups paired together in a duel or binary relationship that is both contrastive and competitive.

You might assume that the chart depicts a chain of historical causality, but it actually characterizes the retrospective identity of the various phases of Chan. The periodization of any set of past events represents an act of reconstruction—not the mere reorganization and ordering of information, but the total remaking of the past as the structured image of our imaginations. Now, there is nothing wrong with creating an image of the past—indeed, I believe it is our task as historians, both professional and occasional, to visualize the past in the best ways we know how. But we should work to remain aware that the ordering of developments from the fifth through the thirteenth centuries inevitably involves this kind of re-creation; we cannot get off the hook with the naive belief that we are merely ordering the information for the sake of convenience, but not really altering it in the process.

This retrospective quality pervades the Chan tradition. Time and again we find we are dealing, not with what happened at any given point, but with what people thought happened previously. We deal not so much in facts and events as in legends and reconstructions, not so much with accomplishments and contributions as with attributions and legacies. The legends and reconstructions, not the supposedly "actual" events, determined later religious and social praxis. This observation may have a broad application beyond Chinese Chan, in describing what it is that makes traditions traditions.[15] But it is certainly applicable to Chan: not true, and therefore more important.

With these considerations in mind, then, and in order to get a better perspective on the subjects to be covered in the remaining chapters, let us look in somewhat greater detail at the phases listed in figure 2. At this point I provide only a few introductory comments to help you become oriented to the material and thus prepared for the more detailed analysis that follows.[16]

PROTO-CHAN

The designation *proto-Chan* refers to the ill-defined activities of a set of practitioners surrounding Bodhidharma and Huike who were known for their dedication to ascetic practices and meditation. Beginning roughly around the year 500 and overlapping with the so-called early Chan phase in the seventh and perhaps even into the eighth century, this group operated in a variety of north China locations. The extent to which the individuals involved conceived of themselves as participating in a single group or movement is unclear, and since they had no way of knowing of the continuity of their activities with any later "Chan school," even the convenient term *proto-Chan* does not bear close scrutiny. (Their activities are "prototypic" only to those who already know what followed.) We know of a small number of figures who studied under Bodhidharma, and a somewhat larger number who were primarily associated with Huike, presumably after his master's death. There is a certain quantity of biographical information about the participants in proto-Chan, and although it attests to the variety of their backgrounds, it imparts only a shadowy image of any shared group esprit.

One important feature of proto-Chan—at the very least, a feature important for the subsequent evolution of the school—was its common focus on a text circulated under Bodhidharma's name, the *Treatise on the Two Entrances and Four Practices (Erru sixing lun)*. As this text circulated, practitioners who identified with Bodhidharma's message appended their own comments to it, making it an expanding anthology of the earliest Chan teachings.[17] Thus, while we cannot describe the scope of proto-Chan

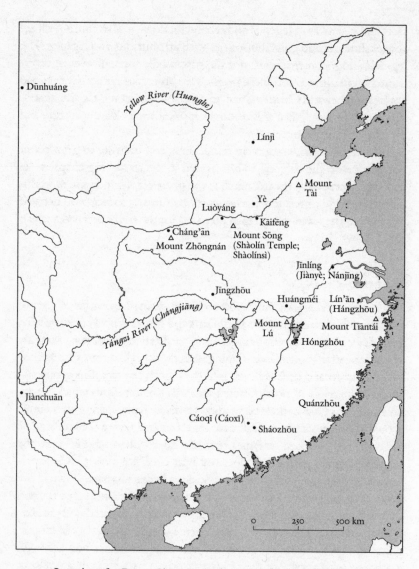

MAP 1. Locations for Proto-Chan, Early Chan, and Middle Chan.

activities with any accuracy, the *Treatise on the Two Entrances and Four Practices* provides insight into precisely those ideas that formed the doctrinal nucleus of subsequent Chan practice ideology. This text describes a fundamental attitude of emphasis on the existence of the Buddha-nature or potential for enlightenment within all sentient beings, as well as an attitude toward how this understanding of Buddhism may be carried out in daily life.[18]

EARLY CHAN

Early Chan designates the phase when the school, or what was to become a school eventually,[19] first articulated its lineage-based ideology in clear and extensive form. Actually, the Dunhuang manuscripts and traditional Chan records include an amazing variety of different formulations from this phase, and it seems evident that a great deal of experimentation was taking place, involving a number of variations on commonly accepted themes, as the Chan movement matured and crystallized over time. Some of these formulations describe specific methods of contemplation practice, sometimes presented in a progressive series of steps. Others describe the role of the Buddha-nature, or "pure mind," within, as well as the behavior of the illusions—the false thoughts, or "impure mind"—that obscure the appreciation of our inner purity. Compared to later Chan texts, these formulations often seem odd but are not particularly enigmatic or difficult; the emphasis at this point was on clarity in expressing this new form of the Buddhist teaching, not on generating entirely different modes of expression.

In contrast to proto-Chan, the early Chan phase manifests a great stability of location: Daoxin and Hongren spent exactly a half-century, from 624 to 674, in the same monastic complex in Huangmei ("Yellow Plum," Hubei Province) and it is not unreasonable to include Shenxiu's quarter-century, from 675 to 701, at the not-too-distant Jade Spring Temple (Yuquansi, in Jingzhou, which overlaps both Hubei and Hunan Provinces) in this phase as well. Matters become more complex with the explosion of Chan into the two imperial capitals of Chang'an and Luoyang during the eighth century. Therefore, whereas investigation of proto-Chan leaves one with the impression of an indefinable will-o'-the-wisp, analyzing the sources for early Chan imparts a sense of continuous community development and a growth pattern that moves from geometric increase throughout much of the seventh century to explosive expansion in the eighth. Also, where proto-Chan refers to a single, albeit incohesive and ill-defined, style of religiosity, early Chan may be understood as a collection of different communities, groups, and factions.

In the most straightforward sense, the label *East Mountain teaching* refers to both the community and doctrines of Daoxin and Hongren, but there is an important sense in which these matters are known solely through information transmitted by their successors. Those successors identified themselves not as purveyors of their own doctrinal innovations, but as transmitters of the East Mountain teaching. We need to recognize that the ideas associated with the names Daoxin and Hongren were primarily those of their followers' later reconstruction; this recognition does not sever the connection between those ideas and the East Mountain teaching figureheads themselves, but it does lend an important retrospective quality to the process. That those successors, who were active in Chang'an and Luoyang in the early decades of the eighth century, came to be known by the label *Northern school* is a curious historical detail. The *Southern school* derives from the mid-eighth-century activities of Shenhui (684–758), although later this label came to be adopted for the Chan school as a whole. The *Oxhead school* is a somewhat later development, a faction or lineage that played an important historical role through its apparent involvement in the composition of the *Platform Sūtra,* the hallmark and culminating text of early Chan.

We will deal with the East Mountain teaching in chapter 2, along with Bodhidharma and proto-Chan. The Northern, Southern, and Oxhead schools, as the most important trends of metropolitan Chan (i.e., those factions that evolved in the two capitals of Chang'an and Luoyang),[20] will be treated together in chapter 3. It is appropriate that the last three schools should be taken together, since they were in dialogue with one another, and the supposed distinctions between them in their original historical identities are not nearly as sharp as the Chan legends would have us believe. It would also be appropriate to mark the East Mountain teaching off as an entirely separate phase, but I hope that adding these comments here—and organizing chart and chapters differently—will be sufficient to show the provisional nature of the boundaries involved. The lack of congruence between the categories "early Chan" and "metropolitan Chan" as used here is intentional.

MIDDLE CHAN

An event of overwhelming significance takes place in the "middle Chan" phase: the emergence of "encounter dialogue," the idiosyncratic manner in which Chan masters are depicted in dialogue with their students.[21] Associated initially with such celebrated figures as Mazu Daoyi (709–88) and his successors Baizhang Huaihai (749–814), Nanquan Puyuan (748–834), and Linji Yixuan (d. 867), as well as Shitou Xiqian and his successors Dongshan Liangjie (807–69) and Caoshan Benji (840–901), this is when Chan appears to have become really Chan, when Chan masters seem to have really behaved like Chan masters. The anecdotes of middle Chan encounter dialogue represent the stories repeated most often in popular books on Chan/Zen as examples of paradoxical but enlightened behavior. Here the locus of religious practice was firmly removed from individual effort in the meditation hall and replaced by a demanding genre of interrogation that sought to destabilize all habitual, logical patterns. Spontaneity was the rule, iconoclastic behavior the norm.

Or so it seems. For here we will have to consider, not only the momentous import of encounter dialogue as the dominant model of religious undertaking, but also the difficult questions of *when* all this spontaneous interaction was actually being practiced and *what* precisely was going on. We will see that there is a substantial gap between when the most famous stories of Chan lore are supposed to have happened, and when we first see them in written form. We will also see that these stories have complex origins, bearing features of both oral and written literature. In the past scholars (myself included) have referred to the middle phase as the "golden age" or "classical period" of Chan. The first of these terms may easily be discarded for its romantic coloring.[22] The latter term may still be used, but only with the provision that what is being referred to is not some collection of activities and events that actually happened in the eighth through tenth centuries, but instead the retrospective re-creation of those activities and events, the imagined identities of the magical figures of the Tang, within the minds of Song dynasty Chan devotees. Mazu and the other Tang figures came to represent a classical age only when their time had passed, when their identities were redesigned to fit the needs of Song-dynasty Chan. Although middle Chan may be considered as a historical phase, "classical" Chan is itself a romantic depiction of activities from that phase within the later texts of encounter dialogue.

SONG-DYNASTY CHAN

The contours assumed by Chan Buddhism during the Song dynasty represent the mature pattern which defines the tradition up until the

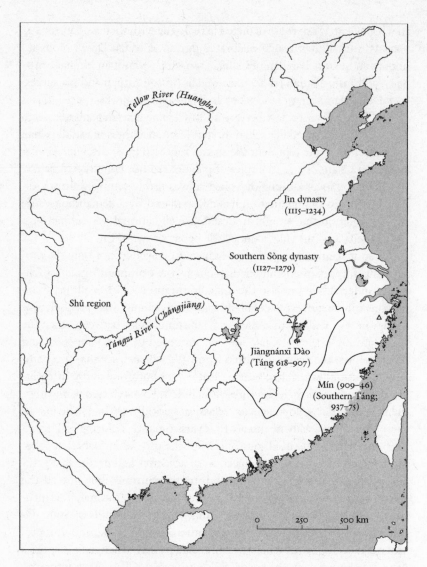

MAP 2. Locations for Song-Dynasty Chan.

modern period. Using an ecological metaphor, I refer to this pattern as a "climax paradigm," which describes the dynamic equilibrium achieved by a mature forest or ecological system. Earlier writers (both scholarly and apologist) have tended to ignore this period, partly out of the wish to explore the more "creative" masters of the Tang, or to jump across the waters to emphasize the emerging Zen school of Japan. The Song has also been denigrated in general textbooks as the beginning of the decline of Chinese Buddhism, its ossification into institutional formalism. This attitude is changing, as Song-dynasty religion has become perhaps the primary focus of the study of premodern Chinese religion, by Euro-American scholars at least. And with this change our impression of Song-dynasty Chan has been transformed as well. It is now increasingly recognized that the Song dynasty witnessed the emergence of a basic configuration of Chan that was disseminated throughout East Asia, and now the world. This is apparent most dramatically in the life and teachings of Dahui Zong-gao (1089–1163), the innovator and greatest exponent of "viewing the critical phrase" or *kōan* practice in the history of Chinese Chan. But the picture of Song-dynasty Chan is not complete without looking closely at the style of meditative introspection advocated by Hongzhi Zhengjue (1091–1157) and other members of the Caodong lineage, evaluating their recommendations on their own terms and not simply in light of the polemical characterization by Dahui as mere "silent illumination." Ultimately, we will see that the Linji and Caodong approaches present an inseparable pair that mimics the sudden/gradual debate of the eighth century, and which resonates with the "two entrances" of the treatise attributed to Bodhidharma. But this is to get ahead of our story. Let us now turn to the legendary account of Bodhidharma himself, to see how Chan Buddhism emerged in the first place.

CHAPTER 2

Beginnings

Differentiating/Connecting Bodhidharma
and the East Mountain Teaching

Bodhidharma, it is said in the traditional accounts, was the third son of
a great Brahman king of southern India, who left home to undertake the
life of a Buddhist monk.[1] Attracted to the profundity of the Mahāyāna,
he eventually became the twenty-eighth patriarch in succession to Śākyamuni Buddha. After traveling by sea to China in order to spread the true
teachings of Mahāyāna Buddhism, he had the following interview with
Emperor Wu of the Liang dynasty (r. 502–549), who was renowned for
building temples, casting images, and supporting the teaching activities
of Buddhist monks:

> *Emperor Wu:* "What is the religious merit of all my efforts on behalf of
> Buddhism?"
>
> *Bodhidharma:* "None whatsoever."
>
> *Emperor Wu:* "Who are you to say such a thing to me!?"
>
> *Bodhidharma:* "I don't know."

Seeing that conditions were not right for him to teach in southern China,
Bodhidharma crossed the Yangzi River by floating across on a reed[2] and
went to Mount Song, just south of the great city of Luoyang. There he
took up residence at Shaolin Temple (Shaolinsi), but instead of joining the
regular activities of the congregation of monks, he spent nine years in a
cave, sitting in meditation while facing a wall. His extraordinary discipline
eventually attracted the attention of a student named Huike, who was to
become Bodhidharma's successor and thus the second patriarch of Chan
Buddhism. But Huike did not achieve this new identity without demon-

strating his total dedication to the Dharma: since the master was absorbed in meditation and would not recognize him, the student knelt behind Bodhidharma in silent supplication, the snow piling up around him in the cold north China winter. Eventually, Bodhidharma broke his silence and asked what Huike wanted—the answer being "instruction in the teachings of Buddhism," of course—only to ignore the student once again. In desperation, to show the depths of his dedication Huike cut off his own arm and placed it before the master. Seeing this, Bodhidharma at last recognized the student's sincerity and allowed him to inquire of the teachings:

> *Huike:* "My mind is not at ease—please pacify it for me!"
>
> *Bodhidharma:* "Bring me your mind, and I will."
>
> *Huike:* "But no matter how I might look, the mind is not a 'thing' I can find."
>
> *Bodhidharma:* "There, I've pacified your mind for you!"

Huike was suddenly awakened at this reply. He continued to study under Bodhidharma and was eventually recognized as his successor.

Bodhidharma later became the target of criticism by jealous monks who did not understand the true teachings of Buddhism. Although they tried to poison him several times, it was only when Bodhidharma himself decided the time was right that he allowed their potions to kill him. Huike supervised his burial along the banks of a river south of Luoyang, but later the master returned to India, leaving only one shoe in his grave; he was seen crossing the Chinese border carrying the other shoe.[3] Huike went on to transmit the teachings to Sengcan, from whom they were passed on to Daoxin, Hongren, and then to the sixth patriarch Huineng.

This, in a nutshell, is the legend of Bodhidharma as it has been passed down within the Chan tradition. There can be no doubt of its utility as a coherent distillation of classical Chan doctrine: Bodhidharma, the enlightened but iconoclastic master, transmits the true teachings of Buddhism to China, where until his time it had only been understood in a superficial and self-seeking manner. The "nine years facing the wall" at Shaolin Temple and the implicit demand made of Huike—or rather, Huike's macabre demonstration of his inner drive for true understanding at all costs—imply both a disregard for conventional representations of Buddhism and the demand that students spare no effort or personal sacrifice in order to achieve enlightenment. How many times this story must have been told in meditation halls in China, Korea, Japan—and now America and Europe—in order to spur practitioners on to greater effort!

The "pacification of the mind" dialogue is in fact an archetypal example of Chan spiritual training itself, which is less an individual endeavor than an interactive event, the interpersonal encounter between master and student set in a genealogical context. The attacks upon Bodhidharma serve to highlight the unique status he held as sole transmitter of the true teachings, and the autonomous control he had over his death and subsequent return to his native land add an occult aura to his extraordinary capabilities. Indeed, the account of Bodhidharma—I should actually refer to the "accounts," since the preceding is but a bare outline abstracted from a number of divergent sources—represents a highly integrated distillation of the Chan message, and as such it has been among the most treasured subjects of Chan sermons and dialogues over the centuries.

But the story is not true.

The Evolving Hagiography of Bodhidharma

It is not that parts of the story are in doubt, or that some of it is accurate and some not, or that it is a false composite of individually acceptable elements. All of these alternatives are correct to some extent, but even in combination they do not accurately represent the true situation. The issue is more fundamental.

The image of Bodhidharma that has been transmitted to us is the result of a long hagiographical process, and it is not "biographical" in some sense of being a more-or-less "accurate" depiction of the man's life. Rather, it is the idealized image of a sage, the human demonstration of enlightened charisma, the life of an Indian saint on Chinese soil. It is ultimately impossible to reconstruct any original or accurate biography of the man whose life serves as the original trace of this hagiography—where "trace" is a term from Jacques Derrida meaning the beginningless beginning of a phenomenon, the imagined but always intellectually unattainable origin. Hence any such attempt by modern biographers to reconstruct a definitive account of Bodhidharma's life is both doomed to failure and potentially no different in intent from the hagiographical efforts of premodern writers.[4] This does not mean that we should disdain examining the sources and evolution of this hagiographical process, of course—only that we should remain firmly aware of the hagiographical dynamic while doing so.

The earliest evidence for Bodhidharma's biography derives from ultimately incommensurable sources. In other words, the hagiographical image of Bodhidharma is fundamentally different from whatever "historical" Bodhidharma may have existed at one point. This understanding of the hagiographical nature of the Bodhidharma who occurs in Chan legends is not just a trivial academic nicety, but a profoundly important key to the understanding of Chinese Chan as a cultural and religious tradition. Before considering the implications of the hagiographical process concerning Bodhidharma, though, we need to establish a baseline, the beginning of the story—not as a kernel of biographical truth, of course, but as the earliest manifestation of mythopoeic creativity about him.[5]

The following chronological assertions can be made with reasonable confidence about the earliest hagiographical image of Bodhidharma. According to sources from the mid-seventh century and earlier, it was thought that he *(a)* arrived in south China by sea sometime in or before 479; *(b)* moved to north China before 495, perhaps by 480 or so; *(c)* was in Luoyang sometime during the years 516–26; and *(d)* died around 530 (i.e., sometime during the years 524–34). In addition, there are a few other characterizations we can make with some confidence about the earliest image of Bodhidharma. That is, he *(e)* was a native of south India, of Brahman caste, and perhaps a member of some royal family; *(f)* professed Mahāyāna Buddhism, taught meditation, and focused his efforts on the Luoyang area; *(g)* had a small number of known students, including Huike—who was the dominant figure in the development of Bodhidharma's following; and *(h)* was the beneficiary (perhaps postmortem) of an editorial contribution by a monk named Tanlin, who produced a text called the *Treatise on the Two Entrances and Four Practices* in his name.[6]

Although all of the eight statements above are based on documentary evidence (of different levels of reliability), we must resist the temptation to accept them as jointly contributing to a single, comprehensive image of the first patriarch of Chan. The eight assertions derive from different sources written at different times and with different authorial agendas. In addition to issues of accuracy, it is not even certain that all of them (especially item *(c)* pertain to the Chan school's founder, rather than to some other figure of the same name. Taking the first four assertions together, we also arrive at the unlikely scenario that Bodhidharma spent a full half-century in China—not impossible, but it would mean that he arrived in China a relatively young man, which is contrary to the legend that he was 150 years old (which occurs in the source of item *c,* for example). Also, given the time frame suggested by the evidence, the story involving Bodhidharma and Emperor Wu of the Liang dynasty is clearly anachronistic, given the latter's reign dates of 502–49. Examining the information available regarding Bodhidharma's life requires dealing with endless subtleties and contradictions. Indeed, his hagiography is a particularly good example of the fluidity of legendary Chan imagery.

The easiest way to understand the dynamics of Chan hagiography is to see how Bodhidharma's image developed over time. The following list of the earliest dates at which each element of his hagiography appeared in written sources reveals an overall pattern of accretion and reinscription. That is, not only does the image of Bodhidharma as Chan patriarch become increasingly detailed over time, but new motifs effectively substitute for earlier ones, changing the very quality of the image as religious icon.[7]

547 Said to have been from Persia and was 150 years old when he arrived in Luoyang sometime during the years 516–26.

645 Described as a Brahman monk from south India who arrived in south China during the Liang dynasty (420–79); Huike's arm is said to have been cut off by bandits/rebels.

667 Depicted transmitting the *Laṅkāvatāra Sūtra* to Huike.

689 Listing of the succession from Bodhidharma to Huike, Sengcan, Daoxin, and Hongren.

ca. 710 Identified with Shaolin Temple on Mt. Song; story of Huike cutting off his own arm;[8] Bodhidharma described as dying voluntarily by poison, then as seen at the Chinese border on his way back to India, leaving an empty grave.

ca. 715 Described as the third son of a Brahman king of south India; identified as second patriarch after Guṇabhadra, translator of the *Laṅkāvatāra Sūtra*.

730 Story of meeting with Emperor Wu; said to transmit robe to Huike after the latter cut off his own arm.

758 or shortly after Specifically labeled "first patriarch"; transmitted the *Diamond Sūtra* to Huike.

801 Described reciting a "transmission verse" before death.

952 Occurrence of the "pacification of the mind" dialogue with Huike.

988 Said to have "faced the wall" in meditation.

ca. 1200 "Relics" (*śarīra,* from a cremated body [!]) venerated by the "Daruma school" in Japan.[9]

1224 Reference to how he "faced the wall for nine years."[10]

Thirteenth century Association of Shaolin Temple with martial arts.

1642 Attribution of a martial arts book to Bodhidharma.[11]

None of the various details of Bodhidharma's life is "true," in the sense of being journalistically accurate, and therefore each is more important than a mere "fact" might be. Presentations of Bodhidharma's biography that are unreasonably detailed—such as the *Encyclopedia Britannica*'s entry for him (written by Heinrich Dumoulin) that identifies him as a "native of Conjeeveram, near Madras"[12]—exemplify the third rule of Zen studies: "Precision implies inaccuracy." Rather than the stark contrast of true/false, of course, it is the overall fabric of creativity within which the hagiography developed that is most impressive.

In fact, if we looked at the matter more closely, we would see that the evolution of Bodhidharma's image functions as a veritable index to the evolution of Chan itself. That is, if we could do analytical cross-sections at different points in time, we would see that the members of the Chan school were reformulating Bodhidharma's identity to fit their own conceptions of religious sagehood in each particular age; each substantive reconfiguration thus implies a qualitative change in the religious identity of Chinese Chan. This is a dynamic process that continues into the present, of course: A 1992 Taiwanese movie account of Bodhidharma's life shows him not only sitting rock-solid in meditation—a full nine years without moving a muscle!—but also as a miraculously gifted martial artist catching arrows in his teeth and flying through the air, his legs churning in the manner of *Crouching Tiger, Hidden Dragon!* The modern martial arts cinema tradition has remade the image of Bodhidharma according to its own needs, just as the medieval Chan tradition did. The results are different, but the process is basically unchanged.

In other words, both medieval Chinese Chan factions and modern martial arts schools have created images of Bodhidharma to fit their own conceptions of enlightened sagehood. These imagined sages serve the need felt by each faction or school for a primal figurehead to personify and thus legitimate its particular style of spiritual and athletic training. To accept any one of the various hagiographical images of Bodhidharma as accurate would be to choose only one legendary image out of a series of continuous change. On the one hand, to tell any version of Bodhidharma's hagiography is to present a Sunday-school image of Chan. Doing so is of course acceptable for participants within the tradition itself, but to present such simplistic stories as historically accurate in works of historical narration is an indefensible commission of the "string of pearls" fallacy. On the other hand, it would be even more egregious to deny the religious and cultural significance of the hagiographical process as a whole, to fixate on the technical accuracy of the images of Bodhidharma produced by generation after generation of Chinese practitioners. Those images are not true, and therefore they are more important. More precisely, those images were used by generations of Chan practitioners and enthusiasts, and therefore they are more important than a simplistic reconstruction of historically verifiable events might be.

Proto-Chan and the *Treatise* on the *Two Entrances and Four Practices*

In all this, there *is* one useful point to hold on to: Bodhidharma's early followers remembered his teachings through a short but extremely influential text known as the *Treatise on the Two Entrances and Four Practices*. The absolute *terminus ad quem* for the appearance of this text is 645, but at this point it already includes some material probably from Huike's life; hence the text no doubt dates back at least to the second half of the sixth century, if not necessarily to the lifetime of Bodhidharma himself. The text does not read like a translation, and the role of the "historical" Bodhidharma in its composition is beyond our knowing at this point. Probably it was written on his behalf by Tanlin on the basis of information about the master's teachings conveyed to him by Huike, so that the text has a kind of retrospective authenticity that is common in the Chan tradition. But the important point is that this treatise was accepted by a community of Bodhidharma's successors as embodying his teachings.

Before I turn to the content of the *Treatise* itself, let me make just a few brief comments about the nature of the "proto-Chan" community that developed in Bodhidharma's name. First, the overall impression one gets from the historical evidence is that Huike, rather than Bodhidharma, was the central figure of this loosely associated group of practitioners. Huike was already a mature adult when he studied with the master, not a fresh-faced trainee, and there is a sense in which Bodhidharma functioned for him primarily as a source of validation of his own level of attainment, a means of legitimation for his own teaching activities. Second, there is a certain range of variation in the individuals associated with Huike and Bodhidharma, including wandering ascetics, Confucian practitioners (of a rather mysterious sort), and eventually specialists in the study of the *Laṅkāvatāra Sūtra*. Third, Huike and the figures associated with him, however distantly in some cases, were identified with various locations in northern China, not only Luoyang. In part this was due to the vicissitudes of time—a significant persecution of Buddhism occurred in the Northern Zhou regime in 574—but, whatever the reason, they did not establish any fixed, lasting base of operations.

Probably the most important characteristic to justify referring to these men (and probably a few women) in one breath as the "proto-Chan" movement was their shared interest in the *Treatise on the Two Entrances and Four Practices*. They discussed this text in letters and used its contents as the framework for written dialogues, which, as time went on, were appended to the text itself. Although I consider only the opening essay proper, the text as it has been transmitted down to us through Dunhuang manuscripts contains a substantial number of additions, which in sum are more extensive than the original essay itself. None of this material is datable, and for all we know the process of accretion may have continued well into the eighth century.[13]

The heart of the *Treatise,* and indeed the doctrinal germ of much if not all later Chan theory, is the following passage:

> The entrance of principle is to become enlightened to the Truth on the basis of the teaching. One must have a profound faith in the fact that one and the same True Nature is possessed by all sentient beings, both ordinary and enlightened, and that this True Nature is only covered up and made imperceptible [in the case of ordinary people] by false sense impressions. If one discards the false and takes refuge in the True, one resides frozen in "wall contemplation," in which self and other, ordinary person and sage, are one and the same; one resides fixedly without wavering, never again to be swayed by written teachings. To be thus mysteriously identified with the True Principle, to be without discrimination, serene and inactive: this is called the entrance of principle.[14]

In the most straightforward sense, this passage is an elaboration of the idea of the Buddha-nature, the potential or actual quality of enlightenment that is latent within all of us, the only difference between buddhas and ordinary people being that the latter do not perceive this inner source of strength due to their foolish discrimination and sensory activity. The terminology used here, with one notorious exception to be discussed in the next paragraph, is not that difficult: the "True Nature," or the Buddha-nature, is a perfect, absolute (if fundamentally nonsubstantial, nonextant) entity, but it is merely obscured from our view by the false conceptualization and mistaken views of ordinary consciousness.

YANAGIDA Seizan, the greatest scholar of Chinese Chan of the twentieth century, has warned that we should not overlook an important clue to the relationship between the Buddha-nature, or True Nature, and the world of sensory discrimination: this is the word "only" toward the end of the second sentence. This inconspicuous qualifier indicates a difference of valence between the two realities—colloquially, we would say a different quantum level of significance—with the Buddha-nature understood as fundamentally more important, profoundly more real, than the constantly changing appearances of our daily lives. In other words, rather than being distracted by the superficial manifestations of our own consciousnesses—though of course these include the attributes of personal identity to which we are usually most closely attached—practitioners should instead emphasize their profound confidence in the existence of the Buddha-nature at the very heart of our innermost being. In Buddhism "faith" is precisely to "reside fixedly without wavering" in one's correct understanding. In Chinese terms this is to be "mysteriously identified with the True Principle," that is, to be united with the Buddha-nature at a level that is inscrutably hidden beneath our ordinary levels of perception, at that level of undifferentiated reality that is obscure yet oddly luminescent.[15]

Although the peculiarly Chinese rhetoric may seem unusual, all this is actually fairly straightforward—except for the notorious exception I alluded to above. This is of course the term "wall contemplation" (biguan), which has bedeviled the Chan tradition ever since its introduction here. Ultimately, no one really knows what the term means. It only occurs in one other more-or-less contemporaneous source, a list of meditation practices recommended for beginners, where it occurs without explanation.[16] The occurrence of the term in this list is not terribly helpful, especially since the estimation of it as a beginner's practice is at odds with the comments made by the historian Daoxuan (596–667) that the "achievements of Mahāyāna wall contemplation are the highest."[17] Eventually, the term came to be interpreted in the Chan tradition as referring to the act of sitting in meditation facing a wall, but as indicated in the discussion of Bodhidharma's hagiographical evolution above, it took some time for this meaning to take hold. (As shown on p. 6, important first references in this process occurred only in 988 and 1224.)

Paul Swanson has recently suggested that the compound biguan might be a combination of two characters that both stand for the word vipaśyanā or "insight meditation." Hence the character bi 壁 is not used in its substantive meaning as "wall" but rather as the transliteration of the first syllable of vipaśyanā, a Sanskrit term usually translated into Chinese as guan 觀, the second character in the compound. The character guan can, of course, be used in different senses in Chinese, but here the compound biguan was thus intended as "the meaning of guan that corresponds to vipaśyanā." Unfortunately, the phonology does not quite work: In medieval Chinese the character for "wall" had a final *k* ending (in modern Japanese the character is pronounced *heki*), and it seems never to have been used for transliteration purposes.[18] Finally, the association of *biguan* with *vipaśyanā* seems off; there is no sense of meditative investigation or discernment about the "entrance of principle."

Zhiyi's magnum opus on meditation theory and practice, the *Great Calming and Contemplation (Mohe zhiguan)*, includes what I suspect is a better possibility: "Concentration *(zhi, śamatha)* is wall concentration *(biding)*, in which the evil perceptions of the eight winds cannot enter. Concentration is pure water, which overflows the eight confusions of lust."[19]

In glossing the term *biding*, Zhanran (711–82) writes that

> a room has four walls, so the eight winds cannot enter. If one is able to stop them, then one has transcended this realm's evil perceptions of internal and external, concordant and discordant. The eight winds are only the four discordant and four concordant. . . . The room's walls also prevent these eight winds [from entering]; hence they are used as a metaphor.[20]

This usage by Zhiyi and Zhanran seems to fit the *Treatise on the Two Entrances and Four Practices* very well: "wall contemplation" in that text might be considered to mean "fixed in *śamatha* or concentration meditation, without allowing the eight winds of good and bad fortune to influence one at all." Whether the specific reference to the eight winds applies to Bodhidharma's treatise or not, the general sense of "wall contemplation" as the solid exclusion of distractions fits well with the "entrance of principle."

Although this metaphoric explanation seems reasonable, it was apparently not transparent to the members of the later Chan movement, who eventually introduced the more graphic image of Bodhidharma sitting in front of a cave wall. The issue is profoundly irresolvable, and we should take clear note of the uncertainty that exists.

In any case, the entrance of principle is Bodhidharma's expression—or, rather, the proto-Chan movement's expression, attributed retrospectively to Bodhidharma—of the fundamental stance of the religious practitioner. It is not altogether clear, unfortunately, exactly how this fundamental stance worked in actual practice. Does this refer to some kind of yogic absorption, some kind of forced mental extinction or tranquilization? The text is elusive on this point, and it remains for the East Mountain teaching phase of early Chan to provide specific details. Now, however, let us look briefly at the structure and content of the *Treatise on the Two Entrances and Four Practices* as a whole.

First, what of the "two entrances"? We should not dismiss this dual-ity as an insignificant convenience of exposition, since in positing two sep-arate types of access to religious truth, the *Treatise* exhibits a bimodality that is endemic to the Chan tradition. This bimodality is often negated, sometimes with polemical vehemence, but its near-universal distribution is noteworthy. In the text of the *Treatise* itself the relationship between the entrances of principle and practice is simultaneously bipolar and uni-tary: each is contrasted with the other, and ultimately they end up being the same thing. This is but the earliest manifestation of a "duel" rela-tionship in Chan. (Recall that the term *duel* is used according to its dou-ble meaning in French, corresponding to both "duel" and "dual" in En-glish; see p. 12.) The earliest description we have of Bodhidharma depicts him in part in terms of his duel relationship with another early medita-tion specialist, Sengchou (480–560); where Bodhidharma was known for the unmatched profundity of his teachings, Sengchou was known for the purity and efficacy of his ascetic endeavors.[21]

The entrance of practice includes the following four increments:

1. Practice of the retribution of enmity: to accept all suffering as the fruition of past transgressions, without enmity or complaint

2. Practice of the acceptance of circumstances: to remain unmoved even by good fortune, recognizing it as evanescent

3. Practice of the absence of craving: to be without craving, which is the source of all suffering

4. Practice of accordance with the Dharma: to eradicate wrong thoughts and practice the six perfections, without having any "practice"

As should be clear from the contents of these four steps, the term *practice* is used here to refer not to spiritual cultivation as an ongoing religious endeavor, but rather to the activities of one's daily behavior.[22] The "four practices" of the second entrance thus represent a progression in which one adopts an increasingly detached perspective on the varying circum-stances of one's own life, culminating in the realization that everything that occurs does so in accordance with the ultimate principles of Bud-dhism. At this point, although attained from different directions or styles of endeavor, the two entrances culminate in the same realization.

The important issue here is the highly contextualized or outer-focused quality of the second entrance, the attention to the details of phenome-nal reality as one actually lives it. There is thus an important contrast between the two entrances: Where the entrance of principle is variously abstract, introspective, and yogic (all of these characterizations being open to reinterpretation, of course, given the allusive quality of the original text), the entrance of practice represents the concrete, extrovertive, and quotidian. Buddhist texts, not only those of the Chan school, often use formulations couched in terms of inner and outer, but the distinction is particularly important here. We will see that the bimodality between principle and practice, or rather between an abstract description of one's inner attitude and the progressive elaboration of one's ongoing activities, is a recurrent theme throughout the Chan tradition—one that will help us to organize the sometimes unruly creativity of later periods.

Hongren and the East Mountain Teaching

The *Treatise on the Two Entrances and Four Practices* came to be ignored in later centuries, no doubt precisely because it was too straightforward, too explicit. Just a little too humdrum in presentation, it simply did not match the image that the Chan tradition wanted to have of its founding patriarch. Given the fundamental Buddhist doctrine that everything changes, it is easy to recognize that everyone and everything is transitory or, in historical terms, transitional. The *Treatise* continued to play an important role, though, through the seventh and early eighth centuries.

This period encompasses the phase of Chan known as the "East Mountain teaching," a term that is based on the location where Hongren (601–74) taught in Huangmei. The reference is to one of the "twin peaks," Shuangfeng, of Huangmei, and even though Hongren's teacher, Daoxin (580–651), resided on the other peak, the name "East Mountain teaching" is used for both masters. Actually, the term was used by Shenxiu (606?–706) and his immediate successors in reference to the teachings they had inherited from Daoxin and Hongren, so it is also appropriate to include Shenxiu's quarter-century of residence at Jade Spring Temple (675–701) in Jingzhou here as well. (See p. 47 for an explanation of the use of the term in association with Shenxiu.)

One of the most basic features of the East Mountain teaching, which distinguishes it clearly from proto-Chan, is that it was centered at a single, fixed location. Of course, this is certainly not to say that *all* Chan-tradition activity during this period occurred at Huangmei and Jade Spring Temple, but that the East Mountain teaching phase included long, uninterrupted periods of community development in one or two fixed locations. This is a radical transition from the unsettled wanderings of Bodhidharma, Huike, and their associates.

Understandably, we have more information about the East Mountain teaching than about proto-Chan, and it is possible to make the following generalizations about the community and its teachers. First, just as Huike was the dominant personality of proto-Chan, Hongren was the central figure of the East Mountain teaching. From the description of their biographies, it appears that Daoxin may have been brought in and installed as the young Hongren's tutor. Hongren is described as being a quiet and unassuming student, who did meditation by day and took care of the cattle by night, so that when he began to teach, everyone was surprised at his brilliance. (This image of Hongren is a clear antecedent to that of Huineng; see the discussion beginning on p. 68.) When Daoxin was about to pass on, he was quoted as saying, roughly, "I guess Hongren would be all right" as his successor—and this half-hearted endorsement is actually an ironic revelation of the real situation, that Hongren was the one and only choice all along. Huangmei was Hongren's native place, where his family was known for its tradition of religious reclusion, but after Hongren's death the community was never heard of again. And, as we will see, when Shenxiu and his entourage moved into Luoyang in 701, they presented themselves as transmitters of the "pure teaching of East Mountain" and circulated a text attributed to Hongren as the content of their teachings.

Second, Daoxin and Hongren taught meditation and nothing else. In all the material we have about them, there is no reference to their advocating or practicing *sutra* recitation, devotion to the Buddha Amitābha, or philosophical analysis—in contrast to the numerous references to them as meditation teachers.

Third, the East Mountain teachers had a gradually increasing number of students. The biographies assert that "eight or nine of every ten" spiritual practitioners in all China practiced under them, but we actually know of only a half-dozen or so individuals who studied with Daoxin and about twenty-five who studied with Hongren. Since the comparable figure for Shenxiu is about seventy, the overall trend is clear.

Fourth, in direct contrast to the single-minded dedication to meditation of their teachers, the students of Daoxin and Hongren included individuals of various religious interests. Whether practitioners of the *Lotus Sūtra,* students of Mādhyamika philosophy, or specialists in the monastic regulations of Buddhist Vinaya, monks traveled to Huangmei to undertake meditation training. Indeed, the East Mountain community at Huangmei seems to have been recognized throughout China by the second half of the seventh century as a specialized training center in the second of the "three learnings" of morality, meditation, and wisdom.

Fifth, as far as we can tell, Hongren's disciples stayed with him for limited periods of time. The most famous case of course is that of Huineng, who is supposed to have stayed at Huangmei for only eight months or so, which was meant to appear to contemporary Chinese as surprisingly brief. The most significant exception to the pattern of short-term residence, on the other hand, is the monk Faru (613–89), who seems to have served as Hongren's attendant or assistant during his sixteen years at Huangmei— which reminds one of the example of the Buddha's cousin and long-time attendant, Ānanda. (Faru is an important transitional figure between the East Mountain teaching and metropolitan Chan phases; see p. 48.) Judging from the biographies, most of Hongren's students were more like Shenxiu, who stayed with the master for six years at the very beginning of his teaching career. Although this information may also be subject to some doubt—six years was the length of time Gautama spent performing austerities before he became enlightened under the *bodhi* tree, and Buddhist hagiography often echoes this figure in order to invoke the Buddha's example—the pattern seems to have been that Daoxin and Hongren's students stayed with them for a few years and then went on to other things.

Sixth, nothing special can be said about the East Mountain community's size, administration, or spiritual lifestyle. The great Japanese scholar Ui Hakuju (1882–1953) suggested that it included five hundred or a thousand members, but the figures he uses actually refer to the attendance figures for Hongren's funeral. There must have been quite a number of lay devotees and admirers present at this event, not to mention some pious exaggeration in the written references. Seeing that we know of about twenty-five men who studied with Hongren in about as many years, even taking into consideration the probability that the number of his students increased as time went on, only a handful of these figures would have been present at any one time. There is no accurate way to estimate the actual number of monks and nuns in training at any one time, which might have fluctuated over time from just a handful to as many as several dozen. *Pace* Ui, there is also no evidence whatsoever that these monks participated in anything other than meditation and ordinary religious services—that is, there is no evidence whatsoever that the famous and probably illusory ideal of Chan monastic labor was known at East Mountain. The famous dictum that "a day without work means a day without food" only appears centuries later, and Hongren's community no doubt had its share of lay workers and tenant agricultural laborers, like other Buddhist centers of the time. Here our best evidence is the *Platform Sūtra,* which depicts the eventual sixth patriarch Huineng as a low-status temple menial. Since this was the image of Hongren's community generated a century afterward, and our first evidence for any special "Chan" style of monastic system does not come for centuries after that, the only possible conclusion is negative: there is no basis for suggesting that Chan had developed a specific lifestyle in which monastic labor was performed as part of spiritual cultivation.

From Proto-Chan to Metropolitan Chan: The *Treatise on the Essentials of Cultivating the Mind*

So, what style of meditation practice did Daoxin and Hongren teach? The usual—almost inevitable—approach is to first explain what we know about the former, then turn to the latter. When this style of presentation is combined with treatments of the earlier patriarchs, as it almost always is, the result is a clear instance of the "string of pearls" fallacy. That is, rather than probing the dynamics of evolution of the Chan movement over time, most authors actually present a static elaboration based on the traditional genealogical configuration of the Chan orthodoxy that developed in the Song dynasty and beyond, a simple form of transposition posing as analysis. In fact, the "teachings of Daoxin" and the "teachings of Hongren" as they are now understood did not exist during the actual lifetimes of these historical figures, but only appeared during the transition from the East Mountain to the metropolitan Chan phase. The time lag was only a few decades, which might seem brief in the overall span of Chinese Buddhist history, but considerable change can occur in such a seemingly brief period. The teachings of Daoxin and Hongren were recorded retrospectively, as written reconstructions of lessons from the past. As it turns out, this retrospective quality of the East Mountain teaching is very significant.

At Huangmei, Daoxin and Hongren would not have needed to present their teachings in writing. In the relatively intimate context of teacher-student interaction, written guidelines might have been useful but would not have been necessary. When their students moved into the much larger arena of the two capitals of Chang'an and Luoyang, though, the situation was entirely different. Chang'an was the greatest cosmopolitan center on earth at the time, with a population of perhaps a million people and enriched by close trading connections across the Silk Road to India, Persia, and the Middle East. Luoyang was a somewhat smaller city, but a venerable center of culture and religion, and the imperial court moved back and forth between the two capitals from time to time. The imperial court and literate society surrounding it were a magnet for intellectual and religious innovations from all over China, and indeed from throughout East Asia, Buddhist India, and Central Asia as well, and this "imperial center" had been the focal point of translation and research activities for Buddhism for centuries, as it continued to be throughout the eighth century. Even though Chan is portrayed in modern writings as having developed in rustic surroundings and as a rejection of merit-oriented activities and imperial largesse, this image of Chan and its fundamental identity developed precisely within the context of the imperial center, rather than on its periphery. We need only recall the legendary encounter between Bodhidharma and Emperor Wu of the Liang, which was concocted in the middle of the eighth century, to realize how these themes played out in medieval China. Just as Chinese nature poetry originally developed among city dwellers, so was the almost barnyard primitivism and anti-intellectualism of "classical" Tang-dynasty Chan created in a highly sophisticated, literate milieu of the Five Dynasties and Song dynasty periods. (Actually, even the encounter between Bodhidharma and Emperor Wu was generated in a context that undercuts the iconoclastic image of Chan; see the discussion beginning on p. 108.)

When Hongren's students moved from the provincial community at Huangmei to the imperial center, one of their first steps was to compile a written record of their master's teachings. This was the *Treatise on the Essentials of Cultivating the Mind*, which includes the straightforward admission that it was compiled not by Hongren himself but by his students, presumably after his demise. Actually, this is the earliest example within the Chan tradition of the composition of texts representing a given master's teachings, that is, of texts that were compiled and edited shortly after the master's death. The *Treatise on the Essentials of Cultivating the Mind* may have been prepared for use by Faru, who taught at Mount Song for a few years prior to his death in 689; the text was almost certainly known to Shenxiu by about the same time, and it was quoted in other texts during the second decade of the eighth century.

Although Daoxin is treated in Chan hagiography as Hongren's predecessor, the written teachings attributed to Daoxin only appeared *after* the text attributed retrospectively to Hongren.[23] One or two of the basic slogans associated with Daoxin may have existed earlier, but the assertions found in scholarly works published to date of a doctrinal evolution from Daoxin to Hongren are impressionistic and thoroughly unconvincing. Moreover, the teachings of this "Daoxin" are composed in an intellectually sophisticated format that belies the supposed succession of ideas. In any case, since "Daoxin's" teachings first appeared in the second decade of the eighth century, we can clearly detect a chronological trend of retrospective attribution. In other words, the members of the Chan movement moved in reverse order through the commonly accepted list of patriarchs, publishing suitable writings first for Hongren, then for Daoxin, and then (in the middle of the eighth century) for Sengcan. Hence any attempt to re-create the evolution of Chan teachings by moving from patriarch to patriarch in a forward order is condemned to failure for methodological reasons that are simultaneously elementary and profound. Such attempts exemplify the "string of pearls" fallacy, which cripples the ability of most authors to deal with the evidence as it evolved instead of how it was designed to look. Therefore, when we look at the *Treatise on the Essentials of Cultivating the Mind,* we are not seeing Hongren himself, but Hongren as he was remembered several decades after his death.

Even so, the *Treatise on the Essentials of Cultivating the Mind* is a masterpiece of religious literature. Concise and unpretentious, it frequently exhorts its readers to make greater effort on behalf of their own enlightenment. It is not merely that life is too short, as we might put it today, but that the opportunity to undertake Buddhist spiritual training in a supportive environment is a rarity that may not happen again for many lifetimes. To complement this vigorous encouragement, the text describes an attitude toward religious attainment that is wonderfully delicate, and the practices it recommends are designed to avoid placing too strong an emphasis on the final goal. (As every beginning student of Buddhist philosophy quickly recognizes, to desire *nirvāṇa* as a final goal contradicts the very desirelessness of *nirvāṇa* itself.) The *Treatise on the Essentials of Cultivating the Mind* manipulates these considerations with a charmingly palpable sensitivity. And it provides a welcome elaboration of the basic themes adumbrated in such deliciously elusive fashion in the *Treatise on the Two Entrances and Four Practices* attributed to Bodhidharma.

The heart of the *Treatise on the Essentials of Cultivating the Mind* is the following dialogue, which includes a made-to-order but spurious scriptural quotation:

> The *Treatise on the Sūtra of the Ten Stages* says, "There is an adamantine Buddha-nature within the bodies of sentient beings. Like the sun, it is essentially bright, perfect, and complete." Although vast and limitless, it is merely covered by the

layered clouds of the five skandhas. Like a lamp inside a jar, its light cannot shine.

Further, to use the bright sun as a metaphor, it is as if the clouds and mists of this world were to arise together in all the eight directions, so that the world would become dark. How could the sun ever be extinguished?

[Question: Without the sun being extinguished,] why would there be no light?

Answer: The sun's light is not destroyed, but merely deflected by the clouds and mists. The pure mind possessed by all sentient beings is also like this, in simply being covered by the layered clouds of discriminative thinking, false thoughts, and ascriptive views. If one can just distinctly maintain [awareness of the mind] and not produce false thoughts, then the Dharma sun of *nirvāṇa* will naturally be made manifest.[24]

The relationship between the "sun-and-clouds" metaphor here and the explanation of the True Nature in the Bodhidharma treatise is obvious, and a similar qualifier is even used to describe how the Buddha-nature or sun of enlightenment is "merely" obscured by one's ordinary psychological identity. In addition to thus adopting the same value structure in this initial formulation, the Hongren treatise describes the fundamental attitude toward spiritual cultivation in terms of "maintaining [awareness of the mind]" *(shouxin)*, which is essentially a posture of nurturing the Buddha-nature as a treasure within one's own person. Rather than aggressively intruding into one's own being to scrape away the clouds of ignorance—which would be rather like reaching a giant claw into the sky to drag away the clouds and mists blocking the sun—the appropriate response is to affirm the ultimate reality of one's beginningless enlightenment, to maintain constant awareness of this pristine condition within oneself, and then to work in an energetic but unharried fashion toward the circumstantial manifestation of the on-going enlightenment experience.

The *Treatise on the Essentials of Cultivating the Mind* describes two specific meditation techniques, which neatly demonstrate the two aspects of this fundamentally vigorous but composed attitude. The first is to visualize the orb of the sun just as it sets, shining back at one from a fixed point on the horizon, large and round as a giant temple drum hanging sideways on a stand. This technique is actually drawn from the *Sūtra of the Contemplation of the Buddha Amitāyus,* one of the major scriptures of the East Asian Pure Land tradition, and although its explicit use here is as an exercise in concentration (one is to focus on the one point of the sun without distraction) it also serves implicitly as a symbolic reminder of the "sun of *nirvāṇa*" within.

The second technique is to focus, not on the Buddha-nature itself, but on the hyperactive mental processes that obscure it:

> Make your body and mind pure and peaceful, without any discriminative thinking at all. Sit properly with the body erect. Regulate the breath and concentrate the mind so it is not within you, not outside of you, and not in any intermediate location. Do this carefully and naturally. View your own consciousness tranquilly and attentively, so that you can see how it is always moving, like flowing water or a glittering mirage. After you have perceived this consciousness, simply continue to view it gently and naturally, without it assuming any fixed position inside or outside of yourself. Do this tranquilly and attentively, until its fluctuations dissolve into peaceful stability. This flowing consciousness will disappear like a gust of wind. When this consciousness disappears, all one's illusions will disappear along with it, even the [extremely subtle] illusions of bodhisattvas of the tenth stage.[25]

Other authorities might object that merely stopping the transformations of consciousness was not equivalent to complete and perfect enlightenment—certainly, this was to become a subject of discussion within Chan.[26] But the important point is the dedicated but undemanding attitude recommended here. Rather than forcing the issue, rather than trying to "achieve" enlightenment, the Hongren treatise counsels the practitioner to simply let it happen. Whether or not this approach is suitable for everyone—and at least one Chan master would openly deride similar approaches as uselessly waiting around for miracles to happen (see p. 135)—the sensitivity of the text in counterposing its two techniques against one another, of demanding energetic patience, if you will, represents a remarkable synthesis.

Indian and Chinese Buddhist Polarities

One of the most prominent features of Chan discussions of meditation is the use of polarities. To be sure, such discussions often include reminders of a fundamental nondualism, the absence of any absolute distinctions. Even so, the frequency of dualistic formulations is striking. Bodhidharma and Sengchou, Huineng and Shenxiu, principle and practice, sudden and gradual, Northern and Southern schools, and Linji (Rinzai) and Caodong (Sōtō): from hagiographical figures to doctrinal themes to lineage divisions, the Chan tradition veritably overflows with dualistic formulations. Given this situation, it is tempting simply to line up the dyads used in different contexts and suggest that they are all essentially the same in some fashion. A better approach, of course, is to remain alert to the possibilities of nuanced differences between the various pairs. At present the question is, what inferences can we draw from comparing the contents of the Hongren treatise with earlier Buddhist meditation theory?

Certainly, the most important pair of themes in Indian Buddhist meditation doctrine is that of concentration (*śamatha*) and insight *(vipaśyanā)*. Very briefly, concentration refers to a set of exercises aimed at developing the mind's ability to focus without distraction on a given object. A variety of objects may be used, assigned by the meditation instructor as appropriate antidotes for the student's particular dispositional tendencies. A trainee given to anger might be instructed to work on the generation of loving-kindness, while one given to pride might be told to perform exercises involving the visualization of corpses. As the practitioner eliminates the hindrances blocking his ability to concentrate effectively, he moves through a set of four stages of *dhyāna,* or "concentration." (The Chinese word *chan* 禪, pronounced *zen* in Japanese, *sŏn* in Korean, and *thien* in Vietnamese, is a transliteration of this Sanskrit word.)[27] According to the canonical descriptions, in the first stage of *dhyāna* the practitioner's mind is characterized by singlepointedness of concentration along with two different types of mental deliberation and a combination of joy and bliss. By conscious decision the practitioner moves from one stage to the next, successively eliminating the two types of mental deliberation and the joy and bliss, which ultimately are considered distractions to the task at hand. With the fourth and "fundamental" stage of *dhyāna* the practitioner's mind is characterized solely by singlepointedness of mind. Although speech and discursive thought are impossible at this stage, it is here that the meditator becomes able to use the supernormal faculties of telepathy, superaudition, levitation, knowledge of his own past lives, and understanding of the karmic fates of others. The Buddha and his disciples often used these abilities for teaching purposes, but the Buddhist tradition considers them potentially hazardous diversions of no value to spiritual cultivation, and there are Vinaya regulations against monks' divulging competence in these powers to laypeople.

In contrast to the great elaboration of concentration exercises, insight or *vipaśyanā* meditation consists solely of the application of the concentrated mind to any object, in order to attain "clear comprehension" of it. In *śamatha* the mind becomes concentrated like a searchlight, while in *vipaśyanā* that searchlight-like mind illuminates the most important issues of the human condition: the transiency and composite nature of the human body, the dependent origination of thoughts and feelings, and the inevitability of human suffering. By using the mind concentrated through *śamatha* to examine these issues, the practitioner sees and understands them through *vipaśyanā*. Thus concentration and insight are not really separate techniques, even though they may be explained separately for convenience. The meditation exercise that is most widely used throughout the Buddhist tradition is that of concentration on the breath, which has the virtue of drawing the practitioner naturally from concentration to insight: as the body settles and respiration slows, one's attention shifts from calming to knowing.

The objects selected for attention in insight meditation by any Buddhist community are congruent with the understanding of Buddhist doctrine within that community. Hence in early Buddhism one was to focus on the body and one's thoughts and feelings in order to recognize their inherent impermanence, causal interrelationship, quality of suffering, and so forth. In Mahāyāna Buddhism, on the other hand, the realization achieved in insight meditation tended to be the fundamental emptiness (*śūnyatā*) of all things, although this and other Mahāyāna themes were expressed in various ways by early Chinese meditators. Although Theravāda and other Mainstream Buddhist sources do adduce stages of progress in insight practice,[28] these stages tend to be increasing gradations of a single achievement of awareness rather than quintessentially different achievements. (In contrast, the explanation of the stages of concentration, or *dhyāna,* include significant conceptual distinctions.) Nor is there any real explanation of how insight happens—only the basic assumption that the mind, when directed at a given subject matter, has the innate capacity to understand. Like the Buddha's enlightenment, the experience of understanding is ineffable, but its impact is liberating.[29] It is axiomatic throughout the Buddhist tradition that the perfect understanding of the human situation yields one's liberation from the deleterious effects of that situation.[30]

To return to matters closer at hand, we may now ask the following question: To what extent do the two entrances of the Bodhidharma treatise or the two practices suggested in the Hongren treatise resemble the Indian Buddhist themes of concentration and insight? I have already introduced evidence to suggest that the entrance of principle might be considered an interpretation of concentration, or *śamatha,* and the same consideration would also apply to the practice of the visualization of the sun. The use of the Buddha-nature idea, the sun of enlightenment within all human beings (indeed, within all sentient beings), the quality of non-discriminatory wisdom that is the sine qua non of buddhahood itself, is a profound innovation that separates proto-Chan and early Chan from early Indian Buddhism. However, it is also a simple concentration exercise, the only peculiarity of which is that the mind is being trained to concentrate on the mind's most quintessential capability of understanding itself. The goal of the practice of "maintaining the mind" in the Hongren treatise is precisely to affirm the existence of that latent wisdom and to allow it to shine forth in unqualified form. Where I tend to describe the concentrated mind of Indian Buddhist *śamatha* theory as a searchlight that may then be focused on specific topics in *vipaśyanā,* in Chinese imagery the enlightened sun of *nirvāṇa* within is an all-encompassing source of illumination. Given this difference in metaphoric construction, though, the Indian Buddhist concept of concentration meditation thus correlates, if only approximately, with the entrance of principle and the visualization of the sun.

However, this is not the case for the comparison between insight meditation and Bodhidharma's entrance of practice and Hongren's focus on the activity of the discriminatory mind. Part of the problem, of course, is that the two specific meditation techniques attributed to Hongren include substantial components of both concentration and insight. (As we have seen just above, of course, the same can be said for many Indian Buddhist meditation exercises.) Hongren's instructions to concentrate on the movement of the discriminatory mind imply both cessation—in that it is expected that the mind's movement will eventually stop in the course of one's practice—and understanding—in that the cause of that cessation is said to be a "wind of wisdom." For the moment, however, we must grant that the second practice recommended in the Hongren treatise is more like concentration than insight.

The problem is that the entrance of practice in the Bodhidharma treatise simply does not fit into this pattern. Rather than being any kind of yogic practice at all, in fact, the four steps within this "entrance" to the path pertain to one's activity in the world. To be sure, the emphasis is on the mental posture with which one approaches one's life experience. However, the emphasis is on action, not realization. This should alert us to the fact that something is going on here that does not fit within the confines of "meditation practice" per se. Instead, we need to look within the Chinese tradition for a suitable analog to the pairing of the two entrances of the Bodhidharma treatise.

As Chinese clergy and laypeople were struggling to understand Buddhism in the fourth and fifth centuries of the common era, they were wont to use a uniquely Chinese formulation: the distinction between essence *(ti,* lit., "body") and function *(yong,* lit., "use"). There is no sharp distinction between essence and function; depending on the perspective, any entity or situation can be approached in terms of either one. Nor is there any sharp transformation in moving from essence to function, since the difference between the two is more in the mind of the beholder rather than in the entity itself. In his *Treatise on the Immutability of Things* Sengzhao (374–414) explains the relationship as follows, based on an initial quotation from an early translation of the *Perfection of Wisdom:*

> The *Light-Emitting* [*Perfection of Wisdom*] *Sūtra* states, "Dharmas are without going and coming, without active transformation." In searching for the operations of inactivity, how could one possibly seek stillness by undoing the active? One must seek stillness within the activities [of things]. Since one must seek stillness within the activities [of things], although active they are always still. Since one should not undo the active to seek stillness, although [things] are still they do not transcend activity. Nevertheless, even though activity and stillness have never varied, the deluded take them as different.[31]

The early-twentieth-century scholar TANG Yongtong (1893–1964) explains that Sengzhao's entire treatise is devoted to showing that active and still are identical. This is not to say that there exists some unmoving fundamental essence that generates the myriad phenomenal manifestations, but that that the fundamental realities and phenomenal permutations are inseparably identical.[32]

Thus it is entirely reasonable that the two entrances of Bodhidharma's text are quite different and yet seem to merge in the fourth practice, where "practicing in accord with the Dharma" so closely resembles the entrance of principle. The two entrances may be separate, but in a certain sense they imply each other, even contain each other. From a more general perspective, this is only the beginning of a broader attention to the similarities and differences between the different types of polarities that are scattered about the Chan tradition. We will have occasion to return to the Bodhidharma treatise again, to recognize its signal role in establishing patterns that recur again and again throughout Chan. At this point, however, let us be content to notice that not all such polarities are identical, that different matchings may harbor substantially different implications. With this simple but important observation in hand, we may turn our attention to the next phase of Chinese Chan.

CHAPTER 3

Metropolitan Chan

Imperial Patronage and the Chan Style

A "Chan Boom" in the Imperial Chinese Capitals

In the first half of the eighth century, the northern Chinese cities of Chang'an and Luoyang were the greatest urban centers in the world. Chang'an had a population of over a million, a number far larger than any city in the Middle East (let alone Europe) would reach for centuries. Originally a safe military headquarters "within the passes" of the mountainous northwest, Chang'an was laid out on an extremely grand scale and in a cross-hatched design of wide boulevards running north-south and east-west. The city walls formed a nearly square rectangle enclosing a neatly ordered set of government centers, market areas, and neighborhoods. With the imperial palace in the north of the city and major thoroughfares connecting to regional highways leading eastward to Korea and Japan and westward to Central Asia, Persia, India, and the Middle East, the emperor could face south towards both city and realm, even as the entire world seemed to face north in paying homage toward this ruler of "all under heaven."

The imperial state was expressed in grand and imposing material form, with massive office buildings and official temples, and it was operated by a bureaucratic organization of ministries, bureaus, and departments manned by officials who achieved their positions through different combinations of hereditary advantage and civil service examinations. The most elite of these bureaucrats were required to attend an imperial audience every morning, some of whom recorded poetic laments of the windy chill of lonely city streets in wintertime as they rode on horseback from their homes to the palace in the far north of the city.

In addition to its majestic official identity as a political center, Chang'an was a cosmopolitan nucleus of trade, literature, culture, and religion. As the major Chinese trading node on the Silk Road, it received imports of rare treasures from India, Persia, and beyond, and its people enjoyed new musical styles, carnival entertainments, and art forms imported one after the other from the "western regions." Polo was a favorite game among men (and some women) of the Chinese upper classes, and some of the latest song styles from the "western regions" shocked the older generations as much as contemporary music does in the United States today. With local populations of traders and their descendants from Sogdiana, Khotan, Korea, and other exotic locations around China, Chang'an was an exciting and lively mix of cultures. In terms of knowledge of both the western regions and Buddhism, the example of the great pilgrim Xuanzang (600?–64), who had traveled through Central Asia to India in the mid-seventh century, was still reverberating throughout the Chinese realm. And, of course, there were dozens of magnificent Buddhist temples (and a smaller number of Daoist ones) throughout the city, with a large population of monks and nuns.

The second capital at Luoyang was not nearly as large, nor was it laid out quite so neatly as Chang'an, but its location some 320 kilometers to the east was within the rich alluvial Yellow River plain and thus in the very cradle of Chinese civilization. Luoyang had been a Buddhist center from the second century onward—one of the earliest and most important in China—and its temples were numerous, venerable, and magnificent. In addition to its reputation as a center of culture, Chinese officials sometimes preferred that the emperor reside at Luoyang because it was easier to supply with grain than was Chang'an in the mountains to the west. For students of Chan, Luoyang is also known as the city just north of Mount Song, the central peak in the quinary configuration (i.e., having points in the center and four corners) of traditional Chinese sacred geography. Bodhidharma had been associated with Mount Song since at least 645, although it was only at the end of the seventh century that Chan monks are known to have taken up residence at the fabled Shaolin Temple there.

At the beginning of the eighth century, in a pivotal event marking the public beginning of Chan as a school of Chinese Buddhism, the Chinese emperor invited a certain monk to the capital at Luoyang. This was not just any emperor, but the only woman to sit on the Chinese throne in her own name: Wu Zetian, usually referred to in English as Empress Wu (r. 690–705).[1] Through an exceptional combination of native intelligence and political acumen, along with good luck and personal beauty, Empress Wu had been able to take over control of the Chinese state when her husband, Emperor Gaozong (r. 656–90), was debilitated by strokes beginning in 670, and then to rule in her own name from the time of his death in 690. Although she is excoriated by orthodox Confucian historians, her efforts to justify her political position by identifying herself as a Buddhist ruler, and even as an incarnate Bodhisattva, are a fascinating subject for students of Chinese religions. For our present purposes, we may merely note that by the turn of the eighth century she was well established in her rule and had no need for further ideological artifice.[2]

And the Chan teacher invited to court by Empress Wu was no ordinary monk! He was Shenxiu (606?–706) from Jade Spring Temple in Jingzhou (Hubei and Hunan Provinces), the preeminent figure in the burgeoning Chan tradition. Two separate texts describe his welcome into Luoyang in 701 as follows:

> Empress Wu Zetian sent a palace messenger to escort Shenxiu to Luoyang. Monks and laypeople spread flowers in his path, and the banners and canopies [on the vehicles of the wealthy and prestigious] filled the streets. He entered the palace riding on an imperial palanquin decked with palm leaves. Empress Wu, following him, touched her forehead to the ground and knelt for a long time in a spirit of reverent dedication and chaste purity. When Shenxiu administered the precepts to the court ladies, all the four classes of Buddhists took refuge in him with the same feelings of veneration that they had for their own parents. From princes and nobles on down, everyone in the capital took refuge in him.[3]

.

> [After his imperial invitation to Luoyang, Shenxiu] accompanied the imperial chariot on its comings and goings, proselytizing in the two capitals and personally becoming the Imperial Instructor. The Great Sage Empress Wu Zetian inquired of him: "Whose teaching is it that you transmit?" He answered, "I have inherited the East Mountain teaching of Qizhou [i.e., Huangmei, the location of Hongren's monastery]." Empress Wu Zetian said, "In considering the cultivation of enlightenment, the East Mountain teaching is unexcelled."[4]

This was a spectacular demonstration of imperial reverence, which Empress Wu emphasized by having Shenxiu sit facing south with herself kneeling in front of him, facing north. Shenxiu's epitaph, which was written by a prominent statesman and literatus of the day, defended this by saying that "he who transmits the Holy Truth does not face north; he with abundant virtue does not follow the protocol of a subordinate."[5] Shenxiu seems to have been a member of the Tang ruling family, but this treatment was exceptional nonetheless. In addition to Empress Wu's sincere reverence, she may even have been making a conciliatory gesture toward those who would replace her in office after her death.[6] The result is that Shenxiu is the first historical member of the Chan tradition whose specific ideas, rather than a retrospective or posthumous image, are known in any depth and detail.

In spite of the use of imperial north/south symbolism to indicate Shenxiu's exalted religious status, there is only a distant connection between this and how his teachings and following came to be referred to as the "Northern school." (See the next section, "Shenhui's Campaign against the 'Northern School,'" beginning on p. 54.) Instead, here we see Shenxiu effectively producing his own history, in the sense of identifying himself in the present by selectively and/or creatively describing his past, by labeling his approach to Buddhism as the "East Mountain teaching" of his teacher Hongren.[7] At about the same time, Hongren's students compiled the *Treatise on the Essentials of Cultivating the Mind;* a little afterward they compiled a suitable set of teachings attributed to Daoxin; and decades later other monks produced the *Treatise on Believing in Mind* and other documents celebrating Sengcan's life. Thus the process of retrospective production of history continued forward through time, even as its focus shifted to successively earlier figures in the lineage. (This subject has been mentioned above; see especially the discussion on pp. 36–38.)

This was the religious environment in which we discover the very first expressions of the Chan lineage scheme. That is, the genealogical presentation of the Chan transmission was first recorded on paper in the early years of metropolitan Chan activity. The earliest recorded instance of this was in the epitaph for a certain Faru, a student of Hongren's who died in 689 (see p. 35), and by the second decade of the eighth century, the later followers of Hongren had produced two separate texts describing the transmission from Bodhidharma to Shenxiu. These two texts, which I do not discuss individually here, are known to contemporary scholarship as early "transmission of the lamp" histories after the title of the defining text in the genre written several centuries later, the *Record of the Transmission of the Lamp [compiled in] the Jingde [period]*, or *Jingde chuandeng lu*.[8] There are differences of content and emphasis between the two "Northern school" texts, but they both express essentially the same doctrine: that the central teaching of Buddhism was transmitted through a sequence of patriarchs reaching Shenxiu and his disciples.

While one of the fundamental implications of the "transmission of the lamp" texts was the unchanging continuity from master to disciple in the

Chan lineage, from a historical perspective it is clear that the transition from East Mountain to the two capitals was accompanied by a profound transformation in the nature of the Chan movement. As environments of rhetorical exchange and religious discourse, there was a radical difference between East Mountain and the two capitals, and Chan was transformed as its members actively sought to move from one setting to the other. Notes and partial transcripts of the masters' teachings might have been made at the East Mountain monastic community in the provincial town of Huangmei, but it was only when Hongren's successors moved into the environment of the two capitals, with its literate society and incomparably larger urban scale, that well-written texts were required for disseminating the teachings. No doubt the creative process of active remembering began in some fashion at East Mountain, but we have no direct evidence of this. Whatever rustic simplicity or sophisticated discourse might have governed life at Huangmei is now largely unrecoverable, since all our sources are retrospective creations of the literate cultural center.

Even granting the complexity of our sources, though, it is clear that Shenxiu's teachings were qualitatively different from those of Hongren as described in the *Treatise on the Essentials of Cultivating the Mind*. Shenxiu was fascinated with a style of radical reinterpretation of the Buddhist scriptures based on his own religious insight, which he referred to as the use of "skillful means" or the "verification of the Chan meaning." This was actually the extensive use of a form of anagoge or metaphor, in which every pronouncement of the scriptures was subject to reinterpretation in terms of "contemplation of the mind."[9] In simple terms, what Shenxiu told his listeners was that the Buddha was not interested in mundane matters, but used each and every utterance to describe the practice of Buddhist meditation. Shenxiu thus advocated, in a fashion distantly reminiscent of the Buddha himself, that Buddhists should work to achieve buddhahood and the salvation of all living beings themselves right now.

Thus we find in Shenxiu's writing a number of parallels drawn so as to redefine conventional religious practices in terms of actual spiritual cultivation. The following are paraphrased summaries of the most instructive of these parallels:

Temple repair: The Chinese transliteration for *saṅgha-ārāma* is defined as a "pure ground," so that the eradication of the three poisons of greed, hatred, and ignorance is described as constituting the repair or "cultivation" of such a monastery.

Casting and painting of images: The Buddha was not interested in the creation of mundane images, but was instructing the true practitioner to "make his body a forge, the Dharma its fire, and wisdom the crafts-man." The three groups of pure precepts and the six perfections become the mold for casting, within the practitioner's own body, the Buddha-nature of Suchness.

Burning of incense: The incense referred to here is not some worldly fragrance but rather that of the true, unconditioned Dharma, which "perfumes" the tainted and evil karma of ignorance and causes it to disappear.

Offering of flowers: The Buddha is said never to have advocated the injury of live flowers, but referred in the scriptures to the "flowers of merit" imbued with the essence of Suchness. Such flowers are perma-nent and never wilt.

Circumambulation of stūpas: The body is equated with the *stūpa,* and circumambulation is defined as the ceaseless circulation of wisdom throughout the body and mind.

Holding of vegetarian feasts: Through the selective use of Chinese ho-mographs, the phrase "to hold vegetarian feasts" is interpreted as the ability to make the body and mind equally regulated and unconfused.

Obeisance: Through the manipulation of transitive and intransitive equivalents of the Chinese characters involved, obeisance is defined as the suppression of errors.[10]

Shenxiu also introduces a short scriptural passage extolling the virtues of bathing and then reinterprets the endeavor as "burning the fire of wis-dom to heat the water of the pure precepts and bathe the Dharma-nature of Suchness within one's body." The following is a summary of Shenxiu's seven "dharmas of the bath":

Clean water: Just as clean water washes away the dusts of this world, so do the pure precepts clean away the defilements of ignorance.

Fire: The fire that heats the bath water is actually wisdom, with which one contemplates or examines one's internal and external being.

Soap powder: The soap powder used to clean away dirt is actually the ability of discrimination by which one can ferret out the sources of evil within oneself.

Toothpicks: The "sticks of willow" used to eradicate mouth odor are nothing less than the Truth by which one puts an end to false speech.

Pure ashes: The ashes or powdered incense rubbed on the body after bathing are endeavor *(vīrya),* by which one puts an end to doubt-laden ratiocination.

Oil: Rather than softening one's skin, the oil referred to here is meant to soften dispositional stiffness, or bad habits.

Underwear: The clothing worn in the bath is actually the sense of shame that inhibits evil actions.[11]

In other words, Shenxiu interpreted every passage of every scripture he considered in terms of its instruction concerning Buddhist spiritual cultivation, and he advocated a manner of living in which even the most prosaic of one's activities became—in every feature and detail—an act of religious practice. There is a definite connection between this style of interpretation and the later Chan emphasis on having one's practice extend to every facet of daily life. We will return to this provocative implication later (see the discussion in chapter 4, pp. 85–86).

The point to be emphasized here is the significance of Shenxiu's innovations for the eventual crystallization of Chan as an independent tradition of Chinese Buddhism. There was, in short, a remarkable "Chan boom" in early eighth-century Chang'an and Luoyang, in which Shenxiu's Chan teaching became wildly popular in the greatest cities on earth, among the world's most sophisticated and cosmopolitan society. As one courtier wrote,

> Students of Buddhism from both capitals and the faithful from all areas of China all come to the [Five-Gated Entrance to the Imperial City to hear his teaching]. They come from a thousand *li* away without any hesitation! The mendicants with their robes and begging bowls crowd into newly built halls like schools of jumping fish; their huts cover the hillside like lines of geese. Gathering like clouds and free as the dew, they go to Shenxiu empty-handed and return fulfilled.[12]

Shenxiu's message was breathtakingly simple, since he in effect told his followers to simply practice contemplation of the mind now, working to be bodhisattvas here and now, in this very lifetime, in every moment of their lives. There are echoes of this fundamental attitude not only in later Chan, but also in the early-ninth-century "enlightenment in this body" doctrines of the Japanese Tendai and Shingon school figures Saichō (767–822) and Kūkai (774–835), whose teachings were clearly inspired by the Chan innovation.[13]

Although his message may have been simple in a certain sense, Shenxiu obviously conveyed it with a commanding personal charisma and a uniquely appealing rhetorical style. His activities in the two capitals at the beginning of the eighth century spawned an explosion of Chan religious creativity. Not only did he have some seventy ordained disciples whose names are important enough to be known, but his major students became imperial instructors themselves. They and their students and friends wrote a number of important texts outlining their doctrines and practices, including not only the treatises attributed to Daoxin and Hongren and the "transmission of the lamp" histories mentioned above, but also a variety of documents that have come down to us through the finds at Dunhuang. Taken together, these texts give the impression of a collective experimental effort, an exploration of just how a still-evolving Chan message might best be conveyed to others. Some of these formulations are genuinely inventive, while others are oddly mechanical in their application of Shenxiu's new style of metaphor, and the diversity of formulations implies that not everyone participating in this new movement understood the practice of Buddhism precisely as he had. But this was an entirely natural course of events.

One of the most intriguing features of this material is that some of these texts describe actual practices of meditation. Although there is tremendous variety, the following passages from the text known as the *Five Skillful Means* and circulated by the "Northern school" provide a good introduction:

> To view the mind as pure is called "to purify the mind-ground." Do not constrict the body and mind and then unfold the body and mind—view afar in expansive release. View with universal "sameness." Exhaust space with your viewing.
> The preceptor asks: What do you see [lit., "What thing do you see"]?
> The disciple(s) answer: *I do not see a single thing.*
> Preceptor: Viewing purity, view minutely. Use the eye of the pure mind to view afar without limit, without restriction. View without obstruction.
> The preceptor asks: What do you see?
> Answer: *I do not see a single thing.*
>
> ▪
>
> View afar to the front, not residing in the myriad sensory realms, holding the body upright and just illuminating, making the true essence of reality distinct and clear.
> View afar to the rear, not residing in the myriad sensory realms, holding

the body upright and just illuminating, making the true essence of reality distinct and clear.

View afar to both sides . . .
View afar facing upwards . . .
View afar facing downwards . . .
View the ten directions all at once . . .
View energetically during unrest . . .
View minutely during calm . . .
View identically whether walking or standing still . . .
View identically whether sitting or lying down . . .

■

Question: When viewing, what things do you view?
Answer: *Viewing viewing, no thing is viewed.*
Question: Who views?
Answer: *The enlightened mind views.*
Penetratingly viewing the realms of the ten directions, in purity there is not a single thing. Constantly viewing and being in accord with the locus of nonbeing, this is to be equivalent to a buddha. Viewing with expansive openness, one views without fixation. Peaceful and vast without limit, its untaintedness is the path of *bodhi*. The mind serene and enlightenment distinct, the body's serenity is the *bodhi* tree. The four tempters have no place of entry, so one's great enlightenment is perfect and complete, transcending perceptual subject and object.[14]

The preceding does not need much elaboration. It clearly asks the students to place emphasis on the enlightened mind at the center of their beings, and it instructs them to train their minds so as to penetrate the entire cosmos and all individual activities. The spatial quality of the instructions is distinctive, but the mental attitudes to be nurtured through such practices resemble those of the later Chan tradition: a sense of release, the recognition of the universal sameness of all experience, recognition of the fundamental emptiness of all things, a quality of profound tranquillity, and above all the innate ability of the mind to illuminate and understand all things. The basic practical orientation indicated here is similar to that of the Hongren treatise in advocating an approach to spiritual cultivation that is energetic and vigorous but entirely without tension or the discriminatory fixation on the goal.

Although the best way to appreciate the meditation exercises just described is in terms of Shenxiu's understanding of the "perfect teaching," to which we will return shortly, it is also easy to appreciate how these instructions to "view afar" could be criticized by someone less disposed to meditation practice himself. It is to just such a figure that we now turn.

Shenhui's Campaign against the "Northern School"

In 730, 731, and 732, a monk named Shenhui staged public "debates" at a town in Shandong, far to the northeast of Luoyang, in which he attacked two students of Shenxiu's for making false claims about their lineage and for teaching an inferior style of practice. In 745 Shenhui took up residence in Luoyang, where he continued his campaign. The written account of the 732 event (actually edited after 745) describes the question posed to Shenhui by his interlocutor, an otherwise little-known monk named Chongyuan, and Shenhui's response:

> Dharma Master Chongyuan asked Shenhui, "The two worthies, Chan Master Puji of Mount Song and Chan Master Xiangmo Zang of the Eastern Peak (i.e., Mount Tai), teach people to sit in meditation and 'freeze the mind to enter concentration, fix the mind to view purity, activate the mind to illuminate the external, and concentrate the mind to realize the internal.' They declare that this is the teaching. Why do you today preach Chan without teaching people to sit [in meditation] and without teaching people to 'freeze the mind to enter concentration, fix the mind to view purity, activate the mind to illuminate the external, and concentrate the mind to realize the internal'? What is 'sitting in meditation'?"
>
> His Reverence Shenhui answered, "To teach people to sit [in meditation this way] . . . is to obstruct *bodhi* (i.e., enlightenment). When I say 'sit' now, [I mean that] 'sitting' is for thoughts not to be activated. When I say 'meditation' now, [I mean that] 'meditation' is to see the fundamental nature. Therefore, I do not teach people to have their bodies sit and their minds abide in entrance into concentration. If it were correct to declare such a teaching, then Vimalakīrti would not have scolded Śāriputra for sitting in meditation."
>
> Dharma Master Chongyuan asked, "Why is it impermissible for Chan Master Puji to use the label 'Southern school'?"
>
> His Reverence answered, "Because when Reverend Shenxiu was alive, all those who study the Path in China referred to these two great masters as '[Hui]-neng of the South' and [Shen]-xiu of the North'—everyone knew this. It is because of these titles that we have the two schools of North and South. Chan Master Puji is actually a student of [Shenxiu of] Jade Springs [Temple]; he actually never went to Shaozhou (Huineng's place of residence) but now falsely mouths off about his being the Southern school. Therefore, this is impermissible."[15]

This was a shocking presentation. Using the format of a public debate, Shenhui staged a dramatic and sharply worded attack on the "Northern school," which was a label he invented himself and applied to Shenxiu and his disciples. The name "Northern school" immediately stuck, even though it was clearly a pejorative and polemical distortion—we can infer from the above (there is other corroborating evidence as well) that certain members of this loose confraternity of practitioners actually used the title "Southern school" to describe their own teachings. Shenhui was actively engaged in reformulating the history of Chan, and it is important to recognize that he borrowed substantially from the so-called "Northern school" even as he criticized it so severely. For example, Shenhui set up his own lineage hall in imitation of Puji, even as he worked to establish the transmission from Bodhidharma to Huineng (and then implicitly to Shenhui himself) as the sole lineal succession of Chan.[16] The "Northern school" had originally generated the basic configuration of the Chan genealogical model, but only with Shenhui was its unilineal quality highlighted so clearly. Shenhui's ideas of meditation practice also inherited perspectives shown in the Hongren treatise and Shenxiu's writings, but he was of course far more explicit about denying the value of mental manipulation.

Shenhui was a unique religious persona within the Chan tradition, in that his vocation was that of an evangelist. He did not fit the standard pattern of the meditation teacher who patiently guided dedicated practitioners as they struggled to work through the various problems and stages of spiritual cultivation. Instead, his life's work was performed on the ordination platform, where he served as inspirational orator, recruiter for the *sangha,* and fund-raiser for both church and state.[17] Shenhui's mission was to inspire believers to generate a sincere aspiration to achieve perfect enlightenment on behalf of all living beings (this is the moment of *bodhicitta,* the primary criterion of being a bodhisattva). He was a master at public preaching, able to draw large crowds with his histrionics and inspiring style.

Here is an example of how Shenhui worked to motivate his listeners to attain the first moment of realization *(bodhicitta)* even as they listened to him preach:

> Friends, you have all been able to come here so that you can all generate the unsurpassable *bodhicitta*. It is extremely difficult to encounter the Buddhas, Bodhisattvas, and true spiritual compatriots. Today you are going to hear something you've never heard before. In the past you never encountered it, but today you have.
>
> The *Nirvāṇa Sūtra* says, "The Buddha asked Kāśyapa, 'Would it be difficult to throw a mustard seed down from Tuṣita Heaven and hit the point of a needle on the earth below?' Bodhisattva Kāśyapa replied, 'It would be extremely difficult, World-honored One.' The Buddha told Kāśyapa, 'This is not difficult. For the correct cause and the correct condition to meet—this is what is difficult!'"

What are the correct cause and the correct condition? Friends, your generation of the unsurpassable *bodhicitta* constitutes the correct cause. For the Buddhas, Bodhisattvas, and true spiritual compatriots to cast this unsurpassable *bodhicitta* into your minds such that you achieve the ultimate emancipation constitutes the correct condition. For the two to meet is excellent. . . . You must each and every one of you generate *bodhicitta!* . . .

Since you have already come to this ordination platform to study the perfection of wisdom, I want each and every one of you to generate the unsurpassable *bodhicitta* both mentally and orally and to become enlightened to the cardinal meaning of the middle way in this very place![18]

One modern Chinese commentator makes much of Shenhui's creation of "a new kind of Ch'an that was no *ch'an* at all," by which he means a new approach to Buddhism that omitted the practice of meditation.[19] But the reason the practice of meditation is so strikingly absent from Shenhui's writings is not that meditation was no longer to be included in the Chan training regimen, but because Shenhui's personal religious vocation was that of an evangelist, recruiter, and fund-raiser, rather than that of a spiritual mentor to dedicated trainees. This is not a reflection of Chan monastic behavior in general, but of Shenhui's distinctive religious identity.

We have no evidence that Shenhui ever concerned himself with the ongoing endeavor of spiritual cultivation, and his lineage was not notably long-lasting. Although the names of a few of his immediate students are known, none of them was historically significant. Even his most famous successors in subsequent generations seem not to have been descended from him, but rather from another monk by the same name. (This is a good example of the second rule of Zen studies: "Lineage assertions are as wrong as they are strong.") The reasons for Shenhui's very substantial impact on the evolution of Chan must be sought elsewhere.

The Oxhead School: Resolving the Factionalist Crisis

Shenhui's attack on Shenxiu's students created a crisis in early Chan, by creating a sharp dichotomy between two newly defined factions, the Northern and Southern schools. This crisis was resolved by the appearance of a third faction, the Oxhead school, and the composition of the *Platform Sūtra*. Shenhui's waspish criticism of other contemporary monks by name was unprecedented, and it stigmatized him even as many of his positions were accepted. His caricature of "Northern school" teachings as gradualist may not have been accepted by everyone, but since the "Northern school" was an artificial creation of Shenhui's imagination, very little energy was expended in defending it. Shenhui's simple value structure, in which sudden enlightenment (especially the first moment of inspiration) was good and gradual enlightenment (or the progressive development toward complete understanding) was bad, was not accepted, but his combative bombast did make everyone else shy away from formulations that might be attacked as either dualistic or gradualist. Hence subsequent Chan texts observed an unspoken "rule of rhetorical purity," avoiding any direct discussion of specific meditation practices—since *any* method was by definition gradualistic in some fashion.

In addition, in the records of the latter decades of the eighth century we find a number of attempts to erase the sharp distinction between north and south, gradual and sudden.[20] Below are a few examples.

First, here is "Eulogy on the Two Patriarchs Huineng and Shenxiu," by the poet-monk Jiaoran:

> The minds of these two men
> were like the moon and sun.
> With no clouds in the four directions,
> they appear in space.
>
> The Three Vehicles share the same path;
> the myriad teachings are one.
> The "division into Northern and Southern schools"
> is an error of speech.

Jiaoran has eulogies to Bodhidharma, Zhiyi (founder of the Tiantai school), the "Northern school" monks Lao'an (d. 708) and Puji, Huineng and Shenxiu, the legendary Baozhi (418?–514?), Shenxiu (individually), and Xuansu (688–752) of the Oxhead school—but none that is dedicated to Huineng individually.

Next, the famous poet Liu Zongyuan's (773–819) epitaph for an Oxhead school monk contains the following:

> The greatest aberration in the diminution of the Buddhist teaching is the term "Chan": Grasping, it defiles things; misleading, it becomes separate from the truth. This separation from the truth and increase of deception is greater than the [entire realm of] space of both present and past. Such stupid errors and deluded self-indulgence only debase oneself, misrepresent Chan [here meaning *dhyāna?*], and do injury to the Buddhist teaching. Those who make this error are characterized by stupidity and moral dissolution. . . . [Master Ruhai (the subject of the epitaph)] has said. . . . [After the transmission reached]

Shenxiu and Huineng, north and south reviled each other like fighting tigers, shoulder-to-shoulder, and the Way became hidden.

Finally, here is a statement by an important Oxhead school figure:

A lay supporter asked: "Are you a follower of the Southern school or the Northern school?" He answered: "I do not belong to either the Southern school or the Northern school. The mind is my school."[21]

So what was the impact of this "Oxhead school"? It arose in the latter half of the eighth century, among monks renowned for their literary creativity who felt a deep connection with the Chan tradition. As a lineage, it defined itself separately from either the Northern or Southern schools, but at least some of its members were enchanted by the image of Huineng, the figure promoted by Shenhui as sixth patriarch. The earliest version of the *Platform Sūtra,* which dates from around 780, makes effective use of Oxhead school ideas in producing a narrative framework for the understanding of Chan (see p. 65 below).

The Oxhead school did not merely soften the edges of contention between the Northern and Southern schools, it created new rhetorical devices by which to overcome the agonizing division that Shenhui had generated. The philosophy that underlay these efforts is demonstrated in the following passage, which is from the *Treatise on the Transcendence of Cognition (Jueguan lun).* This imaginative text is presented as a dialogue between an idealized teacher called Professor Enlightenment and his student, Conditionality. The result is the most meaningful sort of fiction, in which is depicted the spiritual dialogue between master and student that leads to the latter's awakening:

Professor Enlightenment was silent and said nothing. Conditionality then rose suddenly and asked Professor Enlightenment: "What is the mind? What is it to pacify the mind?" [The master] answered: "You should not posit a mind, nor should you attempt to pacify it—this is called 'pacified.'"

Question: "If there is no mind, how can one cultivate enlightenment *(dao)*?"[22] Answer: "Enlightenment is not a thought of the mind, so how could it occur in the mind?" Question: "If it is not thought of by the mind, how should it be thought of?" Answer: "If there are thoughts then there is mind, and for there to be mind is contrary to enlightenment. If there is no thought then there is no mind, and for there to be no mind is true enlightenment." . . . Question: "What 'things' are there in no-mind?" Answer: "No-mind is without 'things.' The absence of things is the Naturally True. The Naturally True is the Great Enlightenment *(dadao).*" . . .

Question: "What should I do?" Answer: "You should do nothing." Question: "I understand this teaching now even less than before." Answer: "There truly is no understanding of the Dharma. Do not seek to understand it." . . . Question: "Who teaches these words?" Answer: "It is as I have been asked." Question: "What does it mean to say that it is as you have been asked?" Answer: "If you contemplate [your own] questions, the answers will be understood [thereby] as well."

At this Conditionality was silent, and he thought everything through once again. Professor Enlightenment asked: "Why do you not say anything?" Conditionality answered: "I do not perceive even the most minute bit of anything that can be explained." At this point Professor Enlightenment said to Conditionality: "You would appear to have now perceived the True Principle."

Conditionality asked: "Why [do you say] 'would appear to have perceived' and not that I 'correctly perceived' [the True Principle]?" Enlightenment answered: "What you have now perceived is the nonexistence of all dharmas. This is like the non-Buddhists who study how to make themselves invisible, but cannot destroy their shadow and footprints." Conditionality asked: "How can one destroy both form and shadow?" Enlightenment answered: "Being fundamentally without mind and its sensory realms, you must not willfully generate the perception of impermanence."

∎

Question: "If one becomes [a Tathāgata] without transformation and in one's own body, how could it be called difficult?" Answer: "Willfully activating the mind is easy; extinguishing the mind is difficult. It is easy to affirm the body, but difficult to negate it. It is easy to act, but difficult to be without action. Therefore, understand that the mysterious achievement is difficult to attain, it is difficult to gain union with the Wondrous Principle. Motionless is the True, which the three [lesser vehicles] only rarely attain."[?]

At this Conditionality gave a long sigh, his voice filling the ten directions. Suddenly, soundlessly, he experienced a great expansive enlightenment. The mysterious brilliance of his pure wisdom [revealed] no doubt in its counter-illumination. For the first time he realized the extreme difficulty of spiritual training and that he had been uselessly beset with illusory worries. He then sighed aloud: "Excellent! Just as you have taught without teaching, so have I heard without hearing . . ."[23]

This text is significant for at least two reasons. First, and most important, it depicts the interaction between teacher and student as the latter begins the quest, attains an intermediate realization that is momentarily mistaken for the goal, and then achieves final enlightenment. This is only one of a number of texts from the latter half of the eighth century that are devoted to explicitly fictional depictions—that is, dramatic scriptings—of this process. It was not yet conceivable that written texts should include the words of actual, historical students. This observation is relevant to the emergence of written transcriptions of Chan "encounter dialogue," and we return to this point in the next chapter.

Second, we should pay attention to the threefold structure of this passage. In contrast to Shenhui's simple, dualistic value system of gradual vs. sudden, here there is a threefold pattern of beginning questions, intermediate hesitation, and final achievement. A close examination of Oxhead school writings suggests that their teachings were frequently written using a threefold logical format, which resembles Zhiyi's scheme of the three truths of absolute, relative, and middle.[24] It is also structurally similar to Hegel's thesis-antithesis-synthesis pattern, but in this case the second element achieves its impact by the application of the fundamental Mahāyāna concept of *śūnyatā,* or emptiness. Indeed, the same tripartite structure is apparent in the thought of at least one important Indian Mādhyamika philosopher.[25] That is, an expression of Buddhism is made in the first element, the terms of this expression are erased in the second element, and the understanding of Buddhism is thereby elevated to a new level of profundity in the third element. The significance of this pattern will only become clear when we examine the greatest masterpiece of early Chinese Chan Buddhism, the *Platform Sūtra.*

The *Platform Sūtra* as the Climax Text of Early Chan

The *Platform Sūtra* appeared in about 780, over a century after the events it describes were supposed to have taken place. Many scholars have struggled to identify the contents of some "original" or "core" version of the text that might date back to Huineng himself, but the utter failure of these attempts has only confirmed the late provenance of the text as we have it. Barring some miraculous discovery, we must consider the text as we first discover it, in its Dunhuang version. But we really should be satisfied with this, for this earliest version of the text is a brilliant consummation of early Chan, a masterpiece that created a new understanding of the past even as it pointed the way to a new style of Chan practice.

The heart of the *Platform Sūtra* is the following story.[26]

Since he was approaching the end of his years, the Fifth Patriarch Hongren instructed all his disciples to compose a "mind-verse" demonstrating their levels of enlightenment. If one of these verses manifested a true understanding of Buddhism, its author would receive the Fifth Patriarch's robe and the status of Sixth Patriarch. All but one of the disciples simply ignored Hongren's instructions, deferring instead to the man they felt would be the next leader of the Chan community: Shenxiu. Shenxiu himself was perturbed by his teacher's request, though, and thought to himself,

> The others won't present mind-verses because I am their teacher. If I don't offer a mind-verse, how can the Fifth Patriarch estimate the degree of understanding within my mind? If I offer my mind to the Fifth Patriarch with the intention of gaining the Dharma, it is justifiable; however, if I am seeking the patriarchship, then it cannot be justified. That would be like a common man usurping the saintly position. But if I don't offer my mind then I cannot learn the Dharma.

In the end Shenxiu did compose a verse, but he was so uncertain about its worth and the propriety of seeking the patriarchship that he inscribed it anonymously on a wall in one of the monastery's corridors, doing so late at night so that no one would see him. Shenxiu's verse read:

> The body is the *bodhi* tree.
> The mind is like a bright mirror's stand.
> At all times we must strive to polish it
> and must not let dust collect.

When Hongren saw this verse on the corridor wall the next morning, he canceled plans to have illustrations from the *Laṅkāvatāra Sūtra* painted there. He praised Shenxiu's verse highly and ordered his students to recite it so as to avoid unfavorable future rebirths. In private, though, he pointed out to Shenxiu that it did not display true understanding, and he counseled his senior disciple to write another verse to gain the Dharma. In the end, Shenxiu was unable to do so.

In the meantime, an uneducated layman from the far south of China named Huineng was at work threshing rice, completely unaware of Hongren's instructions about the future succession. When one day an acolyte passed by the threshing room reciting Shenxiu's verse, Huineng realized immediately that its author did not understand the "cardinal meaning" of Buddhism. The boy explained the matter to Huineng, who asked to be shown the corridor wall on which the verse was inscribed. Since he was illiterate, Huineng requested that someone else record his poetic statement.

Actually, the earliest version of the *Platform Sūtra* contains two versions of Huineng's verse:

> *Bodhi* originally has no tree. The mind is the *bodhi* tree.
> The mirror also has no stand. The body is the bright mirror's stand.
> The Buddha-nature is The bright mirror is

| always clear and pure. | originally clear and pure. |
| Where is there room for dust? | Where could there be any dust? |

Clearly, the editor could not decide which was better! In later versions, this indelicacy is cleared away, and a famous third line is added:

Bodhi originally has no tree.
The bright mirror also has no stand.
Fundamentally there is not a single thing.
Where could dust arise?

According to the basic Dunhuang account, Hongren denigrated Huineng's verse in public, but late that night he privately taught the layman the ultimate teaching of the *Diamond Sūtra*. Huineng was immediately awakened to its profound meaning, received the transmission of the sudden teaching and the Fifth Patriarch's robe, and left the monastery in secrecy that very night.

This is one of the most treasured legends of the Chan tradition. I have introduced only the bare essentials of the story, but even with this minimal detail we can see a number of ways in which the *Platform Sūtra* was producing a new historical account of the evolution of Chan, even as it implied a new religious vision.

First, in some of its details the *Platform Sūtra* account is clearly written as historical allegory. Note, for example, the shift from *Laṅkāvatāra Sūtra* to *Diamond Sūtra* implied in the account (i.e., in the cancellation of the painting commission and Hongren's teaching to Huineng), which parallels the two texts' changes in popularity over the course of the eighth century. The position of the *Laṅkāvatāra* within Chan was always ambiguous, since the text was more revered in the abstract than actually studied. However, it was generally associated with "Northern school" teachers. Shenhui was one of the first monks of his day, but by no means the only one, to favor the *Diamond,* which was becoming more widely popular throughout the Chinese tradition at the time. Hence, in the *Platform Sūtra* the two texts roughly symbolize the Northern and Southern schools. Also, Shenxiu's prominence within Hongren's community and Huineng's inferior status may be taken as indications of the relative strengths of the two factions prior to the composition of the *Platform Sūtra*. In a biography written at about the same time as this text, and in later versions of the *Platform Sūtra* itself, Huineng is depicted as remaining in hiding for sixteen years after receiving the transmission, a more graphic representation of the early weakness of the movement associated with his memory.

FIGURE 3. "Huineng's" verse from the *Platform Sūtra* on the back window of a taxicab, Tainan, Taiwan. Photograph by the author, 1996.

Second, the absence of any reference to Shenhui is significant. Shenhui's own texts never mention the "mind-verses" nor anything like the *Platform Sūtra* story, which is an important indication that the verses were composed after his death. At the very least, the verses could not have been written prior to Shenhui's vigorous campaign on behalf of Huineng as sixth patriarch, nor Shenhui's vigorous espousal of the teaching of sudden enlightenment. One of the most important features of the *Platform Sūtra,* in other words, is that it incorporates Shenhui's innovations while writing him out of the story. As mentioned above, even as Shenhui transformed the understanding of the evolution of Chan, the factionalist cast of his campaign stigmatized Shenhui himself.

But how should we understand the verses themselves? The traditional interpretation, since the time of the great systematic Chan and Huayan philosopher Zongmi (780–841), has been that Shenxiu's verse represents gradualism and Huineng's subitism (the position that enlightenment occurs in a single transformation that is both total and instantaneous). This simplistic explanation cannot be accepted. (Zongmi artificially claimed succession from Shenhui, but given the manifest difference between Shenhui's teachings and the *Platform Sūtra,* Zongmi's interpretation should be recognized as a tactical distortion of the original.) First, the verse attributed to Shenxiu does not in fact refer to gradual or progressive endeavor, but to a *constant* practice of cleaning the mirror. Hence, Zongmi's traditional interpretation is conceptually incorrect. Second, the verse attributed to Huineng could not stand alone (nor could any of the variants attributed to him), since it could not be understood without reference to "Shenxiu's" verse. Since the two verses constitute an indivisible pair—they indicate a single polarity, not two separate teachings—it is inappropriate to use either verse as a key to the religious teachings of the two historical individuals Shenxiu and Huineng.

And how are we to understand the equations made in "Shenxiu's" verse? Thinking of the body as the *bodhi* tree is easy enough, since both sides of the equation are comfortably physical; just as the *bodhi* tree was the location of Śākyamuni's enlightenment, so must the physical body be the site of enlightenment for each human being. But how can the mind be like a mirror's stand? Many English translations of "Shenxiu's" verse omit reference to the stand and say simply that "the mind is like a mirror," but this interpretation is simply erroneous.[27] The solution lies in the following passage from a treatise by Shenxiu:

> Further, lamps of eternal brightness (i.e., votive lamps) are none other than the truly enlightened mind. When one's wisdom is bright and distinct, it is likened to a lamp. For this reason, all those who seek emancipation always consider the body as the lamp's stand, the mind as the lamp's dish, and faith as the lamp's wick. The augmentation of moral discipline is taken as the addition of oil. For wisdom to be bright and penetrating is likened to the lamp's flame (or brightness). If one constantly burns such a lamp of truly suchlike true enlightenment, its illumination will destroy all the darkness of ignorance and stupidity.[28]

There is no specific evidence that the historical Shenxiu ever wrote anything like the verse attributed to him in the *Platform Sūtra,* or even that he made any metaphoric identification between mind and mirror's stand. However, it would have been entirely in character for him to have done so. If we were to speculate how he might have generated such a metaphor, we would presumably conclude that he would have used the logic introduced in this passage. That is, in his use of "skillful means" to interpret all the various elements of Buddhist scriptures as demonstrations of the "constant practice" of the "contemplation of the mind," Shenxiu might have posited the body as the overall setting for enlightenment (i.e., the *bodhi* tree), the sensory and intellectual activity of the mind as the proximate support for enlightenment (i.e., the mirror's stand), and the pure or enlightened mind itself as the illuminative surface of the mirror—and the act of rubbing the mirror clean of dust as a standard maintenance operation similar to maintenance of the Buddhist precepts or monastic regulations.[29] Based on the most comprehensive reading of the texts pertaining to Shenxiu, it is apparent that his basic message was that of the constant and perfect teaching, the endless personal manifestation of the bodhisattva ideal.

Even at a glance we can see that it makes more sense for the anonymous authors of the *Platform Sūtra* to depict Shenxiu's teachings as remarkably profound rather than as an elementary form of gradualism. Since the goal was to show the superiority of Huineng's teachings, the comparison should not be made with something recognizably inferior—as gradualism was considered at the time, especially in this post-Shenhui moment—but rather with something already recognized as superior in itself. If I were to propose a new theory of mathematics, for example, I would not compare it to elementary school arithmetic but to something far more sophisticated.

Huineng's verse(s) exhibit no explicit subitism, but only the reversal or denial of the terms of Shenxiu's verse. The two sets of verses do not, then, represent the alternatives of gradual and sudden, and they certainly do not represent the distinctive doctrines of two opposing lineages. If we compare this to the structure of the Oxhead school's depiction of the interchange between Professor Enlightenment and the student Conditionality, the parallel is clear: The *Platform Sūtra* uses the same threefold structure found in Oxhead-school thought. The constant teaching is first posited as the highest possible expression of the Buddhist teaching *in formal terms,* after which Huineng's verse(s) apply the rhetoric of emptiness to undercut the substantiality of the terms of that formulation. However, the basic meaning of the first proposition still remains, rather like a shadow whose sharp outlines have been removed by the impact of the second proposition. The third and final proposition thus includes both the assumption of the first and the erasure of the second, now shorn of its oversharp outline. In the *Platform Sūtra* this third proposition is implicit in the balance of the text, which contains the expression of the ultimate teaching of Buddhism in ways that do not contravene the "rule of rhetorical purity."

Although somewhat disjointed, the balance of Huineng's sermon in the *Platform Sūtra* is a wonderful mélange of early Chan teachings, a virtual repository of the entire tradition up to the second half of the eighth century. At the heart of the sermon is the same understanding of the Buddha-nature that we have seen in texts attributed to Bodhidharma and Hong-ren, including the idea that the fundamental Buddha-nature is *only* made invisible to ordinary humans by their illusions. There are clear borrow-ings from Shenhui's criticisms of "Northern school" meditation practices, as well as his doctrine of the identity of concentration and wisdom. The Huineng of this text is conscious of Shenhui's proscriptions against du-alistic formulations, and he warns repeatedly that the difference between sudden and gradual lies only in the aptitude of the practitioner. For all this, the sermon as a whole establishes a posture toward the actual prac-tice of meditation that differs from that of Shenhui, and the entire mood of the *Platform Sūtra* regarding the gradual/sudden distinction is not Shenhui's straightforward polemic of inferior vs. superior, but rather a nuanced attempt to describe a notoriously refractory subject, that is, the basic attitude that should be adopted toward Buddhist spiritual cultiva-tion. In addition, the text clearly admits laypeople to full participation in this process, something that the monastic recruiter and fund-raiser Shenhui never did. (For him laypeople were potential converts to the monastic life or, in some cases, prominent scholar-officials who lent pres-tige to his activities.) The *Platform Sūtra* inherits the style of reinterpret-ing conventional Buddhist pronouncements as meditation instructions that had been originally developed by Shenxiu and that was maintained to some extent by Shenhui and to an even greater degree by the Oxhead school.[30]

The sermon Huineng is depicted as delivering in the *Platform Sūtra* has been subjected to various interpretations, and it is worthy of far more extended attention than I can give it here. For the present, we need only notice the open quality of the text. That is, even though this famous scrip-ture serves to cap a certain line of development within the Chan tradi-tion, it does not close off further doctrinal evolution. Indeed, the text it-self was frequently updated in the ensuing centuries, implying that in some sense the devotees of Chinese Chan took some time to become satisfied with the *Platform Sūtra's* presentation of the teaching. (In the future, scholars may be able to explore the accretions to and modifications of this text as something of an index to the evolution of Chan.) However, there is also a sense in which the subsequent evolution of Chan passed the *Plat-form Sūtra* by; that is, the text helped set the stage for the emergence of encounter dialogue as a mode of spiritual cultivation, but it represents more the grand culmination of one era than a scripture for all seasons. The *Platform Sūtra* has enjoyed great attention in the twentieth century because of the Dunhuang manuscript finds, and it is now extremely popular in Chan and Zen communities around the world. We need to remember, though, that it was not nearly so widely used during the Song dynasty in China or during the Kamakura period in Japan.[31]

But there is still more to say about the opening *Platform Sūtra* anecdote itself. The reader might wonder, for example, whether there is any possibility that the events described might have actually happened. Here we can be definitive: there is no such possibility whatsoever, and the account must be accepted as a brilliant and religiously meaningful bit of fiction. How is it possible to be so certain? First of all, Shenxiu studied with Hongren for a few years at the very beginning of the latter's teaching career, so he was nowhere in sight when the events in question are supposed to have occurred. Second, the very notion of selecting an individual successor to serve as "sixth patriarch" would have been inconceivable in the latter years of Hongren's life, since the concept of a Chan "monosuccession"—that there was one and only one orthodox succession of patriarchs—appeared only later, in the teachings of Shenhui.[32] Third, if the matter had been known to Shenhui, who was a master storyteller dedicated to promoting Huineng's identity as sixth patriarch, he certainly would have included it in his writings. We have good evidence to show that in the late 730s Shenhui was ignorant of most of the details of Huineng's life. It is probable, but by no means certain, that Shenhui only thought to contribute to the embellishment of Huineng's life quite late in his own career.[33]

There are also indications that the *Platform Sūtra* verses—*both* those attributed to Shenxiu and to Huineng—were generated utilizing "Northern school" rather than "Southern school" writings. We have already seen references to the "path of *bodhi*" and the body's serenity as the *bodhi* tree in "Northern school" writings above (see p. 53), as well as allusions to not seeing "a single thing." In this context it is significant that a Dunhuang manuscript containing numerous metaphors in the manner of the "Northern school" contains the line "within suchness there originally is really not a single thing." The Chinese for this line is similar to the famous later third line of Shenxiu's *Platform Sūtra* verse, implying that the scripture was modified on the basis of ideas originally transmitted in a "Northern school" style or context. Since "Northern school" refers to a sizeable movement associated with literate court society and Buddhism, while the "Southern school" of Shenhui and Huineng was a minor voice from the provinces to the east and far south, it should not be too surprising that the invention of a tradition associated with the latter used resources derived from the former.[34]

Huineng as Illiterate Sage and the Evolution of Chan

Finally, let us briefly examine the legendary identity of Huineng himself, since it is through this image rather than through doctrines per se that the primary impact of the *Platform Sūtra* was felt.

The historical Huineng seems to have been a member in good standing of that loose confraternity of teachers we have referred to above as the Northern school. That is, his name is mentioned in one of the early eighth-century "transmission of the lamp" texts as one of Hongren's ten major disciples—although one of only regional significance, since he lived in Caoqi in the far south of China. Huineng's name appears one other time in a Dunhuang text dedicated to the memory of Hongren, where, along with other figures, he is briefly quoted in a manner that says nothing about any particular ideas that might have been associated with the historical Huineng. We are told elsewhere that after Huineng's death his residence was converted into a temple, and if this were true, his family must have had a certain degree of local prominence. It is striking, even stunning, how little Shenhui knows about the person who is supposed to be his own master, and it seems that Shenhui may have actually gained rather little more from Huineng than the certification of his own enlightenment. (Here, of course, we can draw a comparison with Huike and Bodhidharma.) It is probably fair to think of the historical Huineng as a reasonably conventional Chinese monk, whose teachings differed only slightly if at all from those of other members of the Northern school.

In contrast to the image just described, the legendary Huineng depicted in the *Platform Sūtra* is an illiterate layman from the far south, whose family had been reduced to such poverty that he had been making his living gathering and selling firewood. Although humble of origin, this Huineng is blessed with the highest of all Chinese moral qualities: he is a filial son taking care of his widowed mother. This image of the humble, unassuming paragon is clearly developed from the hagiography previously associated with Hongren, who was supposed to have sat in meditation by day and minded the cattle at night. In all these qualities, Huineng is the very antithesis of the highly cultured and socially advantaged monks who dominated the Chinese Buddhist *saṅgha* at the time. Shenxiu was in fact one of the prime examples of this type of individual—well educated in both Buddhist and secular literature, from a highly ranked family and perhaps even related to the imperial house, and thus used to the world of social and economic privilege. In this sense the contrast between the historical Shenxiu and the legendary Huineng could not be greater.[35]

But the image of Huineng is only apparently iconoclastic, only superficially populist. In terms of the developing Chan genealogical theory, the goal of his depiction in the *Platform Sūtra* is to show that anyone— even someone so clearly lacking in all the usual qualifications of an elite Chinese Buddhist monk—could be appointed as sixth patriarch as long as he fulfilled the only qualification that really mattered. That is, the particulars were negotiable as long as it could be argued that he was innately enlightened. The story is designed to say that the Chan school would go to any lengths to nominate anyone who fulfilled this one crucial prerequisite, and that as an institution it was unconcerned about anything else whatsoever. On the surface, this seems to make the patriarchate accessible to anyone.

To be sure, there is a universalist aspect to the *Platform Sūtra* account, in its implication that anyone can become enlightened regardless of educational or social background. But in terms of the Chan lineage itself, there was a paradoxical implication. Just as the Chan school would go to any length to find the right appointee, even if he lacked all the "right" social qualities, conversely, one implication of the *Platform Sūtra* story is that each person the Chan school later selected as a lineal successor to its enlightened masters was similarly qualified as an enlightened individual, even though it might seem that considerations of social status, family connection, and other worldly qualities played a role in the selection. Thus a brilliant iconoclastic form can actually serve to maintain a socially conservative orthodoxy.[36] There is no explicit evidence that this paradox was on the minds of the compilers of the *Platform Sūtra*, of course, nor even that it was obvious to the readers of the text. The logic involved here becomes important when we consider the paradoxical role of iconoclasm in Song-dynasty Chan discourse, where it is used within a highly ritualized formal setting. We also need to look at how the imagery of the illiterate sage found in the *Platform Sūtra* resonated through the encounter dialogue anecdotes of the so-called "classical" stage of Chinese Chan. Before proceeding to these issues, however, we should briefly consider certain issues of historical context.

Three Other Sets of Events

Although this book focuses on Chan, we must remember that this one school of Chinese Buddhism did not develop in a vacuum. There are at least three major events, or rather sets of events, that occurred in the eighth century that significantly altered the evolution of Chan.

The first set of events was the appearance of esoteric Buddhism on the

Chinese scene. Although writers who focus myopically on the Chan tradition imply that the Southern school supplanted the Northern school solely through the superiority of its sudden teaching, the attention of the imperial court and metropolitan literati had already been diverted from Chan long before the distinction between the Northern and Southern schools was posited. Śubhākarasiṃha (637–735) arrived in Chang'an in 716 and immediately began to excite the Chinese with a new interpretation of Buddhism that promised both rapid spiritual attainment and unparalleled worldly power. On his heels came Vajrabodhi (671–741), who arrived in Guangzhou (Canton) in 720, and Amoghavajra (705–74), who became a disciple of Vajrabodhi's at age fifteen in China, traveled to India after his master's death, and returned to China in 746. Along with the native exegete Yixing (683–727), a former Northern school monk and protoscientist who collaborated in the translation and teaching work of Śubhākarasiṃha and Vajrabodhi, these men dominated the Buddhist scene in Chang'an and Luoyang throughout most of the eighth century. Here was a religious teaching that allowed one to ally oneself with the greatest spiritual powers of the universe, both for one's own spiritual advancement and for maximum ritual efficacy in worldly affairs, including healing illness, bringing rain or ending floods, and even causing victory on the battlefield. Using a unique combination of profound doctrine, visualization technique, and impressive ritual theater, esoteric Buddhism overwhelmed the Chinese—and indeed East Asian—religious consciousness.

As soon as esoteric Buddhist teachers appeared on the scene, competition for patronage between them and native Chan masters became inevitable. We have a lengthy description of an encounter between Śubhākarasiṃha and Jingxian (660–723), one of Shenxiu's students. What is most interesting about this encounter for our purposes is that the foreign master explicitly criticizes the Chan style of meditation practice, insisting that by "single-mindedly maintaining nonthought (wunian) as the ultimate, the [longer you] search, the more unattainable [is your goal]."[37] Although there are certain similarities between Chan and esoteric Buddhist practice (the importance of the relationship between Chan master and student resembles that between tantric guru and esoteric practitioner, for example), Chan had nothing to match the highly theatrical style and magnificent promise of esoteric ritual. One or two Chan masters were prominent at the imperial court in the last decades of the eighth century and beyond, but none of them attracted the faddish aura of excitement that had surrounded Shenxiu and other Northern school figures at the beginning of the century.[38]

The second set of events is a sequence of civil and political disasters that led to the collapse of the Tang dynasty itself, implying the destruction of what had been a supremely influential model for Buddhism throughout East Asia. The process began in 755–63, with a major rebellion instigated by a military governor in the far north, a man of Sogdian extraction named An Lushan (Roxanna in Sogdian). In most ignominious fashion, the emperor was forced to flee Chang'an, made to abdicate in favor of his son, and compelled to watch the execution of his favored concubine. (She and her brother, a notoriously corrupt official, were blamed by the emperor's military escort for allowing the catastrophe to occur.) After An Lushan's death the rebellion was carried forward by others, and it took some eight years for the Tang imperial government to reestablish itself. In the process, though, China was changed forever: regional governors were effectively given autonomy in many of the outlying regions; the imperial house remained in charge of only the central provinces. Changes in taxation and military conscription that began at this time signaled a major transformation of Chinese society as a whole.

The second event in this series was of course the great persecution of Buddhism by the Chinese government in the Huichang period, beginning in 845. Monastic assets were seized, monks and nuns were laicized, and great restrictions were placed on the activities of the church in general. Most introductions to Chinese Buddhism consider this persecution to have dealt the religion a crippling blow, but its effects were only temporary. The problem was that the Buddhist establishment was hardly given time to recover before the next disaster struck: This was the Huang Chao rebellion of 875–84, which devastated the provinces of northern China, effectively destroying the foundation of aristocratic family domination there, and eliminating the combined wealth of the social class from which Buddhism received its support.

The Tang state limped along for another couple of decades, but in 906 it finally collapsed entirely. The next half-century or so witnessed a succession of regimes that controlled different regions of northern and southern China. The Chinese polity would be reconstituted in 960 with the founding of the Song dynasty, but by then the world had changed forever.

The third set of events is the effective end of the translation of Buddhist scriptures from India and Central Asia. This was not an event that occurred instantaneously, and several different factors contributed to this final result. First, from some time in Amoghavajra's career, or perhaps only shortly thereafter, the only new texts being translated were esoteric ritual manuals. There were a handful of translators active throughout the ninth century, but nothing they produced became important for larger doctrinal or devotional reasons.[39] Second, from 810 on, the Tang imperial court divested itself of all involvement in Buddhist translation activities, ending a centuries-old tradition of central government sponsorship. The result was that from about this year until 980, no Buddhist scriptures were formally entered into the canon.[40] Third, in 1004—by coincidence the year in which the *Transmission of the Lamp* was presented to the Song court—Moslem forces conquered Khotan.[41] Buddhism had long been in decline in its heartland areas of India and Central Asia, and now the transmission of texts across the Silk Road was impossible. There was a flurry of activity in the last two decades of the tenth century, but even though the Song government established a central translation bureau, it soon became moribund.[42] The problem, simply enough, was that there were just no more new texts to work on. The influx of Buddhist ideas from the northwest ceased, and Chinese society became increasingly focused on mercantile activity among the coastal provinces, especially in the southeast.

Although Buddhist scriptural translation had generally been carried out in just a few imperial centers, and only occasionally in provincial cities and alpine retreats, still it would be difficult to overestimate the impact of this change. For centuries the Chinese Buddhist community as a whole had thrived on the constant appearance of new texts, new ideas, and new modes of religious praxis—and now all that simply stopped. It is not enough to point out that Chan's characteristic contrast with the "teachings"—as presented in phrases such as "a separate transmission outside the teachings" and the "unity of Chan and the teachings"—took advantage of this new weakness in its perceived counterpart. Along with the decline in Buddhist scholastic writing in general, there was a vacuum of leadership, a hollowness to the former rhetoric of monastic learning. It is significant that the slogans ranking Chan as an equivalent of the Buddhist doctrinal tradition became widely used just as the tradition of translation and doctrinal study was being profoundly undercut.

The emergence of Chan as the single most dominant Buddhist tradition in China came about, in effect, because it fit so well in the post-Tang world. Certain features of Chan—from the classical style of encounter dialogue to its characteristic institutional patterns—worked effectively within the China that was emerging out of the collapse of the Tang. The remaining chapters in this book are designed to explain what these features are and how this "fit" developed. In chapter 4 we explore the most characteristic element of the new Chan discourse, the distinctive style of spontaneous encounter dialogue between masters and disciples. In chapter 5 we examine how the new posture of Chan religious identity allowed the school's members to dominate the Chinese monastic institution from the tenth century onward. Finally, in chapter 6 we see how Chan was presented to its members and the public at the very pinnacle of its success in China, during the "climax paradigm" configuration of Chan that emerged during the Song dynasty.

CHAPTER 4

The Riddle of Encounter Dialogue

Who, What, When, and Where?

"Classical Chan" and Encounter Dialogue

Consider the following anecdotes:

> A monk asked Zhaozhou, "What was the patriarch's (i.e., Bodhidharma's) intention in coming from the west?" Zhaozhou said, "The cypress tree in the front garden."[1]

> ■

> A monk asked Zhaozhou, "Does a dog have the Buddha-nature?" Zhaozhou answered, "No."[2]

> ■

> A monk asked Dongshan, "What is 'Buddha'?" Dongshan replied, "Three pounds of hemp."[3]

Passages such as these should be readily identified by most readers as quintessentially Chan- or Zen-like. For decades, we have been offered such stories as the primary means by which Chan is presented. This is especially true in the writings of D. T. Suzuki, whose most cherished methodology seems to have been to describe some aspect of Zen as beyond ordinary explanation, then offer a suitably incomprehensible story or two by way of illustration. Obviously, Suzuki's approach captured the imaginations of generations of readers. However, while this approach substantiated Suzuki's authority as one with insider access to the profound truths of the tradition, another result was to increase the confusion in readers' minds. To question such accounts was to admit one did not "get it," to distance oneself even further from the goal of achieving what Suzuki termed the "Zen enlightenment experience."

Let us look at these stories, for the moment, as students of East Asian religious history rather than as prospective practitioners. From this perspective we can make a number of observations about them, none of which is individually very earth-shaking, but which, in sum, lead to some meaningful inferences about the Chan tradition. First, the stories involve figures who lived in the ninth century. (Zhaozhou's dates are 778[?]–897, and Dongshan's 807–69.) This is in part the result of my selection, since there exist numerous similar stories involving figures both before and after. However, in addition to keeping the selection of exchanges limited for simplicity, the choice of these particular anecdotes is based on the general recognition that a new style of dialogue emerged around the beginning of the ninth century. Second, each of the exchanges above involves a question by an anonymous monk and response by a known teacher. Actually, there are many similar dialogues in which the names of both participants are known, especially when the questioner went on to become a famous teacher himself. However, the genre of Chan literature from which these exchanges derive is notable for including, not only the doctrinal pronouncements of great teachers, but also the specific questions of individual students. Third, no contextual clues or stage settings are provided. Here again it would have been possible to choose anecdotes that contain some such information, but in general Chan dialogues of this genre are stated without much effort at contextualization. Our attention as readers is directed automatically at the broader religious implications of the exchanges, whatever they may be.

Fourth, most readers would probably add, the teachers' responses are nonsensical. This certainly seems to be the case for the first dialogue. That is, for a student to ask why the founding patriarch of Chan Buddhism, Bodhidharma, came from India to China was in effect to inquire whether Buddhism had not already existed in China before that date. Or, the purpose was to solicit the teacher's comment on the concept of the transmission of the Buddha-mind, which in standard Chan theory was recognized as a nontransmission. However, the issue of whether or not animals possessed the Buddha-nature, the potentiality or actual presence of enlightenment within the ordinary psychology of illusion, was in fact hotly debated in late-eighth- and ninth-century Chinese Buddhism. The selection of the single answer "no" for emphasis thus represents a collective choice by the members of the Chan tradition.[4] The answer to the third question above, about the meaning of the word "Buddha," has also generally been considered an example of the performative use of Chan illogicality, a nonsensical answer meant to knock the student off his accustomed spot and into a different realm of understanding. That this was the ultimate goal is not really in question, but the answer "three pounds of hemp" was not illogical at all in its original context, merely metaphoric: In the Tang dynasty this was the standard allotment of cloth for a set of monk's robes—a colloquial usage that was forgotten by the Song, leading to amusing errors by the Japanese Zen master Dōgen (1200–53) and others, who labored to explain Zhaozhou's apparent reference to "three pounds of sesame seeds"! In other words, when asked the meaning of the word "Buddha," Zhaozhou responded, more or less, "A set of monk's robes is all it takes."[5]

Thus, instead of inferring that the teachers' responses are all illogical, a better fourth observation would be that they are all performative utterances based on contemporary culture—"performative" in the sense of being designed to act as catalysts for the students' understanding. In the process of considering these anecdotes, though, we have entered into a new phase in our examination of the Chinese Chan tradition, one in which we must deploy analytical perspectives not required for the earlier phases of our inquiries. The key to understanding how our task has changed in this phase lies in the appreciation of the terms *classical Chan* and *encounter dialogue*.[6]

In contrast to *middle Chan*, which refers to a specific period of time, from the appearance of the *Platform Sūtra* in 780 to the beginning of the Song dynasty in 972, the term *classical Chan* refers first and foremost to a particular style of behavior displayed by Chan masters in the course of their interactions with students and other masters. Rather than explaining the Dharma in straightforward expository language, such masters are depicted as being more inclined to demonstrate it by means of paradoxical replies and inexplicable counterquestions, gestures and physical demonstrations, and even the shocking and painful tactics of shouts and blows. Precisely when this classical style of religious practice emerged is not clear. Thus to use the term *classical* in direct reference to events that took place during the middle period, that is, to conflate the two terms, would be to make a naive assumption about Chan history, to accept at face value stories such as those introduced above, which have been transmitted in texts of the Song dynasty. Here I will use *classical Chan* only in reference to the *image* of the activities of middle Chan figures as it occurs in the texts of Song-dynasty Chan—just as, with a different nuance, the term *Hīnayāna* is legitimately used when working solely within the context of Mahāyāna doctrine, but not in reference to actual Buddhists of either ancient India or modern Southeast Asia. The distinction may seem elusive at first, but it is important to remember that *classical Chan* refers not to a historical period but to an image seen through historical sources.

Curiously, no clearly stated definition of encounter dialogue appears in the scholarship on Chinese Chan. Part of the reason for this, no doubt, is that the very nature of the subject matter militates against concise definition. Not only is Chan encounter dialogue an unruly topic, difficult to characterize, but one of its primary features is the rejection of simplistic logic. Previous authors, especially those who cite excerpts from encounter dialogue most frequently in their explanations of Chan, have refrained from giving it any clear definition so as to avoid reducing it to a neat set of characterizations and forestall any potential criticism that they do not understand it.

Any working definition of Chan encounter dialogue must include three features. First, it consists of dialogue that occurs in texts identified as containing encounter dialogue, primarily "transmission of the lamp" texts and individual "recorded sayings" or "discourse records" texts. This feature of encounter dialogue is clearly circular in logical form, but it does represent how scholars—and members of the East Asian Chan/Sŏn/Zen/Thien traditions themselves—actually approach the subject. That is, the first step in the definition of encounter dialogue is the identification of a set of Chan texts in which it is found. As explained below, the manner in which encounter dialogue transcription appears in the written record has major implications for how we understand encounter dialogue itself.

Second, Chan encounter dialogue is presented as the written transcription of actual oral dialogues between historically identifiable teachers and students. This is not to say that every participant represented in the literature of encounter dialogue can be identified with full biographical information—far from it. Many of those involved are identified solely as anonymous students present in a given master's training community. In spite of this lack of detail, it is extremely important that the genre presents all such individuals as real and all encounters as having actually occurred.

I must emphasize that these qualities of apparent historical realism are literary effects, characteristics of the genre, and not facts about the dialogues and their participants. One of the ways encounter dialogue texts achieve these effects is through the use of vernacular speech, which gives the impression that the dialogues are presented in precisely the form in which they originally occurred. Whether or not the dialogues ever happened the way they are recorded is of course highly questionable. This is a subject to which we will return soon enough (see the discussion beginning on p. 83); at this point it is important to note that, for encounter dialogue texts as a genre of religious literature, it is of paramount importance that the participants and exchanges are represented as non-fictional realities.[7]

Third, Chan encounter dialogue eschews the straightforward exchange of ideas; it is characterized by various types of logical disjunctions, inexplicable and iconoclastic pronouncements, gestures and physical demonstrations, and even assaultive behavior such as shouts and blows with hand, foot, or stick. The best way to understand such features is as a function of the fundamental mismatch of intention between the students and masters as depicted in these texts. The students are generally depicted as requesting assistance in ascending the path of Buddhist spiritual training toward enlightenment. The masters, for their part, are represented as refusing to accede to their students' naive entreaties, instead deflecting their goal-seeking perspective and attempting to propel them into the realization of their own inherent perfection. This is an oversimplification, of course, and we find numerous cases of interactions that cannot be accommodated within this larger pattern. (It is difficult to define patterns in a genre dedicated to the transcendence of patterns!) Nevertheless, since our task is to understand encounter dialogue exchanges as a religious genre—and not to "solve" the riddles they present as religious practitioners ourselves—it is helpful to recognize this basic intellectual framework.

The encounter dialogue style of religious behavior is well-known in the literature on Chan and Zen in every language, since it is the primary feature of the archetypal image of the Zen master as depicted in both popular and scholarly literature. The central figures by whom this classical Chan is described may include those as early as Bodhidharma and Huineng, and often much later figures from both China and Japan as well, but invariably the focus is on the fabled great masters of the Tang: Mazu Daoyi, Shitou Xiqian, Nanquan Puyuan, Zhaozhou Congshen, and the incomparable paragon, Linji Yixuan.

The hallmark of classical Chan is thus the practice of encounter dialogue. Indeed, the two concepts are so thoroughly interconnected as to be virtually interchangeable: classical Chan refers to those masters who interacted with their students using encounter dialogue, and encounter dialogue is the unique style of interactive teaching utilized by classical Chan masters. It is thus both a natural and customary conclusion to conceive of classical Chan as a phenomenon or set of events occurring at a specific period in the evolution of the religion, lasting roughly from the last few decades of the eighth century until the middle of the tenth. More specifically, encounter dialogue is believed to have first been used by Mazu

Daoyi and his disciples—and this interpretation fits like a glove with Mazu's doctrine that all human actions, even those so seemingly trivial as the slightest movements of eye or hand, are the manifestation of the Buddha-nature:

> The arising of mental activity, the movement of thought, snapping the fingers or moving the eyes—all actions and activities are the functioning of the entire essence of the Buddha-nature. Since no other kind of functioning exists, greed, anger, and folly, the performance of good and bad actions, and the experiencing of their pleasurable and painful consequences are all, in their entirety, Buddha-nature . . . [8]

But the picture just described is too simple. One of the first hints of the complexities involved is that the written transcriptions of encounter dialogue do not appear until the compilation of the *Anthology of the Patriarchal Hall* in 952—around a century and a half after encounter dialogue was supposedly first practiced. This text enters the scene, in effect, as a sudden apparition. It is a massive treasure chest of Chan anecdote and repartée, a highly elaborated written demonstration of the Chan genealogical schema. The contents of the *Anthology of the Patriarchal Hall* are so rich and substantial that they imply a significant accumulation of tradition, and the easiest recourse would be to regard them as the straightforward documentation of classical Chan that they are claimed to be. This is certainly the manner in which the stories in the *Anthology,* or rather the variants in the far more popular—and effectively authoritative—*Record of the Transmission of the Lamp [Compiled in] the Jingde [Period]* of 1004, have been used within the meditation hall, from the premodern period down to the present.

The goal of this book, though, is different from that of the meditation hall. Here our purpose is to analyze Chan, not merely recapitulate its innovative style. This chapter on encounter dialogue is thus different from the two preceding ones, in that it does not treat a specific historical phase in the evolution of Chan, but discusses a component or dimension of Chan practice that was of crucial importance in several different periods. In the next chapter we return to questions of temporal development, so that through both chapters we will see, first, how encounter dialogue evolved and, second, how the image of the classical Chan masters of the Tang is the retrospective creation of several generations of their successors. This will help us recognize the point being emphasized here: that the classical style is not a temporally identifiable historical period of Tang-dynasty Chan, but an image that occurs within Five Dynasties and Song-dynasty texts, which was projected retrospectively by the Chan practitioners of those periods onto their predecessors. Even more significant, along the way we will learn how Chan encounter dialogue implies a paradigm of spiritual cultivation that is profoundly different from earlier Chinese Buddhist practice.

The Story of Mazu's Enlightenment

The following is the traditional account of Mazu Daoyi's enlightenment, drawn from the *Transmission of the Lamp* entry for Nanyue Huairang (677–744):

> During the Kaiyuan period (713–41) there was a monk Daoyi (this is Great Master Mazu), who resided at Transmission of the Dharma Chapel and spent all his time in seated meditation. Understanding him to be very capable, the master [i.e., Huairang] went to him and asked, "Great worthy, what are you trying to do by sitting in meditation?" Daoyi answered, "I am trying to achieve buddhahood." The master then picked up a piece of tile and started rubbing it on a rock in front of the chapel. Daoyi said, "Master, what are you doing?" The master said, "I'm grinding this into a mirror." Daoyi said, "How could you possibly make a mirror by grinding a tile?!" [Huairang replied], "And how could you achieve buddhahood by seated meditation?"
>
> Daoyi said, "How does one do it right?" The master said, "If you're riding a cart that isn't moving, is it right to hit the cart, or is it right to hit the ox?" Daoyi had no response.
>
> The master then said, "Are you training in seated meditation, or training in sitting as a Buddha? If you are training in seated meditation, then meditation is neither seated nor lying down. If you are training in sitting as a Buddha, then the Buddha is without fixed characteristic. You should neither grasp nor forsake the non-abiding Dharma. Your sitting as a Buddha is to kill the Buddha; if you are attached to the characteristic of sitting you have not penetrated the principle involved." When Daoyi heard this manifestation of the teaching he felt as if he had drunk ghee.[9]

This is an archetypal example of encounter dialogue. Mazu, the student, is trying to achieve enlightenment by his own meditative efforts. Rather than simply explain the problem to him, Huairang acts in a way that disturbs Mazu from his misdirected toils, then engages him in a dialogue that inspires the student to penetrate the ultimate paradox of his striving for an impossible goal. This redirection of Mazu's efforts is a direct result of his initial insight. If we imagine this as a primal moment of interaction between a great Chan master and his gifted student, the account can be truly inspirational.

But let's step back for a moment, and consider this account as text, as literary product. This is not to deny its value as religious instruction, but merely to look under the hood, as it were, and see how the engine works.

First, we should look at the earliest version of the anecdote, which occurs in the *Anthology of the Patriarchal Hall*:

> Reverend Ma was sitting in a spot, and Reverend Rang took a tile and sat on the rock facing him, rubbing it. Master Ma asked, "What are you doing?" Master [Huairang] said, "I'm rubbing the tile to make a mirror." Master Ma said, "How can you make a mirror by rubbing a tile?" Master [Huairang] said, "If I can't make a mirror by rubbing a tile, how can you achieve buddhahood by sitting in meditation?"[10]

Even in this shorter and more primitive account, we can clearly hear echoes of other legendary events in the meditation tradition. The first of these, of course, involves Vimalakīrti scolding Śāriputra for sitting in meditation in the forest. In the *Vimalakīrti Sūtra* Śāriputra recounts the experience to the Buddha as follows:

> I remember once in the past, when I was sitting in repose beneath a tree. At the time Vimalakīrti came and said to me, "O Śāriputra, you need not take this sitting [in meditation] to be sitting in repose. Sitting in repose constitutes not manifesting body and mind in the triple world—this is sitting in repose. To neither generate nor extinguish concentration while manifesting the deportments—this is sitting in repose. Not to relinquish the Dharma of enlightenment and yet manifest the affairs of [ordinary] sentient beings—this is sitting in repose. To have the mind neither abide internally nor locate itself externally—this is sitting in repose. To be unmoved by the [sixty-two mistaken] views yet cultivate the thirty-seven factors of enlightenment—this is sitting in repose. Not to eradicate the afflictions yet enter into *nirvāṇa*—this is sitting in repose. Those who are able to sit in this fashion will receive the Buddha's seal of approval." At the time, World-honored One, I simply listened to this explanation in silence and was unable to respond.[11]

And there is an implicit echo of the "mind-verses" of the *Platform Sūtra* as well. (See the anecdote beginning on p. 60 above.) "Shenxiu" and "Huineng" discoursed in verse on the subject of dust upon the mirror and whether or not one had to polish it clean, but in the Mazu account the subject matter is played out in action, with the focus not simply on cleaning some preexistent mirror but actually fabricating one out of impossibly inappropriate material.[12] In fact, the text that immediately follows the dialogue with Mazu in the *Anthology of the Patriarchal Hall* contains other references to the mirror, which implies some sort of unified editorial posture. In comparison to the version in the *Transmission of the Lamp*, though, this rendition is distinctly primitive: neither location nor time is specified, and there is no follow-up dialogue. All we have is the simple nucleus of the words, with no effort to establish the context. It is in fact the editorial policy of the *Anthology of the Patriarchal Hall* to require its readers (including teachers who lecture from it) to use their imaginations to provide their own context; in Marshall McLuhan's terms, this is a "hot medium," like radio, that makes readers or listeners actively imagine what is happening, rather than a "cold medium," like television, that gives viewers just enough sensory input to turn off their minds.[13]

This story is often cited as Mazu's enlightenment story, or at least to indicate his identity as Huairang's student, but although this earliest version includes several lines of subsequent dialogue between the two men, it does not explicitly make either of these claims. This story is also used as the justification for Mazu's traditional identification as Huairang's successor, with Huairang simultaneously understood as a successor to the Sixth Patriarch Huineng. However, when we look more closely at the available sources, we see that Mazu studied with other figures as well, and that Huairang's connection with certain Northern school figures is much more substantial than his problematic connection with Huineng.

In the case of Huairang, the little that is known about his biography definitely undermines the historicity of the filiation between him and Huineng. First, Huairang's epitaph was written in the year 815, some seventy years after his death, at the request of two of Mazu's disciples, so it can hardly be used to suggest that the connection between Huineng and Huairang was historical rather than legendary. In addition, the paucity of detail concerning Huairang's biography—he is said to have been a mountain practitioner who did not "open the Dharma" to others— suggests that he was historically insignificant. And, needless to say, nothing like the story introduced above occurs in the epitaph. In fact, the *Transmissions of Treasure Grove [Temple] (Baolin zhuan)*, the Hongzhou school's important contribution to the "transmission of the lamp" genre of Chan literature, written about 801, describes Huairang's enlightenment as having been gained under the guidance of the Northern school monk Lao'an. Actually, none of the men traditionally recognized as Huineng's most important successors—Huairang, Qingyuan, Yongjia Xuanjue, and Nanyang Huizhong—are mentioned in the Dunhuang version of the *Platform Sūtra*.

And Huairang was hardly Mazu's only religious influence.[14] He became a monk under a second-generation successor to Hongren named Chuji (also known as Reverend Tang; 648–734, 650–732, or 669–736) of

Sichuan. Mazu was probably also acquainted with a charismatic Korean monk named Musang (Chinese: Wuxiang; also known as Reverend Kim [Chinese: Jin]; 684–762). And, when Mazu left Sichuan about 735, he traveled to Jingzhou, where he practiced meditation before going to Nanyue. We could of course try to track down the religious identities and probable teachings of all these men, but to do so would only complicate the picture even further. Ultimately, our main conclusion would be that Mazu had a typically variegated life of religious training, so that even if the interaction between Huairang and Mazu was historical in some sense—and it would be rash to deny this possibility out of hand—this would not be enough to make Mazu Huairang's successor, let alone a direct second-generation successor to Huineng.

The point to be made here is that, from whatever may have happened during Mazu's religious training, from some unknown point in time the Chan community developed this image of an encounter between him and Huairang. Whatever did or did not happen, the news of that encounter was dramatized and circulated in oral and/or written form. What we have in the *Anthology of the Patriarchal Hall* is something like the core of the story, with the reader, listener—or perhaps the teacher—left to supply the details. As Timothy Barrett has suggested, this process of editorial evolution resembles nothing so much as the circulation of joke books at roughly the same time.[15] As with the formulaic notation of the *Five Skillful Means,* which seems to have provided the liturgical skeleton on which Northern school teachers could superimpose their own flourishes and interpretations, the written transcriptions of Chan encounter dialogue were prepared as skeletal notations upon which teachers and students could improvise. The emergence of this genre of literature, though, required a shared conception of Buddhist spiritual practice, some of whose elements we have seen in the preceding pages.

The Eightfold Path to the Emergence of Transcribed Encounter Dialogue

Mazu's Hongzhou school displays an interesting pattern of geographical and stylistic growth, and I take up those matters in the next chapter. Here I want to present what we know about the background and historical emergence of encounter dialogue as a rhetorical pattern of Chan practice. I avoid considering doctrinal issues, such as the concepts of *śūnyatā, prajñā,* the impact of Mādhyamika dialectic, and so on; these general background conditions to the emergence of Chan encounter dialogue have been discussed widely in previous writings. Nor do I consider more distant background elements within Chinese culture, in particular the frequent use of the dialogic mode of exposition from Confucius and Zhuangzi onward.[16] There can be no doubt that Chan dialogue reverberates with the rhetorical wit and humanistic perspective (or, rather, the rejection of all fixed perspectives) personified so exquisitely in the *Zhuangzi*. Indeed, these features and the notion of a style of virtuosic concentration on the activity at hand represent the primary legacy Chan inherited from the native tradition of philosophical Daoism. However, the simple fact of that inheritance is not sufficient to explain why Chan encounter dialogue emerged when it did, more than a millennium after the *Zhuangzi,* and in a social environment that did not even exist in Zhuangzi's day, the Chinese Buddhist monastic community.

Instead, I suggest below that Chan had to develop a rationale for *socially oriented* practice prior to, or perhaps simultaneously with, the perfection of oral dialogue techniques. The following is a set of characteristics by which the social dimensions of this new type of religious interaction may be understood. The following enumeration must still be considered a provisional explanation; obviously, none of these characteristics is shared throughout the entire early Chan movement, and there are almost certainly others not yet identified.[17]

THE IMAGE OF THE CHAN MASTER
RESPONDING SPONTANEOUSLY TO HIS STUDENTS

Early Chan teachers are frequently described as having special abilities of teaching, which they exercised in an unstructured moment-to-moment manner. Some of the earliest known expressions concern Hongren, the central figure of the East Mountain teaching and so-called fifth patriarch. Hongren forms the original nucleus of the hagiographical persona of the unlettered sage, in being described as spending his days in meditation and his nights tending the monastery cattle. As soon as he was appointed successor to Daoxin, the previously silent Hongren was immediately able to understand the problems of his students and teach them with a fluid, spontaneous style that combined an appreciation of the ultimate truth with complete expertise in the expediencies of religious practice.[18] Faru, who was unique among Hongren's students for spending so many years with the master, is described as having unique abilities in his interactions with his students, so that he could remonstrate with them strongly without incurring resentment: his anger is described as being like two empty boats hitting each other in the middle of a lake, which would make a hollow sound signifying an absence of attachment or resistance. Several members of the Northern school were also the subjects of anecdotes depicting their occult charisma,[19] although the primary examples of this religious type are of course Bodhidharma and Huineng. Huineng in particular—as depicted in various works, not just the Dunhuang version of the *Platform Sūtra*—is a figure who responds to situations with remarkable élan and spiritual brilliance, making mysteriously profound pronouncements and posing miraculous challenges to individual seekers. In spite of the fact that he is supposedly quite untutored in the literary arts, he also composes insightful poetry. In all these cases, Huineng is represented as enlightened, not by any doctrine he pronounces or essay he produces, but rather in his interactions with the figures around him.

"QUESTIONS ABOUT THINGS" IN THE NORTHERN SCHOOL

How did early Chan teachers interact with their students? The hagiographical images of Hongren and Huineng are not our only clues: we do not know how the students responded, but at least we have some evidence for the types of questions early Chan masters placed before them.

An important early-eighth-century "transmission of the lamp" text generated by the Northern school, the *Record of the Masters and Disciples of the Laṅkāvatāra,* contains an intriguing set of rhetorical questions and short doctrinal admonitions, which it refers to as "questions about things" (literally, "pointing at things and asking the meanings").[20] Such questions and admonitions are attributed to several of the early masters, as shown in the following examples.

> The Great Master Bodhidharma also pointed at things and inquired of their meaning, simply pointing at a thing and calling out: "What is that?" He asked about a number of things, switching their names around and asking about them again differently.
>
> He would also say: "Clouds and mists in the sky are never able to defile space. However, they can shade space so that the sun cannot become bright and pure. . . ."

■

> The Great Master Hongren said: "There is a single little house filled with crap and weeds and dirt—what is it?"
>
> He also said: "If you sweep out all the crap and weeds and dirt and clean it all up so there is not a single thing left inside, then what is it?" . . .
>
> Also, when he saw someone light a lamp or perform any ordinary activity,

he would always say: "Is this person dreaming or under a spell?" Or he would say: "Not making and not doing, these things are all the great *parinirvāṇa*."

He also said: "When you are actually sitting in meditation inside the monastery, is there another of you sitting in meditation in the forest? Can all the mud, wood, tiles, and rocks also sit in meditation? Can mud, wood, tiles, and rocks also see forms and hear sounds, or put on robes and carry a begging bowl?"

■

Shenxiu also said: "Is this a mind that exists? What kind of mind is the mind?"

He also said: "When you see form, does form exist? What kind of form is form?"

He also said: "You hear the sound of a bell that is struck. Does the sound exist when the bell is struck? Before it is struck? What kind of sound is sound?"

He also said: "Does the sound of a bell that is struck only exist within the monastery, or does the bell's sound also exist throughout the universe in all the ten directions?"

Also, seeing a bird fly by, he asked: "What is that?"

He also said: "Can you sit in meditation on the tip of a tree's hanging branch?"

He also said: "The *Nirvāṇa Sūtra* says, 'The Bodhisattva with the Limitless Body came from the East.' If the bodhisattva's body was limitless in size, how could he have come from the East? Why did he not come from the West, South, or North? Or is this impossible?"[21]

At least one scholar has suggested that these "questions about things" resemble the "precedents" or *gong'ans (kōan)* of later Chan.[22] Obviously, we cannot jump immediately from these questions to the "precedent anthologies" of the eleventh century and beyond; we must instead take into account the intervening efflorescence of encounter dialogue. However, it *is* reasonable to infer that these represent something like the same sort of questions posed by masters to students in that later genre. In contrast to encounter dialogue, here we have only one side, the masters' questions; in contrast to precedent anthologies, there is no context or literary structure to explain how such questions were intended. In addition, based on the content of some of these questions, we may infer that Northern school masters were involved in the extension of spiritual cultivation to all the activities of daily life.

THE "CHAN" STYLE OF EXPLANATION IN EIGHTH-CENTURY SOURCES

In addition to these "questions about things," there are various hints in texts from this period and slightly later of what seems like the idiosyncratically "Chan" style of discourse glorified in the later tradition. It is not always clear, to be sure, that one unified style of explanation is indicated, but the references are enough to suggest that something interesting is being reported, but not yet recorded in full.

The central figure in this respect is Shenxiu, who had a special role as "Chan commentator" on the meaning of the *sūtras* as translated by Śikṣānanda during the first few years of the eighth century. One longs to know what the "Chan meaning" of any scriptural term might be, but no doubt Shenxiu's style of interpretation was largely identical to his style of metaphor introduced in the previous chapter (see p. 49). Another clue to the prevalence of unconventional "Chan-style" dialogue occurs in the epitaph for Yifu (661–736), one of Shenxiu's most important successors, in which the author recounts that he and another literatus collected the departed master's sayings as they were remembered by his students. The two men were apparently unable to write down all of those sayings, presumably because of their great number. Even though they recognized the value of these sayings, neither of their epitaphs for Yifu contains anything that might correspond to the subject of such a collection.[23] Although the convention of disciples collecting a master's sayings is known from the earliest days of Chan (witness the material associated with *Treatise on the Two Entrances and Four Practices* and *Treatise on the Essentials of Cultivating the Mind,* the latter of which declares explicitly that it was compiled by Hongren's students), the statements associated with Yifu imply that a special kind of pronouncement was involved.

As time went on, the epitaphs of members of the Northern school and other figures important in the development of Chan began to include precisely this sort of material. For example, note the following exchange and commentary from the epitaph for Puji's student Fayun (d. 766):

> "Has the Buddha's teaching been transmitted to you?"
> "I have a sandalwood image of the Buddha to which I pay reverence."
> This reply was profound yet brief, and those listening felt chills of loneliness. The day after [the questioner, a prominent official,] left, Fayun died without illness while sitting cross-legged on his chair.[24]

After all the hyperbole about Shenxiu's being equivalent to a buddha and Puji's being the religious teacher of the universe (themes stated in documents from the first half of the eighth century as part of the Northern school's campaign for public recognition), it is perfectly natural to find a slightly later master deflating the idea of the transmission altogether.

The epitaph for Huizhen (673–751), who was more closely affiliated with the Tiantai and Vinaya schools than with Chan, includes a more explicit reference to what seems like encounter dialogue, along with several examples:

> "When people do not understand, I use the Chan style of teaching."
>
> Question: "Are not the teachings of the Southern and Northern schools different?"
>
> Answer: "Outside the gates of both houses is a road to everlasting peace."
>
> Question: "Do the results of religious practice vary according to the extent of realization?"
>
> Answer: "When a drop of water falls from the cliff, it knows the morning sea."
>
> Question: "How can one who is without faith achieve self-motivation in spiritual endeavor?"
>
> Answer: "When the baby's throat is closed (i.e., when choking), the mother yells to frighten it loose. Great compassion is unconditioned, but it can also make a student whimper."[25]

A confirmed skeptic might suggest that Huizhen is merely answering in easily understood metaphors, rather than in some genuinely new "Chan" style of teaching. If this is the case, then we must infer that a new type of metaphorical or metagogic usage became the vogue in Chan Buddhism during the second half of the eighth century, for such usage is also apparent in the biographies of Faqin (714–92) and Xuanlang (673–754), well-known representatives of the Oxhead and Tiantai schools, respectively.[26] The *Transmissions of Eminent Monks [Compiled During the] Song [Dynasty] (Song gaoseng zhuan)* and *Transmission of the Lamp* contain several examples of encounter dialogue involving Northern school figures, although of course these exchanges may be later fabrications.[27] The practice of this prototypic encounter dialogue may have had a much wider currency than the extant body of literature suggests, and the members of the Northern school may have been only the first to legitimize its use within the Chan tradition.

DOCTRINAL BASES FOR THE SOCIAL ORIENTATION OF EARLY CHAN PRACTICE

What were early Chan practitioners doing when using paradoxical interrogation, dialogue, and interactive training methods? Since they do not tell us explicitly,[28] we must turn to the voluminous writings they did bequeath to us and explore them for clues. Obvious methodological problems arise in this approach, which involves interpretive leaps and projections, but given the present state of the evidence, we have no other recourse.

One of the most important features of the *Treatise on the Two Entrances and Four Practices* is its bimodal structure, which consists of one abstract and one active "entrance" or "access" to accomplishment of the Dharma. Although one can read this text in several different ways, it is both appropriate and useful to take the two entrances as introvertive and extrovertive, respectively. That is, the "entrance of principle" refers to interior cultivation, mental practice undertaken deep within the individual's psyche, and the "entrance of practice" refers to practice undertaken actively and in interaction with the world.

Other than dialogue per se, the other important question to be considered here is the extent to which the doctrinal formulations of the Northern school's *Five Skillful Means* may have provided justification for the emergence of encounter dialogue. Here I am not thinking of encounter dialogue as an oral practice so much as a *social* practice. That is, is there anything in the *Five Skillful Means* that provides justification for the outward, social dimension of Chan religious practice?

In fact, there is a basis for answering this question in the affirmative. The key passage is the following:

> Bodhisattvas know the fundamental motionlessness of the six senses, their internal illumination being distinct and their external functions being autonomous. This is the true and constant motionlessness of the Mahāyāna.
>
> Question: What do "internal illumination being distinct" and "external functions being autonomous" mean?
>
> Answer: Fundamental wisdom is "internal illumination being distinct." Successive wisdom is "external functions being autonomous."
>
> Question: What are fundamental wisdom and successive wisdom?
>
> Answer: Because one first realizes the characteristic of the transcendence of the body and mind, this is fundamental wisdom. The autonomous [quality of] knowing and perception and the nondefilement [associated with the enlightened state] are successive wisdom. . . . If realization [of the transcendence of body and mind] were not first, then knowing and perception would be completely defiled. Know clearly that the autonomous [spontaneity of] knowing and perception is attained after that realization and is called successive wisdom.
>
> When the mind does not activate on the basis of the eye's perception of form, this is fundamental wisdom. The autonomous [spontaneity of] perception is successive wisdom. When the mind does not activate on the basis of the ear's hearing of sounds, this is fundamental wisdom. The autonomous [spontaneity of] hearing is successive wisdom. The nose, tongue, body, and consciousness are also the same. With the fundamental and successive [wisdoms], the locations (i.e., sensory capacities and realms of sensory data) are distinct, the locations are emancipated. The senses do not activate, and the realizations are pure. When successive moments of mental [existence] are non-

activating, the senses are sagely (i.e., characterized by the enlightened menta-
tion of the buddhas).[29]

Although the terminology used here is no doubt unfamiliar to most readers, it is relatively simple to unpack. "Fundamental wisdom" refers to the
first moment of enlightenment, when the mind attains perfect clarity. At
this point one is said to have transcended both body and mind, that is, to
have gone beyond all ordinary distinctions of physical and mental reality.
Although the text never makes the connection, it is reasonable to understand this basic attainment of mental clarity according to the entrance of
principle in the text attributed to Bodhidharma. The rhetoric of innate
entitlement is not used in this specific location, but elsewhere the *Five
Skillful Means* discusses the "enlightened mind" in a fashion that implies
such an understanding.

Here "successive wisdom" refers to what happens immediately after
that first moment of "fundamental wisdom," both in the very next and
all succeeding moments. Other texts might have deconstructed the
artificiality of this moment-by-moment sequence, to point out that true
realization happens all at once, but the *Five Skillful Means* is firm in its
dualism. It is not precisely clear what it would mean in real life for one's
various sensory capacities to be non-activating and autonomously spontaneous in their functioning, not to mention the distinct identity and
emancipated quality of both sensory capacities and the realms of sensory experience. However, to continue with the analogy to the *Treatise
on the Two Entrances and Four Practices,* we may note that these various
qualities pertain to how the practitioner interacts with the world at large.
In terms of religious self-cultivation, this attitude would involve a certain
level of forbearance toward all one's circumstantial conditions; in terms
of the on-going activities of an enlightened master, the result would be a
style of perfect responsiveness to the needs of one's students.

Scattered throughout the same section of the *Five Skillful Means* we
find various statements involving similar dyads referring to inner realization and outward-directed activity:

> If the mind does not activate, the mind is suchlike. If form does not activate,
> form is suchlike. Since the mind is suchlike, the mind is emancipated. Since
> form is suchlike, form is emancipated. Since mind and form both transcend
> [thoughts], there is not a single thing.[30]

■

> The transcendence of mind is enlightenment of self, with no dependence on
> the five senses. The transcendence of form is enlightenment of others, with no

dependence on the five types of sensory data. The transcendence of both mind and form is to have one's practice of enlightenment perfect and complete and is equivalent to the universally "same" *dharmakāya* of the Tathāgata.[31]

■

The transcendence of thought is the essence, and the perceptive faculties are the function. Serenity is the essence, and illumination is the function. "Serene but always functioning; functioning but always serene." Serene but always functioning—this is the absolute corresponding to phenomena. Functioning but always serene—this is phenomena corresponding to the absolute. Serene yet always functioning—this is form corresponding to emptiness. Functioning yet always serene—this is emptiness corresponding to form. . . .

Serenity is unfolding; illumination is constriction (lit., "rolling up"). Unfolded, it expands throughout the *dharmadhātu*. Constricted, it is incorporated in the tip of a hair. Its expression [outward] and incorporation [inward] distinct, the divine function is autonomous.[32]

■

The meaning of enlightenment is that the essence of the mind transcends thoughts. Transcending the characteristic of craving, it is equivalent to the realm of space, which pervades everywhere. This is called enlightenment of self. Transcending the characteristic of anger, it is equivalent to the realm of space, which pervades everywhere. This is called enlightenment of others. Transcending the characteristic of stupidity, it is equivalent to the realm of space, which pervades everywhere. The single characteristic of the *dharmadhātu* is the universally "same" *dharmakāya* of the Tathāgata. This is called complete enlightenment.[33]

These examples, which could easily be supplemented from later sections of the *Five Skillful Means* and other works, reveal the basic Northern school concern for describing not only how one understands the abstract truth of the Buddhadharma, but also how one puts it into practice on behalf of sentient beings. Although the specific expressions are new, this bimodal structure is certainly indebted to the *Treatise on the Two Entrances and Four Practices* attributed to Bodhidharma and may be taken as a basic characteristic of early Chan Buddhism.

It would be more convenient for our purposes, I suppose, if this bimodal structure explicitly involved masters and students, and if it stated clearly that one was first to become enlightened oneself and then inspire the enlightenment of others. Instead, as with all Chan literature at this time (not to mention the texts of other schools), the aspiring student is still invisible, and from the moment of successive wisdom onward, the recipients of the enlightened master's grace are anonymous sentient beings. However, the emphasis on the importance of activity in the social or interpersonal realm (which is implicitly seen as temporally subsequent but equal in value terms) is firmly established with these formulations.

THE USE OF RITUALIZED DIALOGUE
BETWEEN TEACHERS AND STUDENTS

The mechanical formulations given above are not the only interesting feature of the *Five Skillful Means*. The text seems to have been a set of teacher's notes for holding initiation and training meetings according to an approved Northern school program, in which context it includes several examples of ritualized dialogue. We have already seen one example of this above (see the quotations beginning on p. 52). Here is a second:

> The preceptor strikes the wooden signal-board and asks: Do you hear the sound?
> Answer: *We hear.*
> Question: What is this "hearing" like?
> Answer: *Hearing is motionless.*
> Question: What is the transcendence of thought?
> Answer: *The transcendence of thought is motionless.*
> This motionlessness is to develop the skillful means of sagacity out of meditation. This is to open the gate of sagacity. Hearing is sagacity. This skillful means can not only develop sagacity, but also make one's meditation correct. To achieve this motionlessness is to open the gate of wisdom, to attain wisdom. This is called the opening of the gates of wisdom and sagacity.[34]

Here we find transcribed segments of ritual dialogue from a specific Northern school doctrinal context. When looking for antecedents for transcribed dialogues in early Chan texts, we should not be misled by preconceptions about the original spontaneity of such dialogues and thus overlook this type of material.

The question is, to what extent did encounter dialogue grow out of a monastic training and ritual context in which students responded to monkish ritual celebrants in a thoroughly formalized manner? Elsewhere in the *Five Skillful Means* are other portions of this catechistic ritual, which demonstrate the same form of scripted recitation-and-response pattern. This material skillfully weaves Northern school doctrine into an intriguing mix of ritualized initiation, teaching catechism, and guided meditation practice.[35] Here I would like to focus on the following possible reading of the implications of this material: that Chan encounter dialogue derived not (or, perhaps, not solely) out of *spontaneous* oral exchanges but (perhaps only in part) out of *ritualized* exchanges. Given arguments already made by other scholars that spontaneity is merely "inscribed" within the heavily ritualized context of Song-dynasty Chan,[36] this interpretation allows us to wipe out the distinction between the "classical" age of Tang-dynasty Chan when encounter dialogue was spontaneous and the subsequent ritualization of dialogue within Song-dynasty Chan. At the least, the examples of transcribed dialogue introduced above should break us loose from the preconception of "event" and suggest we look elsewhere for the origins of encounter dialogue as "text."

THE WIDESPREAD USE OF ANECDOTE AND DIALOGUE IN TEACHING

One factor that should not be overlooked is the widespread tendency within the developing Chan movement to use anecdotal material and dialogue transcriptions for teaching purposes. One could chart the anecdotal content of Chan literature as a sharply ascending curve. From Bodhidharma's treatise through the texts of early and middle Chan, there is a treasure trove of anecdotes, parables, metaphors, dramatizations, and other narrative material that becomes increasingly central with time.

The most important individual contributor to this dimension of Chan was Shenhui. Shenhui's activities, ideas, and rhetorical style transformed Chinese Chan. Whatever the doctrinal significance of his teaching of sudden enlightenment, whatever the factionalist impact of his outspoken criticism of the Northern school, one of the ways in which he changed Chan was in the extreme caution he made his colleagues feel about describing their doctrinal formulations. I have labeled this impact the standard of "rhetorical purity," which mitigated against any expression using dualistic or gradualistic formats. That is, even though the long-range impact of nondualism may have been ultimately liberating, Shenhui's vigorous attack on the dualism and gradualism of Northern school teachings must have had a chilling effect on other teachers.

Simultaneously, Shenhui was a master storyteller and public speaker. Many of the most famous stories of Chan appear first in the transcriptions of his sermons and lectures: Bodhidharma and Emperor Wu, Bodhidharma and Huike—but not, curiously enough, many stories about his own teacher Huineng. There is also a substantial amount of transcribed dialogue within the Shenhui corpus, either between Shenhui and his designated Northern school foil Chongyuan or between him and various famous laymen of his day. There is a palpable sense of fictional creativity here, such that some of the dialogues with famous laymen may well have been made up out of whole cloth. On the other hand, the dialogues do not quite conform to our expectations of encounter dialogue, in that they are too clearly structured and have too much of a logical pattern to represent genuinely spontaneous exchanges. Every historical figure is transitional in some way, and although he was apparently not a practitioner of full-fledged encounter dialogue himself, Shenhui's career pushed the Chan tradition forward in the use of anecdote.

THE FABRICATION OF ENLIGHTENMENT NARRATIVES

Another characteristic of early Chan writings is the tendency to compose fictionalized accounts of enlightenment experiences. Let me discuss several examples of this tendency before turning, in the next section, to the case of Huineng.

We have already encountered the Oxhead-school text *Treatise on the Transcendence of Cognition* (see the passage quoted beginning on p. 58), which is the prime example of an openly fictional dramatization of a Chan master-student encounter. There are other examples of fictionalized enlightenment narratives in eighth-century Chan literature: a pair of texts, the *Treatise on the True Principle* and *Essential Determination,* which share the same rhetorical structure.[37] In each case, a single proponent of Buddhist spiritual cultivation is depicted as both enlightened Chan master and sincere lay seeker. That is, the author depicts himself as both asking and answering questions concerning spiritual cultivation, in his dual identities as monk and layman. I have always been amused by the openings of these texts: after introducing himself as both teacher and student, when the first question is posed, by himself in the guise of the student, the author switches to his guise as teacher to praise it as the most profound inquiry he's ever received in all his years as a monk!

The narratives found in the *Treatise on the Transcendence of Cognition, Treatise on the True Principle,* and *Essential Determination* are manifestly fictional, but they must somehow have modeled ideal teacher/student interactions and may have resembled actual exchanges that took place between living meditation masters and practitioners. Their authors must have had some knowledge of such encounters — either by direct participation or monastic hearsay — in order to generate their literary images. Rather than speculating on the precise nature of such events, the point to emphasize here is that these texts represent an innovative use of text in the Chan tradition.

More distantly, of course, the Chinese Buddhist apologetic tradition has a certain history of creating fictitious authorities to serve as rhetorical tools. Mouzi, a patently fictional character created to explain the validity of Buddhism for China through references to indigenous Chinese culture, is clearly the best example of this.[38] Here, though, the goal is not to convince a skeptical reader of the validity of Buddhism for China, but to model Chan practice and enlightenment for would-be practitioners.

THE GENEALOGICAL STRUCTURE OF CHAN DIALOGUE

Here let me add one other point about the example of Huineng, based not on the fictionality of the story per se but instead on the character of the protagonist. The following is a famous passage from the Lotus Sūtra:

> Then the daughter of the dragon king presented to the Buddha a jewel worth the great manifold cosmos, and the Buddha accepted it. The daughter of the dragon king spoke to the Bodhisattva Prajñākūṭa and the noble Śāriputra saying:
>
> "I offered a jewel and the Bhagavat accepted it. Was that done quickly or not?"
>
> They answered saying: "It was done extremely quickly!"
>
> The daughter said: "Through your transcendent powers watch me become a Buddha even more quickly than that!"
>
> Then the assembly there all saw the daughter of the dragon king instantly transform into a man, perfect the bodhisattva practices, go to the Vimalā world in the south, sit on a jeweled lotus flower and attain highest complete enlightenment, become endowed with the thirty-two marks and eighty excellent characteristics, and expound the true Dharma universally for the sake of all sentient beings in the ten directions.[39]

I suggest that there is a profound similarity between the story of Huineng and that of the dragon king's daughter in the Lotus Sūtra. Consider their total lack of the conventional accoutrements of spiritually gifted persons. The dragon king's daughter was female, nonhuman (although of high nonhuman birth), and underage—yet in a single moment she was able to transform herself into a male, pass through all the trials and tribulations expected of bodhisattva practitioners, and achieve perfect enlightenment. For his part, Huineng was illiterate, from the very fringes of civilization in the far south, lowborn (although his father had been an official, albeit a banished one), and not even a monk—yet his intuitive genius qualified him to be selected as the sixth patriarch.

In the story of Huineng we find the last key to the emergence of encounter dialogue transcriptions. The problem was not whether or not such dialogues were actually occurring between masters and students, and if so how and to what extent. Rather, the problem was the reluctance to transcribe what may have been virtually an everyday occurrence in the back rooms of China's monastic compounds.[40] There had to be some epistemic change that made it acceptable to transcribe, not only the words of the gifted and famous master, but those of the student as well. The example of Huineng may have been a significant factor in generating this epistemic change, but the time was still not at hand.

Encounter dialogue is generally believed to have flourished initially in the faction of Mazu Daoyi, which is known as the Hongzhou school. Mazu and his disciples are depicted in Chan records as engaging in spontaneous repartée in what is almost a barnyard atmosphere of agricultural labor and other daily tasks. There are enough dialogues concerning a large enough number of figures that it would seem heresy to suggest that nothing of the sort "really" happened, that the encounters were all "fictional." I will certainly not go that far here, but we cannot avoid a certain problem, already introduced above: Whereas the encounters involving Mazu and his disciples are supposed to have taken place in the latter part of the eighth century and beginning of the ninth, they are not found in transcribed form until the year 952, with the appearance of the *Anthology of the Patriarchal Hall*.

We do have a much earlier text from the Hongzhou school, the *Transmissions of Treasure Grove*. Only certain parts of this text are extant, and scholars have generally assumed that the lost portions (which were devoted in part to Mazu and his immediate disciples) must have been incorporated into, and thus were not substantially different from, the corresponding sections of the *Anthology of the Patriarchal Hall*. Unfortunately, this assumption is untenable, for the simple reason that the extant portions of the *Transmissions of Treasure Grove* do not contain encounter dialogue transcriptions. There is a great deal of dialogue transcribed in this text, virtually all of which is fictionalized representation of enlightened masters. However, none of this dialogue has the same lively feel as the exchanges of the *Anthology of the Patriarchal Hall*.

There is one feature of the *Transmissions of Treasure Grove*, though, that I believe to be of crucial importance: the rigid narrative structure of the text. This text describes the lives, and to a lesser extent the teachings, of the Chan patriarchs from Śākyamuni through Bodhidharma to Mazu, and in each case the patriarch in question is described twice, first as a gifted student discovered by the current patriarch and second as a fully vested patriarch out searching for his own successor. It is curious that in no case (with a partial exception in the account of Huike) is the enlightenment experience of the patriarch in question described; we have only the "before" and "after" images, not any reference to or depiction of what we would think to be the most crucial event in the entire process. What is central for our purposes, though, is the great emphasis placed on the patriarchs as students. That is, this text creates a structural symmetry, even an implied parity, between the student as incipient patriarch and the patriarch as realized student.

This structural parity may well have played a role in making the transcription of encounter dialogue possible—that is, in making the transcription of *both sides* of encounter dialogue exchanges possible. However, this was not yet possible when the *Transmissions of Treasure Grove* was compiled in 801, and the reticence of this text to describe enlightenment experiences may imply that it was used for popular teaching in the spread of Buddhism throughout the newly developing areas of Jiangxi, rather than for training within the context of the monastic meditation hall.

The Chan genealogical model requires some form of mutual interaction, some confrontation, between teacher and student. In some cases, as in the account of Mazu sitting in meditation introduced at the beginning of this chapter, the student implicitly represents a "Chinese *mārga* paradigm" (*mārga* is the Sanskrit word for the spiritual path from ignorance to enlightenment), and the teacher responds in terms that force the student to reorient himself in terms of the "encounter paradigm" of spiritual cultivation. That is, the student thinks in terms of what was conventionally referred to in the post-Shenhui world as the gradual teaching, in which he moves progressively through a series of exercises and stages toward the goal of enlightenment. Here the spiritual quest is somewhat like a board game such as "chutes and ladders," in which each player moves by rolls of the dice from the bottom of the board to the top. (In this particular game for young children, certain positions on the board send the player down a slide or up a set of steps, either losing or gaining multiple spaces in the process.) In the spiritual quest, of course, movement of one's token is accomplished not by rolls of the dice but by mastering different spiritual techniques. The focus of each player is on the progress of his or her own token, which requires skills that are akin to those of the mechanic or craftsman.[41]

In Chan practice the teacher reacts to such assumptions by forcing the student into dialogue, into engaged interaction. Thus the unipolar game-piece style of practice is changed into a bipolar encounter, in which a sudden insight can be achieved by a fundamental change of perspective. Since preconceptions are sturdy things, this transformation is easier described than achieved, of course, but with the advent of the Chan school, the model under which real spiritual progress is made shifts to a bipolar framework of interpersonal collaboration. Rather than moving one's piece across a gameboard, this sort of bipolar interaction is less rule-driven and more intuitive, or at least more open to creative innovation—like learning how to dance or an initiation into lovemaking.

Actually, the best metaphor might be the Chinese game of *weiqi*, better known as the Japanese game *go*, or the ancient and medieval Chinese game of *liubo*. In contrast to the board games of Indian culture, in which one moves a single piece along a path of spaces from bottom to top of the board, in the Chinese games one places multiple pieces, not on spaces, but on the intersections between horizontal and vertical lines. While the Indian game can be played by any number of players, one or more, the Chinese game is for a pair of opponents—a duel, we might say. The two opponents compete for control of territory, and the very simple set of rules governing where pieces may and may not be played allows for a very sophisticated calculus of risk and benefit.[42]

Of course, Chan is not precisely like the game of *go*—like all metaphors, this one is empowered by the approximation of its fit, not its precise match. However, the classical examples of Chan master-student interaction are indeed subject to forms of analysis similar to those applicable for *go*, and they do exhibit distinctive and complex types of patterning. The goal of these patternings, however, is to depict masters responding to students in ways that appear to be unstructured and creative, spontaneous and immediate. To put it differently, the collision between the Chinese *mārga* and encounter paradigms that takes place in the context of every master-student interaction is the real echo of the gradual/sudden distinction in post-Shenhui Chan.[43]

To understand the emergence and functions of encounter dialogue within the Chan tradition, we must consider a number of different factors and their complex concatenation. Even more, we must also be aware of the conjunction of entirely different realms of culture, for example, the institution of the monastery, the structure of oral discourse, and the creation of a new genre of religious literature.

Encounter dialogue emerges from a style of oral exchange that seems to have been practiced within the "back rooms" of the meditation hall, abbot's quarters, and other private areas of the monastery, from perhaps as early as Shenxiu's residence at Jade Spring Temple in the last quarter of the seventh century. Perhaps it was a style of interaction and instruction already known at East Mountain, and perhaps it was even in part a legacy of Tiantai Zhiyi's earlier residence at Jade Spring Temple. Perhaps it was practiced more widely throughout the Chinese Buddhist monastic institution as a whole, in meditation halls and training facilities of various styles and configurations. Whatever its original currency, it was originally restricted to the back rooms, and not presented in writing at first. It is entirely likely that some of the excitement that Shenxiu, Lao'an, and other Northern school figures attracted in Chang'an and Luoyang at the beginning of the eighth century was due to their revelation of this backroom style in elegant public occasions. Whether this was the case or not, until the appearance of the *Anthology of the Patriarchal Hall* in 952 the written texts of Chan demonstrate a palpable reluctance, even an inability, to include the words of mere students. It was as if, prior to 952, only the words of the celebrated masters and their imperial or literati interlocutors could be transcribed in the formal mode of literary Chinese texts. After 952, though, the situation changed dramatically. From this point on it becomes not only allowable but expected, even required, to include the words of students in Chan texts. Indeed, the identity of Chan masters cannot be seen any other way except through their interactions with often anonymous students. We examine the *Anthology of the Patriarchal Hall* in more detail in the next chapter, but at the moment it is useful to notice what a major social and conceptual transformation its appearance represents.

What we have before us, of course, are texts, the written transmutation of an oral tradition. How significant was the shift from oral to written medium? Most readers approach Chan recorded sayings literature quite naively, taking the words as simple and basically accurate transcriptions of what was actually said during the event depicted. But the impression of vivid immediacy that we gain through reading these texts is primarily a literary effect, a direct result of their rhetorical style. In fact, Chan dialogues have gone through a number of stages before being presented to us in their present form:

1. *Initial transcription:* The act of transcribing spoken Chinese into written form should not be taken for granted, but rather represents the first step—actually a certain type of translation—in a complex process of oral-to-written transformation. On the basis of historical linguistics, we

know that all transcriptions were done into a standard form of colloquial Chinese that was based on the spoken dialect then current at the
capital of Chang'an. The ability to render this standard colloquial form
was only achieved with some difficulty, and not only were actual vocal
utterances cleaned of the usual verbal "noise" that characterizes actual
speech and simplified for written use, but any dialect peculiarities were
omitted in the translation into the medieval Chang'an standard. Thus,
even when southerners are depicted talking to southerners, their dialogues are shown in the form of Chang'an Chinese even though the
texts could just as well have used southern language forms.[44]

2. *Circulation, evaluation, and selection:* We have a number of examples
   where the same stories are recounted with different actors, or where
   similar stories imply some process of internal development. In other
   cases a student will ask a teacher about a dialogue or pronouncement
   by some other master. In other words, these stories were clearly
   passed around and subjected to repeated reevaluations and modifications. This seems to have occurred in a complex environment of both
   oral and written transmission, with the reputations of different masters growing or fading based on the ability of their circulated dialogues
   to attract interest from both students and other teachers.

3. *Editorial modification:* As discussions continued, and especially after
   the written publication of encounter dialogue material began in
   earnest, there is a clear tendency for editors and compilers to modify
   their texts in order to increase the perceived religious utility of the dialogues. Ironically, this meant making them seem more like direct oral
   transcriptions than they had before, by making them more colloquial
   as time went on. The best example of this involves one of the most
   important Chan texts of all time, the recorded sayings of the legendary
   Linji Yixuan. It is important to recognize that the vivid immediacy of
   Chan literature, the feeling of "being there," is a literary effect con-
   trived through literally centuries of combined effort.[45]

The texts of encounter dialogue are thus several steps removed from
the actual participation in encounter dialogue itself. Before considering the
age in which those texts were published—the Song dynasty—we should
consider the institutional transformations that occurred in Chinese Buddhism from the Tang to the Song.

CHAPTER 5

Zen and the Art of Fund-Raising

Religious Vitality and Institutional
Dominance in the Song Dynasty

Against the "Zen of Anything"

Once or twice at formal academic meetings I have introduced papers with a dramatic reading of forty or fifty book titles that include the word "Zen." The most widely known example nowadays is Robert Pirsig's novel *Zen and the Art of Motorcycle Maintenance,* but this is merely one member of a very large genre. Beginning with Eugen Herrigel's classic, *Zen and the Art of Archery* (which has recently become the subject of some dispute),[1] such works include *Zen and the Art of the Macintosh, Zen and the Art of Windsurfing, Zen and the Art of the Internet, Zen and the Art of Cubing: In Search of the Seventh Side* (whatever that subtitle might mean!), and *Why Toast Lands Jelly-Side Down: Zen and the Art of Physics Demonstrations.* In addition to landmark works by D. T. Suzuki and Alan Watts such as *The Zen Doctrine of No-Mind, Zen and Japanese Culture,* and *The Way of Zen,* there are also any number of "The Zen of" books, such as *The Zen of International Relations, The Zen Teachings of Jesus,* and *The Zen of Oz: Ten Spiritual Lessons from Over the Rainbow.* A single author has written books entitled *Zen Computer* and *Zen Sex: The Way of Making Love*—I have not actually seen either of these, but I hope they are very different in style! The late Bhagwan Shree Rajneesh (1931–90), who adopted the name "Osho" toward the end of his life in misinformed deference to the Zen tradition,[2] wrote a number of books explaining the ideas and texts of Zen, one of which is a lengthy tome with the snappy title of *Zen, Zest, Zip, Zap, and Zing.* And recently there has appeared *The Complete Idiot's Guide to Zen Living,* by two medical and mental health professionals without any apparent contact with the Zen tradition at all.

Some of these "Zen and whatever" volumes are good books in their own rights, but taken as a whole they perpetuate a perfectly banal misapprehension of one of the world's great religious traditions. It seems that virtually anyone can claim authoritative understanding of Zen, or at least be comfortable in using the word *Zen* in works totally unrelated to the tradition. It would not do to become too indignant, since this sort of exploitation is but the inevitable side-effect of D. T. Suzuki's missionary success, through which Western interest in Zen and other matters oriental was initially piqued. Nevertheless, we may recognize that, in contrast to its usage within East Asian Buddhism, the word *Zen* has a very different and much more limited range of meaning in contemporary world popular culture. The popular usage implies that Zen is simply an attitude of undistracted concentration that can be applied to any human endeavor. If you get fully involved in the task at hand, become one with it, and allow yourself to flow according to its natural rhythms, then your performance of that task will improve accordingly—which is a discovery of substantial benefit to professional athletes, creative writers, and many others. I have also seen the word *Zen* used to describe home electronics projects and lines of cosmetic products, in which the word is used in the sense of a bare-bones simplicity and ease of use; of course, the latter may also include some "oriental" aesthetic sense for all I know. No doubt there is an exotic cachet to invoking Zen in all these contexts as well.

Although undivided concentration and bare-bones simplicity are legitimate messages of Chinese Chan as a mode of self-cultivation, the Chan tradition, as we have already seen, involves far more than this. This chapter differs from most of the titles just introduced, in that it really *is* about the art of fund-raising as practiced within the Chan tradition. But this is not a "do-it-yourself" book. Though I discuss a Chan approach to making money, I leave the application of this approach to life in the postmodern world to others. (This decision is ill-advised financially; it would no doubt be much more profitable for me to write a book on "how to raise money the Zen way"!)

In the following pages we explore a possible scenario for how members of the Chan lineage managed, from the ninth to the eleventh centuries, to take control of the Chinese Buddhist monastic institution, or at least its highest leadership positions. The hypothesis presented here is intended to explain how the encounter model of Chan religious praxis worked as a public ideology, how Chan responded to the persecution of Buddhism and the economic tribulations of ninth-century China, and how the mythology of Chan monastic labor served an important function, even though most of the productive labor in Buddhist monasteries—including supposedly Chan temples—was performed by lay workers and tenant farmers. In contrast to the conventional viewpoint that the fund-raising efforts of Chan abbots during the Song dynasty indicate the degeneration of both Chan and the Buddhist tradition as a whole, I suggest precisely the opposite: that the institutional success of Chan was made possible by—and in fact represents proof of—its vitality as a spiritual discipline. To put it most succinctly, Chan developed a unique approach to fund-raising that allowed its advocates to create for themselves an identity of moral uprightness and detachment from worldly profit even as they worked openly to gather financial support for their institutions.

Chan Buddhism in Chinese History

Readers familiar with writings on Chan (in either European or East Asian languages) may be surprised at the scope of the reinterpretation just introduced. But the payoff of this different perspective is even greater than one might imagine at first glance: What is at stake here is nothing less than our global understanding of the role of Buddhism in the sweep of Chinese history. Early-twentieth-century studies of Chan had a major impact in shaping how most English-language writings interpret the cultural and intellectual transitions from the North/South Dynasties period (220–589)[3] to the Song dynasty, that is, from the third through the thirteenth centuries. Conversely, those standard interpretations of the contours of Chinese intellectual history for the same lengthy period have profoundly influenced how writers describe the Chan tradition. There has been a palpable circularity at work, with historians of China building comprehensive theories based in part on a romanticized image of Chan, and apologists for Chan buying into those theories because they served the missionary agenda. Our understandings of Chinese Buddhism, Chinese intellectual and religious history, and Chan itself have been impoverished as a result.[4]

The fallacies and contradictions deriving from this circularity are starkly apparent in the writing of Heinrich Dumoulin. His work is an extreme but representative example, which has become the sourcebook for countless popular and semischolarly accounts. His work is also especially useful here because it is so strongly derivative of earlier research—Father Dumoulin was if nothing else a systematic and voracious reader. He describes the great masters of the Tang dynasty as rustic spiritual virtuosi, geniuses of untrammeled spontaneity who lived in a basically uncluttered world of master-student interactions and diligent spiritual cultivation. We see them working in the fields and vegetable gardens along with their students, unburdened by any mundane problems of monastic administration or relations with local officials and landed gentry, let alone the state bureaucracy and imperial court. The locus of their activity is somehow removed from conventional Buddhist monasteries that fulfilled ritual, festival, and pilgrimage functions within Chinese society, neither blessed with the financial resources that such human services provided nor saddled with the headaches and hassles of involvement with ordinary human society. Within such Chan training temples a new spirit of monkish involvement in manual labor developed, according to this idealized portrait, partly out of the refusal to participate in ordinary fund-raising activities and partly through the more profound need to have the effort of spiritual training permeate every instant and activity.

It is within this quaintly naive depiction of Tang-dynasty Chan that Dumoulin describes the monastic regulations legendarily ascribed to Baizhang Huaihai. For him Baizhang's authorship is unquestioned fact; the lack of any contemporary enumeration of the rules Baizhang supposedly implemented poses no problem. Indeed, the religious context of the earliest version of these rules (which dates from the beginning of the twelfth century) is entirely beyond the concern of Dumoulin, who has already shifted his attentions to Kamakura Japan.[5] Instead, as the Tang dynasty went through the throes of the Huichang persecution, and other Buddhist schools were critically wounded by the removal of material assets and laicization of many clergy, Dumoulin suggests that it was the pure spirit and unselfish ethic of Chan based on Baizhang's rules that allowed the school to survive relatively unscathed.

With regard to the Huichang persecution in particular, Dumoulin devotes a page or two to its political background in the Chinese antipathy to celibacy and corruption within the Buddhist establishment itself. He details the different phases of the persecution, its prelude of hostile but low-impact measures beginning in 842, the increase in the pace of decrees in 844, the climax in 845, and the end after Emperor Wuzong's death early in 846. Immediately following this summary, Dumoulin writes,

> Economic factors also played a clear and determinative role in sustaining the persecution, as the Buddhist community, with the fortunate exception of Zen, contributed little of economic benefit to Chinese society. Zen monks worked their farmlands and cultivated their fields productively; if the information we have about the East Mountain teaching is correct, they were doing so already from their early years in China.[6]

This is a clear statement of the romanticized image of Chan, the notion that it represented a special subset within the Buddhist community, a group of sincere practitioners who had retired from worldly activities and devoted themselves to the simple endeavors of farming as part of their own efforts at self-cultivation. We have already seen that the East Mountain community was probably no different from other Chinese monastic training centers at the time in its use of lay laborers, and that even when the *Platform Sūtra* appeared, more than a century after the end of the East Mountain period, around 780, there was no evidence whatsoever for such an idealized image of Chan monastic labor. The treatment of Huineng as a temple menial no doubt realistically portrayed the manner in which an illiterate wood-gatherer from the far south would have been treated—thus setting up the dramatic surprise to follow. (See the story beginning on p. 60, and the discussion on p. 68.)

After describing the destructive yet temporary quality of the persecution, Dumoulin comments on its lack of real impact on Zen:

> The short duration of the persecution is one reason why Zen suffered so little. The greatest damage was done in the major cities and in the northern provinces. Located principally in the South and in the countryside, the Zen movement was fortunate to find itself far from the fray. Moreover, Zen monasteries struck a rather unimposing image in the eyes of the religious powers. The Zen masters of the T'ang period kept their distance from the imperial court and were not at all engaged in academic or public activities that might have attracted attention. As a result, they were able to sustain their minor losses without consequence.[7]

This is simply an elaboration of the same idealized image. Immediately following this passage, however, Dumoulin introduces broader historical issues:

> The Buddhist persecution during the T'ang period signaled a turning point in the history of Chinese Buddhism. The main thrust of the persecution lasted only about a year. How was it possible that in such a short period the broadly based institution of Buddhism could suffer wounds that would leave it permanently crippled? One would have thought that after the storm had subsided the numerous temples and monasteries so beloved by the people would have had the strength to renew themselves. Or had Buddhism—despite its beautiful façade and imposing edifices, its complicated doctrinal systems and impressive rituals—been dealt a blow that exhausted its inner energies? Was there more to the picture than the external damage that was so evident, especially in certain monasteries and convents? Did the debilitation and devastation reach into the very marrow of Buddhism?[8]

Dumoulin's answer to this rhetorical question is, predictably, in the affirmative: he goes on to describe how the example of the Zen movement and its unhampered rural setting confirmed for him the suspicions that Buddhism had indeed reached such a profound state of debilitation.

This depiction of the fate of late Tang-dynasty Buddhism needs to be substantially rewritten, but at this point we need to focus squarely on the goal of Dumoulin's attentions to these issues. His presentation is largely a setup for the discussion of the non-Buddhist glories of the Song:

> During the Sung period, Chinese civilization attained heights it had known before only during the time of classical antiquity. One may properly speak of a "renaissance," since the general cultural growth was accelerated by a return to the classics. . . .
>
> The dominant intellectual movement of the time, known in the West as Neo-Confucianism, contributed to this renaissance by adopting the naturalistic and rationalistic orientation of the classics to confront modernity. The golden age of Buddhism, whose numerous schools had attracted large segments of the Chinese population for half a century [sic] with their metaphysical speculations, elaborate rituals, and mysticism, was clearly over. . . .
>
> After Emperor Wu-tsung's great persecution (845), Buddhism lived on in only two movements, the meditational school of Zen and the mainly popular school of the Pure Land. To the Zen monasteries of this period fell the responsibility of representing the Buddhist heritage at a higher level, and from them flowed intellectual and artistic currents greatly enhancing the culture of the Sung period.[9]

Here we can easily detect the echoes of the modern positivist historian Hu Shih's (1891–1962) interpretation of Chinese history, including his specific theory of the "Chinese renaissance." Dumoulin has uncritically imported Hu's ideas into his own work, virtually unchanged.

Hu Shih believed that ancient Chinese culture was a basically just and rational society, with little use for superstition or indeed religion of any kind. Following the disintegration of the Han dynasty, though, just when Chinese civilization was at its weakest point, Buddhism arrived as a pernicious foreign system of superstitious theories and practices. China was sick, and Buddhism infected it like an uncontrollable virus. At one point, Hu even refers to China during the North/South Dynasties period as an "intellectual colony" of India. Given this perspective, the rise of Chan Buddhism was interesting to Hu for only one reason: he believed that the doctrine of sudden enlightenment represented the surgical tool by which China excised the Buddhist sickness from its own corporate body, leading eventually to the rise of Neo-Confucianism in the "Chinese renaissance" of the Song dynasty.

The errors in Hu's understanding of the role of Buddhism in Chinese history are simply too numerous for us to treat them all here.[10] I discuss the philosophical implications of his approach for the understanding of the Chan enlightenment experience in the next chapter; here we must remain focused on issues of historical process. Let us note, though, that his projection of China's early-twentieth-century plight onto the past is blatant, especially in his use of the rhetoric of colonization and liberation. And his rhetoric of renaissance, of the "flowering" of the Song Neo-Confucian tradition and the positive value of its emphasis of the ancient classics, is echoed almost word for word in Dumoulin's text.

The Five Factors of Institutional Takeover

What alternative is there to the style of interpretation represented by Hu Shih and Heinrich Dumoulin? Let us concentrate on five different factors, which taken together represent a preliminary delineation of an alternative hypothesis.

SHENHUI'S RHETORIC FOR CHAN FUND-RAISING

The monk Shenhui occupied virtually all of Hu Shih's attentions in Chan studies. In contrast to Hu's description of him in military terms as the leader of the Southern school's assault against the Northern school, and in contrast to our conventional image of Chan masters as meditation instructors or spiritual guides engaged in intimate religious encounter with their students, Shenhui is actually best understood as a public evangelist. That is, he operated as a public exponent of the "good news" of Chan. His religious vocation was not in the private sanctuary of the meditation hall but on the very public venue of the ordination platform, where he made exciting and highly theatrical public presentations that inspired his listeners to begin the path of Buddhist spiritual cultivation. Not only did this result in men and women taking ordination to become monks and nuns (thus adding to the numbers of Chan practitioners in China), it also added hard currency to the coffers of both church and state. Each man undergoing ordination had to pay a sizeable sum to the government—which gained the ordinand a lifetime tax exemption as a member of the clergy. (We do not have similar information about the nuns, since women were not directly subject to taxation.) After the An Lushan rebellion began in 755, Shenhui was enlisted by the Tang ruling house to raise money in this fashion, and later he was commended for his contributions to the defense of the government. We do not have any financial details about donations received by the *sangha* through Shenhui's activities, but Chinese archaeologists have discovered a gold ingot whose markings testify to the profitability of such ordinations to the state. All of this activity was shortsighted, of course, for both church and state, resulting in increased state control of ordination and the erosion of the government's tax base. The entire story is a fascinating episode in Chinese religious history.[11]

What is significant here is that Shenhui achieved his success as a fundraiser not in spite of any other-worldliness of the Chan tradition, but *by means of* his iconoclastic rhetoric. For example, the famous encounter between Bodhidharma and Emperor Wu of the Liang (see p. 22 above), which on the surface seems like a clear denunciation of merit-oriented activity, in fact occurs for the first time in Chan literature in the written transcript of Shenhui's presentation at a large-scale Buddhist fund-raising gathering. In other words, Shenhui found an appealing and effective way to tell his listeners, in essence, "Your donations on behalf of the *sangha* are empty and ultimately of no religious merit. However, through your aspirations to achieve enlightenment on behalf of all living beings and your undertaking of this basically simple path of Chan practice, you should go ahead and make those donations anyway." Iconoclastic language was used, not to undercut the action of contributing to the *sangha,* but to nuance the manner in which the fund-raising request was made. Judging from Shenhui's career as a fund-raiser, this paradoxical appeal for donations *worked*.

Although I have paraphrased the underlying message of Shenhui's mission here in stark and simple terms, this should not be taken to imply a cynical or corrupt ploy on his part. There is an overly ambitious side to Shenhui's vigorous factionalism that created an identity crisis in early Chan (see p. 56), but we do not have enough information to accuse him of anything really seamy. It seems better to accept his abilities as a public evangelist as based on a real ability to move his listeners to moments of transformative religious inspiration. In the process, though, he articulated the Chan message in a way that was eminently suited to successful fundraising activities.

EXPANSION OF MAZU'S HONGZHOU SCHOOL

Mazu Daoyi and his two or three generations of successors, collectively known as the Hongzhou school, are always described as the very paragons of the Chan ideal. These are the "great masters" of the Tang: Nanquan,

Baizhang, Zhaozhou. The basic problem with this depiction is that it is entirely based on texts beginning with the testimony of the *Anthology of the Patriarchal Hall,* which only appeared in 952, a century and a half or so after the flourishing of the Hongzhou school. We consider this important Chan "transmission of the lamp" text just below; for the moment let us use contemporaneous sources to examine certain aspects of Mazu's faction. Here the subject is not the famous stories involving these figures and their spiritual practice, but rather three intriguing aspects of the school's public face.

First, the epitaph written for Mazu shortly after his death states that, at least at the beginning of his time in Hongzhou, he resided in the "government office." Nothing like this is mentioned in the sources available for any Chan monk before this time, which makes it uncertain exactly what the arrangement was. At the time, Hongzhou was in an area of economic, agricultural, and population growth that was of increasing relative importance to the Tang government. That is, after the An Lushan rebellion removed many of China's more outlying regions from de facto central government control, the rice-growing areas of the central southeast became the primary source of in-kind taxation. Hence the location of Mazu's first local residence—he eventually took up residence at the Kaiyuansi, the officially sponsored temple in Hongzhou—implies some kind of collaboration with the central government's tasks of administration.[12]

Second, the Hongzhou school after Mazu exhibits a strikingly clear pattern of expansion throughout Jiangxi (a region geographically similar to modern Jiangxi Province). Over the first three generations there is a steady and progressive expansion of the places throughout Jiangxi at which Hongzhou monks resided. A similar pattern exists for the lineage of Shitou Xiqian (710–90) in Hunan, the progenitor of the Caodong (Sōtō) school and a figure almost equal in stature to Mazu in Chan mythology. Although we do not have enough information to say much that is relevant here to Shitou's lineage, the similarity of the two patterns of geographical expansion implies a regional policy of government support for the new Chan factions.[13]

Third, the earliest text produced by the Hongzhou school, the *Transmissions of Treasure Grove* of 801, uses a format that seems designed for public lectures for laypeople rather than master-disciple discussions in the meditation hall and private quarters. Usually this text is explained within the generalized context of Tang-dynasty Chan practice, or with regard to its inferred enumeration of the Chan lineage in terms of twenty-eight patriarchs from Śākyamuni to Bodhidharma. The closing portion of the text, presumably devoted to Mazu himself, is missing, and YANAGIDA has suggested that the text was no longer needed after the appearance of the *Anthology of the Patriarchal Hall* in 952. Hence, lacking its potentially most interesting sections, the *Transmissions of Treasure Grove* itself has not been widely studied. (On the narrative structure of the *Transmissions of Treasure Grove*, see p. 96.)

The unique format of the *Transmissions of Treasure Grove* is intriguing. As mentioned briefly above, the story of each patriarch's career is presented in two portions, depicting him first as a gifted student who is recognized by the current patriarch and then as an enlightened master seeking his own successor. The reduplication implies a popular storytelling context, a frame structure used to keep the audience entertained and always coming back for more. The lay orientation of these presentations is also implied by the lack of any reference to how any of the patriarchs actually attained enlightenment, a reticence probably based in part on Vinaya proscriptions against monks making false claims regarding their spiritual attainments to laypeople.[14] Although this reticence was modified, or circumvented, in later years, at this stage in the development of the written transcription of encounter dialogue, it is understandable that such restrictions would still apply. It was only a century and a half later, with the *Anthology of the Patriarchal Hall*, that the words of mere students and even brief allusions to the enlightenment experiences of actual people would be included in Chan literature.

It might seem strange that the government would have had any interest in supporting Chan Buddhism, but the reason is straightforward. Scholars to date have written frequently about the "sinicization" of Chinese Buddhism, the process by which it was influenced by and adapted itself to Chinese cultural and political conditions, but no one has addressed the involvement of Chinese Buddhism in what we may call "sinification." Rather than the passive process of sinicization, sinification refers to the long-range enterprise of Han Chinese civilization to overwhelm, incorporate, and pacify the peoples within its ever-increasing cultural sphere. Sinification was a massive historical event, whereby Han culture spread from north to south, and then to the southwest and far west. Beginning sometime in the first millennium before the common era, this process continues down to the present in the increasingly intense efforts going on in Tibet and Xinjiang, the scenes of ongoing Buddhist and Islamic tragedies we will have to pass by without further discussion here.[15]

What has not been realized thus far is the extent to which Buddhism contributed to the process of sinification. Here just a few comments will have to suffice. Fotu Deng ("Buddha" Deng, or Cheng; d. 349), a magic-working Buddhist advisor to an early non-Chinese ruler of northern China, is remembered among other things for having converted the Rong and Mo "barbarians," two non-Chinese ethnic groups of northern China. Rather than interpret this, as Chinese historians have done, in terms of the compatibility between Buddhism and non-Chinese ethnic groups—their only link would be that of an origin considered foreign by Chinese eyes, a link presumably far less salient to the two groups themselves—I suggest that this represents the government use of Buddhism to sinify those groups, to make them more easily governable within a Chinese administrative system. Scholars of religious Daoism have long known that, from the third century at least, Daoist priests worked hand-in-hand with various Chinese governments, providing religious legitimation of their rule.[16] One of the aspects of this collaboration was the use of Daoism to control or suppress popular religious cults that threatened government stability, and there was a collaborative effort against so-called "licentious cults" in southern China during the third and fourth centuries.[17] We do not know specifically how the Hongzhou school may have collaborated with local officials, but the spread of officially sanctioned Buddhist monasteries could well have been part of a program for the social control of local populations.

IMPACT OF THE LATE-TANG CATASTROPHES

In addition to the new interpretation just given of Buddhism's participation in the long-term process of sinification, we also need to reevaluate the impact of the Huichang persecution and Huang Chao rebellion on Chan. As Stanley Weinstein relates in his important study of the political dimensions of Chinese Buddhism under the Tang dynasty, the Huichang persecution may have been temporarily damaging, but the church seems to have recovered fairly quickly. Of greater economic significance was the Huang Chao rebellion of 875–84, which devastated north China and thereby destroyed the social infrastructure on which Buddhism depended for its institutional existence. Professor Weinstein writes:

> Unlike the Hui-ch'ang suppression which in its most destructive phase covered a period of approximately two years, Huang Ch'ao's insurrection raged for nine years and devastated almost every major region of China. Although there is no conclusive evidence that the rebels were specifically hostile to Buddhism, the damage suffered by the church proved to be irreversible . . . the

losses were nothing less than catastrophic and in the long run were probably more detrimental to the maintenance of Buddhist traditions than even the blows of the Hui-ch'ang suppression.[18]

We should also consider adopting a new understanding of the psychological impact of these events, especially the Huichang persecution, on the Buddhist *sangha*. Whether or not the persecution was caused in part by any real degeneration of the clergy, it must have intensified everyone's sensitivity to the rhetoric of such a decline. In her book *Once Upon a Future Time,* Jan Nattier has shown that in India the rhetoric of the demise of Buddhism (known in Chinese as *mofa,* "end period of the Dharma") developed not due to persecution of Buddhism by antagonistic rulers, but rather when the Buddhist church enjoyed excessive material success. Worldly success implied a loss of the original spirit of Buddhism, which involved at the least some distance from ordinary human luxuries, if not their outright rejection.[19] To apply this logic to the Chinese case, if part of the reason for government persecution was that Buddhist monks had violated the other-worldly spirit of their religion by enjoying excessive individual prestige and personal wealth, then the reaffirmation of the religion's lofty ideals would have been an important consideration in the rehabilitation of Buddhism after 845. After the Huang Chao rebellion, the fall of the Tang, and the chaos of the Five Dynasties, the need to justify the fund-raising efforts of the Buddhist monastic institution as a whole would have become even more important. What Chinese Buddhism needed was a way to convince both government and laity that it was firmly committed to higher spiritual goals and therefore deserved their continuing financial support.

THE *ANTHOLOGY OF THE PATRIARCHAL HALL* AS PUBLIC DOCUMENT

The answer to this dilemma of Chinese Buddhism was presented to the court of the Five Dynasties regime of Min (in what is now Fujian Province, directly opposite the island of Taiwan), in the form of the *Anthology of the Patriarchal Hall.* This epoch-making text, which survived only in Korea, is notable in a number of respects. First, it contains transcriptions of massive quantities of Chan encounter dialogue, a genre of discourse which appears here virtually for the first time. Since this dialogue material is presented in colloquial language, the text marks an important milestone in our understanding of the evolution of vernacular Chinese.

Although compiled in the far southeast, one of the curiosities of the text is that it represents its figures using speech forms of the capital at Chang'an. Second, beyond its substantial linguistic value, the *Anthology of the Patriarchal Hall* is a priceless source for the earliest versions of Chan's most famous anecdotes, and as such it is almost always used to describe how Chan master-student interaction took place, how the great Tang patriarchs taught, and how different Chan teaching styles developed. (We have already exploited the text in just this way; see the anecdote introduced on p. 81 above). Third, the text is the first one to present the entire Chan genealogical system of the "transmission of the lamp" genre of texts, so that it presents not only a body of stories but a clearly articulated understanding of the evolution of Buddhism as well. With its extensive treatment of the seven Buddhas of the past, the twenty-eight Indian patriarchs, and the successive generations of Chinese patriarchs from Bodhidharma onward, the *Anthology of the Patriarchal Hall* presented a thoroughly documented framework for understanding the overall evolution of Buddhism from India to China according to the Chan transmission scheme. (See the discussion beginning on p. 2, as well as figure 1.) Although the *Anthology of the Patriarchal Hall* was superseded in only a half-century by the *Transmission of the Lamp*, its compilation was an important step in the evolution of Chan literature.

I suspect that the *Anthology of the Patriarchal Hall* was compiled in part due to a sense of impending loss.[20] Social and military chaos dominated most of China, and the many monks who escaped to the south shared their stories so that this new approach to Buddhism might be preserved. There may have also been a positive sense of self-discovery, as refugee monks realized that the stories they exchanged in their own monasteries were being avidly discussed in so many other locations as well. Hence this text represents an important milestone in the evolution of the Chan community's self-awareness as a "school," and it represents the first manifestation of its interest in and ability to transcribe colloquial Chinese dialogues in written form. For all these reasons, this text gives us an unprecedented access to the world of Chan religious praxis in the mid-tenth century and before.

Given all of this, at this point let us focus on another dimension of the *Anthology of the Patriarchal Hall:* its identity as a public policy document. For it is one of the most notable features of this and the succession of "transmission of the lamp" texts to follow that they were formally submitted to the throne for official recognition and inclusion in the Chinese Buddhist canon. This official sponsorship was not merely a recognition of the overall popularity of Chan Buddhism within the Chinese realm, nor just a natural outgrowth of the role of the imperial court in Chinese religious affairs, but also an indication of the use of these texts *outside* the realm of seated meditation, teacher/student dialogue, and ongoing spiritual cultivation. To be used for these intimate religious purposes, a text would need only to exist, to be circulated and discussed within the confines of the meditation hall community. The government's formal recognition of the "transmission of the lamp" texts was the hallmark of their utilization within a broader institutional framework.[21]

So the question is, Within the context of the Chinese polity as a whole, how would the format and contents of the *Anthology of the Patriarchal Hall* and subsequent "transmission of the lamp" texts serve the needs of the monastic community?

When the question is posed in this fashion, the answer is really quite simple: These texts legitimated the spiritual identity of Chan monks and provided a straightforward cognitive framework for the management of power and patronage within the monastic establishment. To explain this, we need to return to the structure of Chan's genealogical system.

There are really two major sections of the Chan lineage scheme. In chapter 1 we considered the implications of only the first section, that from the seven Buddhas of the past down through the first six Chinese patriarchs. Here the lineage is unilineal, a feature that has significant implications for the homologization of religious charisma within the identity of the Chan patriarch. Each patriarch is essentially equivalent to every other patriarch, meaning that Chinese patriarchs are said to have the same religious authority as Indian Buddhas. In addition, each patriarch/successor account is a paradigm for teacher/student interaction. The varieties of presentation represent only the diversity of human types rather than any absolute religious differences.

But after the sixth Chinese generation the lineage branches out, first in two major divisions, then in a handful of smaller groupings, and ultimately, in the true arboreal fashion of a flourishing family tree, in a veritable thicket of ever more extensive sublineages. Or, to change metaphors, the single river of the transmission flowed undivided through twenty-eight Indian and six Chinese patriarchs to Huineng, after which it branched into two major currents and then a cascade of streams and rivulets. The picture is complicated even further by the successive additions to the "transmission of the lamp" genre, published in close succession in 1004, 1036, 1101, 1183, 1204, and 1252.[22] It was not merely that new figures deserved recognition by their prominence; the differing lineage emphases of these various texts (the specifics of which are not significant here) suggest that strong contestation was involved.

Just as the essentially unilineal first section of the Chan lineage implied homogeneity and equivalence, so must the complex multiplicity of its second section imply heterogeneity and differentiation. Each individual in the massive family tree of Chan was still connected directly to the Buddha and conveyed the full transmission of the Buddha's teachings. At the same time, however, all such individuals were separated into different groupings, a nested set of lineage identities of ever-increasing complexity. Each individual's lineage identity thus traversed a unique set of subdivisions and branches, but eventually connected him to a primordial unity: first one's own teacher and various regional and intermediate figures, then the Tang-dynasty greats such as Linji, Caoshan, Mazu, and Shitou, and ultimately the twenty-eight Indian patriarchs and the Buddha himself.[23]

INSTITUTIONAL FUNCTION
OF THE CHAN LINEAGE SYSTEM

Why did Chan authors record sublineage distinctions in such detail? No doubt there were important doctrinal and even spiritual factors at play. Without denigrating the importance of cognitive modeling, I believe that much more mundane considerations played a major role. The answer can only be that those distinctions mattered in some real and tangible way in how Song-dynasty Buddhists lived their lives and administered their common institutions.

A number of gifted scholars have provided detailed explanations of how the Chinese monastic institution operated during the first half of the twentieth century, and they have shown that the modern patterns of monastic administration are generally continuous with those of the Song dynasty.[24] The picture these scholars describe involves two different types of monastic institutions: large public monasteries known as "forests of the ten directions" (shifang conglin) and a variety of smaller institutions referred to collectively as "disciples temples." There were probably two or three hundred public monasteries during the Song dynasty, some 90 percent or more of which were labeled "Chan" and the rest "teaching" or "Vinaya." Although there were many more similarities than differences between the various public monasteries, since a broad range of Buddhist activities — not limited to either Chan meditation, Tiantai doctrinal instruction, or maintenance of the Vinaya or Buddhist monastic regulations—took place in all such institutions, for the purposes of this discussion I consider only the Chan ones.

Although they are not central to our discussion, for comparative purposes it is important to note some of the features of the disciples temples. Some of these were also sizable institutions, but most were small establishments housing only a single teacher and a handful of novices and trainees. Some were effectively owned by wealthy lay families, while others were under the control of the monks themselves. Often such local temples were controlled by a single succession of teacher and students—but here the succession was simply one of initiation into the Buddhist order (not all of the "disciples" were even formally ordained as novices), not the "mind-to-mind" transmission of Chan. Holmes Welch has shown how, for twentieth-century Buddhism, the human relationships established at the beginning of a trainee's career might continue throughout his life, even for those who went on to gain full ordination and take part in the lifestyle of the public monasteries. We may imagine that a similar overlap of associations was in place during the Song dynasty. One of the tasks of future scholarship of course will be to chart the institutional evolution of Chinese Buddhism, which will certainly result in increasing the sophistication of distinctions drawn between the Song and twentieth-century systems.

Thus there simply were no independent "Zen monasteries" as imagined by Dumoulin. They are a figment of a romantic imagination, and such rose-colored stereotyping always goes hand-in-hand with cynical dismissal. In short, it is the falsely positive image of the Tang that has led to the pervasive disdain for the "degenerate" Song. In Zen studies, and no doubt other fields, "romanticism breeds cynicism."

The important point here is that public monasteries imposed specific, lineage-based restrictions on who could hold the position of abbot. In those public monasteries carrying the designation "Chan," this position was naturally held by a member of the Chan lineage; in the much smaller number of public monasteries labeled "teaching" or "Vinaya" institutions, a Tiantai or Vinaya school affiliation was required. There was also a highly significant rule governing the succession from one abbot to the next: the new abbot had to belong to a sublineage different from that of his predecessor. This was one of the primary distinctions between the public monasteries and disciples temples: the greater prestige of the former carried with it the requirement that power be shared among different sublineages.

In other words, abbots' appointments were determined in part through reference to the micro-level sublineage identities established in the "transmission of the lamp" genre. Hence in very concrete terms, the Chan lineage schema provided a framework within which to negotiate the distribution of power within the monastic institution. This is by no means to suggest that all monks were power-hungry, or that we should ignore the real spiritual dimensions of their lives. Many twentieth-century Buddhist monks are known to have felt that their administrative roles were a burden, and they only participated in monastic administration out of a sense of loyalty and responsibility.[25] No doubt this was true in medieval times as well.

The "success" of Chan in the Song dynasty was thus not the creation of a new monastic institution, but rather the conquest by members of Chan lineages of the highest administrative positions in the vast majority of the largest establishments within that institution. The succession of "transmission of the lamp" texts that appear in the tenth century and beyond were written not just to document the further growth of Chan as a tradition of self-cultivation, but to provide justification for changes, either de facto or proposed, in the balance of power between the various Chan sublineages.

The success of the Chan lineage scheme seems to have taken the other schools of Buddhism by surprise. Or, it would be better to say that the Chan success led to a new understanding of the very definition of a Buddhist "school." Never before in the history of Chinese Buddhism had the theoretical identity of a particular school been associated so closely with monastic administration. To be sure, the Tiantai school had been strongest at its original center on Mount Tiantai, but by the Song (actually, by at least the ninth century), Chan practitioners had come to dominate many of the monasteries on the mountain. Scholars used to talk about Vinaya and Tiantai school monasteries as if they were separate types of institution, but with a few trivial exceptions this simply was not the case. On the contrary, public monasteries incorporated activities of all the so-called "schools" within their precincts—devotions to Amitābha Buddha, lectures on the *Flower Garland* and *Lotus Sūtras,* repentance rituals, and so forth— and it was only in the abbot's position and the meditation hall that such a monastery was in any way "Chan." The "teaching" monasteries of the Song and later were essentially identical, except that the abbot was from a Tiantai lineage, the meditation hall might (but did not necessarily) emphasize Tiantai Zhiyi's instructions on meditation, and there might be regular instruction in the doctrinal taxonomy and other unique teachings of the Tiantai school.

To understand how unprecedented this development was, we should ask ourselves the following question: Why should meditation specialists become abbots of the most important monasteries in early premodern China? Given the preferences of recent American converts to Buddhism, who consider meditation to be the sine qua non of Buddhism itself and ignore almost entirely the cultural role played by the religion in its ethnic communities, this question may not seem obvious at all. Meditation teachers have founded and led most if not all elite American Buddhist communities, after all. But in the medieval and early premodern Chinese context, as well as in other Asian Buddhist contexts from ancient times until now, the question is very much an apposite concern. Why should meditators be good administrators? Why would meditators actively seek, or at least accept, administrative power? Although several other factors require further examination (e.g., what role did specialists in esoteric Buddhism play in this process?), the administrative success of Chan was no doubt predicated on the vacuum created by the end of scriptural translation as the primary focus of attention in the monastic community (see p. 71). However, it was also made possible by a style of religious rhetoric and a shared image of enlightened sagehood disseminated through the newfound medium of woodblock printing. In the next chapter we will see how these factors combined in the Chan school's period of greatest success, the Song dynasty.

CHAPTER 6

Climax Paradigm

Cultural Polarities and Patterns
of Self-Cultivation in Song-Dynasty Chan

Song-Dynasty Chan as Climax Paradigm

After a forest has been devastated, whether by fire or the excessive harvesting of lumber, it immediately begins to grow back. First to sprout are quick-growing grasses, followed by wildflowers whose seeds are carried on the winds. Erosion from rainfall and runoff carve new channels in the earth, sometimes changing the topography forever, but eventually a network of roots develops to stabilize the ground. Given the variations of climate, birches or other softwoods may climb to the sky first, but they will eventually be crowded out by taller species of trees that are able to reach through to the sun. Although it may take several decades, or even centuries, in the absence of new catastrophes a kind of stability will eventually emerge. Subject to a complex dynamic of forces and processes, individual plants and animals will grow and die within the mature forest, which has now become what ecologists refer to as a *climax community*. Although change still occurs within the forest on the basis of different natural cycles—the days, seasons, and years—the overall system has stabilized. Individual plants and animals are born, grow to maturity, and die within that system, but the major components of the forest community function interdependently. The overall configuration of those components, the subcommunities, colonies, and niches within the larger climax forest community, will also change, sometimes quickly and in some cases almost imperceptibly, over time. However complex and dynamic it may be, the forest as a whole has taken on a relative stability that allows its analysis as a single (if multidimensional) system.[1]

In the Song dynasty (960–1279), Chinese Chan Buddhism reached something of a climax paradigm.[2] By "climax paradigm," I mean a conceptual configuration by which Chan was described in written texts, practiced by its adherents, and, by extension, understood as a religious entity by the Chinese population as a whole. As with the forest climax community, this is not to say that all change within Chan Buddhism ceased—far from it!—only that the basic conceptual parameters of the school's self-conception and approach to spiritual cultivation had become well established. Previous events in Chan were interpreted through the lens of the Song-dynasty configuration, and subsequent developments in China, Korea, Japan, and Vietnam were evaluated, even as they occurred, against what was known of the standards established during the Song. Thus the romanticized image of the great Tang-dynasty masters—Mazu and his students, Caoshan, Dongshan, and their students, and of course Linji—was generated by Song-dynasty authors and functioned within Song-dynasty texts. Similarly, even where subsequent figures throughout East Asia—Hakuin Ekaku (1685–1769), the famous reviver of Japanese Rinzai, is the best example—evoke the examples of Bodhidharma, the Sixth Patriarch Huineng, Mazu, and the others, they do so through the conceptual filter of Song-dynasty Chan. The individual images of Bodhidharma, Huineng, and other early Chan figures no doubt continued to change as time went on, but the overall framework in which their examples were used was based on the conceptual paradigm that matured in the Song.

This interpretation is radically different from earlier understandings of the evolution of Chinese Chan. As we have seen, Dumoulin treated Tang-dynasty Chan as the golden age of the tradition and dismissed Song-dynasty Chan as a period of decline. I have cited Dumoulin's work extensively in the preceding pages, but only because he is the most convenient example of a general style of interpretation. China historian Arthur F. Wright espoused a similar approach, extolling the "everyman" quality of the Sixth Patriarch Huineng, then dismissing everything that follows without even serious consideration. Kenneth K. S. Ch'en, whose textbook on Chinese Buddhism is still widely used, characterizes *all* of Chinese Buddhism from the Song dynasty onward in terms of "decline." And the interpretations of Jacques Gernet and Wm. Theodore de Bary echo this same pattern.[3] A number of different historiographical factors have concatenated to create this situation, ranging from Hu Shih's scholarship, Confucian prejudices, overemphasis of the novelty of "popular" or vernacular religious developments in the post-Song period, and the misapplication of Japanese sectarian models to the Chinese subject matter. These topics are far too involved for discussion here, but their cumulative effect—the image of Song-dynasty Buddhism as a religion in decline—is persistent.

In spite of this commonly held misunderstanding, recent scholarship on both Chan and Chinese Buddhism is unanimous in holding that the overall activity level of Buddhism in China actually rose to a peak during the Song. Scholars of Chan now argue that the school really took shape only in the Song, and that its image of a "golden age" during the Tang is just that, an image in the minds of Song devotees. During the Song dynasty, Chan monks became abbots of most of the great monastic establishments in China, moving by imperial invitation from one position to the next, often carrying imperially bestowed titles and purple robes along the way. Similarly, it was during this period that the Tiantai school reorganized itself, albeit through a process of sometimes acrimonious debate. And the Pure Land school developed from a diffuse style of devotional and ritual endeavor into the most widely accepted vehicle for the salvation of ordinary monks, nuns, and laypeople, producing new types of social organizations that promoted mutual assistance for their members during the trials of illness and death.

It is important to recognize, of course, that not all the successes and shortcomings of Chan occurred in a single pattern of congruent features. One of the major goals of this book, indeed, is to suggest that we avoid reducing the subject matter to simplistically encyclopedic parallels. I hope that the ecological metaphor used here will help us appreciate the complexity, even the chaos, of the phenomena with which we are dealing. We have scattered evidence about Bodhidharma and his associates in the proto-Chan phase, but not really enough to know how, or even whether, all that evidence pertains to one definable group or movement. Our knowledge of the East Mountain teaching phase is better, but still involves substantial retrospective inference. There seems to be a stable central community, but it is known only through limited evidence and later projections. At the beginning of the eighth century the self-described successors to this community exploded on the national scene, and in the process they described themselves as an identifiable religious movement using the lineage model. No matter how diverse and multifaceted the Chan movement was at this point in time, no matter how fuzzy the boundaries were between it and other realms of Chinese religious life, from this point onward Chan had achieved a significant level of sectarian identity. To continue the ecological metaphor, it was as if the various disparate elements of the earlier phases had generated a set of relationships, patterns of interaction (whether dependency, symbiosis, or even parasitism) that were relatively stable even as the elements continued to change. The emergence of encounter dialogue in the middle period brought with it a substantial change in those patterns of interaction, resulting in major changes within the Chan community as a whole. Here "Chan community" refers not just to a community of individuals, but more importantly to a conceptual set of different lineage groups, styles of practice, and rhetorical forms.[4] It was during the Song dynasty that the genealogical, practical, and rhetorical forms of Chan attained their most lasting configuration; even as those separate forms continued to evolve and interact, their overall network of interrelationships attained a stable "climax community" pattern.

I do not devote any significant space to the description of the Song dynasty monastic establishment; let us await the appearance of Foulk's detailed and penetrating analysis.[5] However, one important feature must not be overlooked: Chan was not nearly as separate from these other types of Buddhist activity as one might think. In our discussion of Chan's administrative success in the preceding chapter, we saw that the monasteries of which Chan monks became abbots were comprehensive institutions, "public monasteries" that supported various types of Buddhist activities other than Chan-style meditation. The reader should bear this point in mind: In contrast to the independent denominations of Sōtō and Rinzai that emerged (largely by government fiat) in seventeenth-century Japan, *there was never any such thing as an institutionally separate Chan "school" at any time in Chinese Buddhist history.*

In spite of this absence of any demonstrably separate institutional identity, Song-dynasty Chan—even allowing for its conspicuous variations over time and space—represents the climax paradigm of the tradition for the following reasons. First, it was during this period that the most lasting forms of Chan practice emerged. By "Chan practice" here I mean both the monastic conventions of meditation hall life (the social practice of Chan as a whole) and the styles of religious introspection and self-cultivation discussed below. Second, these forms of practice were the basis for the dissemination of Chan throughout East Asia, that is, not only in China but in Korea and Japan as well. Actually, the ecological metaphor used here suggests how improper it would be to portray Song-dynasty Chan with a single brush: from its climax paradigm repertoire came quite an array of species, phenotypes, and niche configurations that were to be transplanted and evolve across East Asia. Although it would be impossible to quantify the overall popularity of Chan in comparison with other types of East Asian Buddhist religious activity, it is undeniably the case that during the Song dynasty Chan attained an unprecedented plateau of ascendancy throughout Chinese and eventually all East Asian culture. Indications of this ascendancy may be seen in the increased percentage of Chan specialists covered in the standard biographical collections from before the Tang to the Song,[6] the flood of Chan publications, and the frequent references to Chan in the secular literature. Third, it has been through the lens of Song-dynasty understandings that both the members of the school in subsequent centuries and its interpreters in the twentieth and twenty-first centuries have experienced Chan Buddhism. Here I need mention only that D. T. Suzuki's twentieth-century exposition of Rinzai Zen as *kōan* practice finds its roots in the innovations of the twelfth-century Dahui Zonggao, to be discussed just below.

These chapters have been devoted primarily to outlining the evolving Chan ideology of spiritual cultivation, not the details of the school's institutional history, and this final contribution is no exception. That is, in defining the climax paradigm of Song-dynasty Chan, I would like to focus, for simplicity, on two well-known but very different approaches to Chan meditation practice, known by the convenient shorthand labels "viewing the phrase" and "silent illumination" Chan. Readers who are already familiar with Zen will quickly recognize the association of these terms with the Linji (Rinzai) and Caodong (Sōtō) schools.

The Exemplary Career of Dahui Zonggao

Although there were many eminent Chan monks during the Song, the one with the most lasting importance was certainly Dahui Zonggao (1089–1163). His accomplishments clearly derived from his training under great masters, particularly Yuanwu Keqin (1063–1135), compiler of the "precedent anthology" known as the *Emerald Cliff Record (Biyan lu),* but Dahui added new emphasis and energy of his own to the contemporary understanding of Zen practice. It is no exaggeration to say, in fact, that in Dahui's life and teachings we find exemplified the very pinnacle of Linji Chan.

Dahui's Buddhist training was unexceptional for his times.[7] Tonsured at age sixteen and given the Dharma name Zonggao (meaning roughly "brilliance of truth"), he became formally ordained the next year. He was soon drawn to Chan writings, especially those of the innovative Yunmen Wenyan (864–949).[8] At the same time, he is said to have had an inspirational experience while reading a Mahāyāna scripture. The following year he began his wanderings to study under different teachers, sometimes sampling the styles of several teachers in a single year. (At this stage, it seems that most of his teachers were actually in the Caodong lineage.) In 1116 Dahui met the retired prime minister and lay Buddhist scholar Zhang Shangying (1043–1122), and soon after that Han Zicang (d.u.). These two prominent laymen were to be important influences in his life.

From relatively early in his training, Dahui had received recommendations to study under Yuanwu, but it was only in the fourth month of 1125 that he was finally able to enter Yuanwu's assembly. After only six weeks or so, on the thirteenth day of the fifth month of that year, Dahui had a decisive moment of awakening during one of Yuanwu's sermons. Miriam Levering recounts the event as follows:

> Yuanwu cited an exchange in which a monk asked Yunmen, "What is the place like where all the Buddhas are born?" Yunmen answered: "The East Mountain travels on the water." Yuanwu continued, "If today someone were to ask me what the place is like where all the Buddhas are born, I would reply: 'The *xun* wind comes from the south, and the palace has a slight coolness.'"
>
> On hearing these words, Dahui experienced a marvelous end to all his doubts, and a feeling of great peace, joy and release. When he went to report his breakthrough to Yuanwu, the teacher made Dahui an attendant without duties in the quarters where court guests were entertained, a spot where Yuanwu could supervise his progress personally every day. Seeing that his enlightenment needed further refinement, Yuanwu gave Dahui another *huatou* ("critical phrase") to work on. Every day for half a year Dahui worked on this *huatou* under Yuanwu's supervision. Finally one day Dahui asked Yuanwu to tell him how his teacher Wuzu Fayan had replied to Yuanwu's asking about that same *huatou* once in the past. When Yuanwu complied, Dahui experienced a complete and certain enlightenment. Yuanwu tested it by posing other *huatou* to Dahui and found that Dahui could answer them all without the slightest hesitation. Yuanwu then gave Dahui a residence of his own at Heavenly Peace Temple (Tianningsi) and allowed Dahui to share in the teaching and preaching duties as a fellow teacher.[9]

Not long after this, Dahui and his teacher had to flee the north in advance of the conquering Jin dynasty forces. They parted ways in 1127, were together again briefly from the end of 1128, and then were separated again when Yuanwu went off west to Sichuan. Dahui spent the next five or six years in comparative isolation in a couple of locations in Jiangxi and Hunan, with only twenty monks in attendance, continuing his practice and coauthoring poetic commentaries on famous Chan precedents.

In 1133 Dahui responded to a letter from Han Zicang, bemoaning the decline of Chan in the world and entreating Dahui to stop "sitting alone on his peak, wearing grass and eating roots." We may safely avoid taking seriously Han's stereotypical denigration of religious practice during his day: Just as appeals by Indra and Brahmā were necessary to get Śākyamuni off his seat under the *bodhi* tree, so Dahui had to be convinced to take up his natural mission as a teacher![10] After a half-year living in Han's house (apparently more than a simple letter was required!), Dahui began to act and write more publicly. He began to attack other teachers and teachings he considered to be heretical, especially those who avoided aiming vigorously at a moment of awakening in favor of a more passive approach to meditation. From 1134 on, Dahui began to attack the advocates of "silent illumination," perhaps because he was in Fujian near the Caodong monk Zhenxie Qingliao (1088–1151), who was then the abbot of a monastery with more than fifteen hundred people in residence.[11] Dahui's targets included members of his own lineage, and his propensity for public criticism of others earned him the nickname of the "one who bawls out heaven"!

But Dahui did not devote all his energies to such acrimony. It was also in 1134, in his role as spiritual instructor of a nun named Miaodao, that Dahui finalized his unique method of Chan practice known as "viewing the phrase" (*kanhua;* J. *kanna),* which is discussed below. While this technique may have been designed specifically to counter the Caodong upsurge with a new contrasting slogan, there is a parallel between the teaching style Dahui developed and his approach to other liturgical responsibilities. That is, Levering notes Dahui's uniquely personal style in the use of funerary memorials and other sermons. Rather than merely repeating generalizations and commonplace truths, Dahui's sermons are the earliest known examples in which the doctrines emphasized were specifically related to the patrons' individual situations. In other words, although he cannot have been the first Chinese Buddhist monk to have used these occasions to develop close personal connections with his supporters, he seems to have done so with an innovative personal touch. The practice of *kanhua Chan* also emphasized the close personal interaction between teacher and student.

Dahui's first major appointment came in 1137, as abbot of Śākyamuni Temple (Nengrensi), also known as Jingshan, near Lin'an, the Southern Song capital. There for almost six years he attracted more than two thousand students while reviving the glory of the Linji line and continuing his attacks on "heretical" teachings. In 1143 he was banished for criticizing government policy—probably for being too outspoken in recommending military action to retake northern China from the Jin—a lost cause, given the sad state of preparedness of Southern Song troops. Although he was not allowed to maintain his clerical status during this time, Dahui's sixteen years in exile were comparatively pleasant. He continued teaching and writing, and he took the opportunity to travel to the Sixth Patriarch's temple in Caoqi. In 1156 he was released from his exile but spent nearly a year traveling, only accepting an imperial invitation to become abbot of Mount Aśoka Temple at the end of 1156. During his year or so there Dahui taught twelve hundred students, and even though dormitories and a water pond were built, the facilities were not adequate for his following. In 1158 he returned to Jingshan, where he stayed for the next four years, with a thousand monks studying under him.

After retiring from the abbacy of Jingshan in 1161, Dahui performed various teaching duties. In 1162 he was invited to preach before the emperor, and only then did he receive the name Dahui ("Great Wisdom"), by which he is best remembered. After traveling about a bit, he returned to Jingshan in the seventh month of 1163. On the ninth day of the eighth month he announced that he would die on the morrow, then sent farewell letters to the emperor and several friends. On the tenth, still clear and calm, he wrote out the following verse before dying peacefully:

Life is just this,
death is just this.
To have a verse or not—
why should it matter?[12]

Dahui had more than 110 ordained Dharma heirs and scores of lay disciples. As Levering observes, it is incredible that he was able to be so productive in spite of the many years in exile, with only ten years of teaching in large public monasteries.

The "Viewing the Phrase" Chan of Dahui Zonggao

The preceding description of Dahui's enlightenment experiences under Yuanwu used the term *huatou (watō)*, "critical phrase," and Dahui's method is referred to as *kanhua Chan (kanna Zen)*, "viewing the [critical] phrase Zen." The "critical phrase" is the most crucial part of a *gong'an*, or "precedent," often its very last sentence. But the meaning of these expressions is not self-evident.

First, let us consider what Dahui meant by "viewing." This was no passive state of observation, nor a kind of intellectual contemplation. Dahui disallows any use of rational processes, any attempt to make ordinary sense of the subject matter. He enjoined his students against attempting to understand the precedent logically, or according to Buddhist doctrine, or using the specifics of its wording, or by clues inferred from a teacher's gestures. Any specific method students might come up with was rejected. For example, Dahui taught his student Miaodao as follows:

> I cited Mazu's "It is not mind, it is not Buddha, it is not a thing" and instructed her to look at it. Moreover, I gave her an explanation: "(1) You must not take it as a statement of truth. (2) You must not take it to be something you do not need to do anything about. (3) Do not take it as a flint-struck spark or a lightning flash. (4) Do not try to divine the meaning of it. (5) Do not try to figure it out from the context in which I brought it up. 'It is not the mind, it is not the Buddha, it is not a thing; after all, what is it?'"[13]

The only possible recourse was a form of total surrender:

> You must in one fell swoop break through this one thought—then and only then will you comprehend birth and death. Then and only then will it be called accessing awakening. . . . You need only lay down, all at once, the mind full of deluded thoughts and inverted thinking, the mind of logical discrimination, the mind that loves life and hates death, the mind of knowledge and views, interpretation and comprehension, and the mind that rejoices in stillness and turns from disturbance.[14]

Attaining this type of awakening was no easy matter, of course. Dahui expected his students to exert themselves with a type of effort that exceeded their normal capabilities.[15]

There is a striking difference between Dahui's intense, even ferocious, attitude toward meditation practice and the nuanced exertion portrayed in the *Treatise on the Essentials of Cultivating the Mind* attributed to Hongren. Of course this may simply be a difference of literary style; by Dahui's time it may have become fashionable to portray one's personal energies more explicitly. Leaving aside the possibility that Hongren may have had his fiercely demanding side as well (the text attributed to him does include numerous exhortations to energetic effort), we may simply note that Dahui demanded total dedication from his students. The list of requirements given above is of course impossible to achieve—and this is no doubt one of his points, that one must throw oneself so completely into the endeavor as to go entirely beyond the boundaries of personal effort and accomplishment.

Second, what is a "critical phrase"? The Chinese compound *huatou* simply means a "bit of speech" or a "topic." In Chan usage, however, it refers to the most crucial (and usually final) line in a *gong'an,* which means roughly a "legal case" or thus a "precedent."[16] The *gong'an* was invariably taken from some transcription of encounter dialogue, usually from the *Transmission of the Lamp.* In the Song dynasty it became fashionable for Chan teachers to compile anthologies of their favorite examples of Chan dialogue, which they then used in oral instruction with their immediate students and commented on in characteristically idiosyncratic Chan language for publication. The most famous example of this process, of course, is the *Emerald Cliff Record* compiled by Dahui's teacher Yuanwu, which includes a hundred such precedents with poetic introduction and commentary by Yuanwu and his own teacher, Xuedou Zhongxian (980–1052). Dahui seems to have had some misgivings about the literary goings-on that accompanied Chan practice, and there is a famous legend that he actually burned his copy of the *Emerald Cliff Record* at one point relatively late in his career. Whether or not this is true (the event is not mentioned in the chronological record of Dahui's life) is of course less important than that many people thought the story was true, or at least believable.

To understand "viewing the phrase" Chan, we must first consider the identity of the critical phrase within the context of an entire precedent. The following is my favorite example, case 63 from the *Emerald Cliff Record,* known as "Nanquan Cuts the Cat in Two." The text includes a brief "pointer" or introduction by Yuanwu, the case itself, and a concluding verse by Yuanwu's teacher Xuedou. The case and concluding verse are graced with Yuanwu's comments, presented here in smaller type to imitate their appearance in most Chinese editions as interlineal glosses (that is, a double column of half-sized characters below each full-sized phrase of the case and verse).

Pointer

What is beyond thinking must be the topic for serious discourse. What transcends words should be the subject of earnest investigation. When lightning flashes and shooting stars fall, you should display the power to drain the deepest lakes and overturn mountains. Has any of you acquired such ability? See the following.

Case

ONE DAY NANQUAN SAW THE MONKS OF THE EASTERN AND WESTERN HALLS QUARRELING OVER A CAT. This was not just this one day's argument, but a regular waste of time. HE HELD UP THE CAT AND

SAID, "IF YOU CAN SAY IT, I WON'T KILL IT." A direct command that should be carried out. [Everyone in] the ten directions just sits there. This old man has an arm that can distinguish dragons from snakes. NO ONE SAID ANYTHING. What a lamentable error! A whole bunch of lacquered dolls—what are they able to do? Fake Chan monks, like hemp or chestnuts! NANQUAN THEN CUT THE CAT IN TWO. Joy, joy! If he hadn't done this it would have been like a man playing with mudpies. To stretch one's bow after the bandits have gone. This is already the second head—he should have hit them before they even brought it up.

Verse

HOW USELESS THE MONKS OF BOTH HALLS; A parent's words come from a parent's mouth. One word and he's said it all. The judgment was decided on the basis of the case. RAISING DUST AND SMOKE, UNABLE TO DO ANYTHING. See, what kind of resolution could you achieve? The precedent of manifest creation (*xiancheng gong'an*; J. *genjō kōan*). There are still a few. FORTUNATELY, NANQUAN GAVE THE ORDER; Raising his whisk and saying, "One like this." Old Master Wang (i.e., Nanquan) is a little like this. To use this excellent precious sword of the vajra king to go cut mud! WITH A SINGLE [SLICE OF THE] KNIFE [HE CUT THE CAT] IN TWO WITHOUT INEQUITY. Smashed in a hundred pieces! Suddenly a man wields a knife, and what do you think he did? Don't make a mistake, or I'll hit you![17]

Dahui's instruction is then to concentrate on understanding the line "Nanquan then cut the cat in two," precisely the most brutal and inexplicable point in the entire case. What sort of a spiritual practice is this?

My own students, especially in the university classroom, are always stunned by the notion that a Buddhist monk could actually kill a cat. Avid Zen practitioners may have had the same reaction at one time, but they eventually become quite blasé about such violent examples. After all, they have long since heard stories about Linji recommending that one kill the Buddha or one's parents, so the radical bifurcation of a feline inevitably seems less of an issue. How sad! In my own mind there is of course no possibility whatsoever that the incident ever happened as written—Buddhist monks simply do *not* carry knives about, nor do they cut off their own arms or dismember other living beings! (The sacrifice of a finger or arm—a highly ritualized act of devotion and asceticism—is a different story, of course.[18]) However, the story was selected from the vast trove of encounter dialogue literature precisely because of its shock value, so as to get students to consider why exactly something like this might have happened.

By considering the line "Nanquan then cut the cat in two," the trainee is forced to wonder just what the monks were arguing about in the first place. Were they debating whether or not their small domestic animal had the Buddha-nature, as a dog might (or might not)? Or were the monks of the two different halls, east and west, claiming ownership of the cat due to its contributions as mouser? In either case, does it matter that the Eastern Hall probably housed the monastery's administrative services and the Western Hall its meditation center? In the McLuhan sense, once again, since so little background detail is provided, the topic of contemplation here demands that the contemplator visualize its original circumstances for himself.

This process of visualization is, in fact, exactly the point.

What was the meditator visualizing, and what would come of it? The trainee was instructed to contemplate images of enlightened behavior, couched so as to be perplexing and beyond ordinary human under-standing, but by this very opacity recognized as harboring some greater truths. At the same time, the attention to the enlightened activity of the ancient patriarchs served as a mirror to one's own inner identity. In this sense it is significant that one was taught to use written accounts of the legendary masters of one's own lineage rather than the Chinese Buddhist tradition as a whole: the subjects of the stories in the *Emerald Cliff Record* were of course the legendary masters of the Tang and Five Dynasties pe-riods, virtually all of whom were portrayed as lineal predecessors of Xue-dou, Yuanwu, Dahui, and by extension Dahui's students. One looked at the enlightened activities of one's lineal forebears in order to understand one's own identity. An encounter with one's spiritual ancestry was the key to understanding the present.

Dahui's own enlightenment experiences occurred when he and Yuanwu played with such dialogues, taking the roles of the participants and en-gaging in dialogue in their stead. Yuanwu's commentary on his master Xuedou's verse and the case itself impart the sense that he was attempt-ing to use the medium of writing to accomplish the same function. That is, he writes as if attempting to enter into the dialogue, to live within the idealized Tang-dynasty realm of spontaneous interaction. Actually, the *Emerald Cliff Record* was not a text that Yuanwu "wrote," but the tran-scribed product of his lectures on the one hundred cases and his own mas-ter Xuedou's verses. The literary impact of this written by-product is cer-tainly intriguing: In at least the one instance introduced above, Yuanwu's commentary sharply demarcates a line between masters and students, as he roots for the actions of his would-be peer Nanquan and condemns the incompetence of the ordinary monks, all from the literary sidelines of interlineal gloss—or, primordially, from the high seat of his sermons. Yuan-wu's comments contain no hint of indecisiveness or question, nor even any inquiry into the deeper implications of Nanquan's action. Was this lack of curiosity some form of intellectual or religious shallowness? Or, was Dahui's supposed difficulty with the text merely that it seemed to fix specific meanings to the cases, when the primary intention of Yuanwu's teaching had been to catalyze an attitude of openness in his students and audience? We will never know why Dahui became frustrated with this text (if in fact he did), but we may speculate that he realized the written text had closed off its subject matter in a way unworthy of his teacher's creativity.[19]

In an important article on the evolution of Chan spiritual cultivation, Robert Buswell explains the emergence of "viewing the phrase" Chan in terms of the school's creation of a truly subitist approach.[20] In his presentation, "viewing the critical phrase" Chan emerges as the result of the school's almost self-conscious quest for a technique to match its subitist rhetoric. To be sure, suddenness acted as a constraint on what could be said about meditation practice, and perhaps even as a guide to what kinds of approaches were considered preferable. However, there were simply too many possible approaches that could be called "sudden" in one way or an-other—if not an infinite number, then certainly an indefinite plurality. In my own estimation, more important than any subitist rhetorical impera-tive was the genealogical framework of "viewing the phrase" Chan—the formulation of the practice in terms of the student's examination of mod-els of enlightened behavior within his own ancestral lineage.

Dahui's "viewing the phrase" Chan developed largely through his in-teraction with educated literati, and it evolved into a form that captured their collective imaginations. It was not precisely the case that Dahui's literati clientele manufactured his ideas for him, but that he happened, through a combination of lineage tradition and individual skill, to pro-duce an approach to Chan practice that conformed to literati expectations. This is by no means to downplay the innovativeness of Dahui's new ap-proach, but even to highlight it by comparing its fate to that of numer-ous other Chan teachers whose ideas did not capture the imagination of the world in the way his did.

What were the most important elements of Dahui's approach? We have already noticed these features above:

1. stress on both effort and enlightenment, since without the former the goal would be belittled and without the latter there would be no in-ducement for training

2. reduction of the genealogical encounter implicit in encounter dialogue to the practice of meditative introspection, by using contemplation on snippets of dialogue as a substitute for engagement in actual dialogue

3. creation of a backward-looking model of enlightened sagehood that fit the Chinese style of "ancestral time," in which the pure simplicity of a golden age is attributed to the age of one's primordial ancestors

4. unification of past and present practitioners into a genealogically defined "consociation," an association of individuals unrelated by birth or marriage that presents an outer face of unity under one figurehead but within which its members actively compete for status.[21]

We can see in these patterns the manner in which "Zen spontaneity" lived in the Song-dynasty context. Rather than actually live their lives in untrammeled spontaneity, as the Tang figures Hanshan and Shide were supposed to have done, for example, Song-dynasty Chan practitioners inscribed spontaneity within clearly demarcated limits. They talked about spontaneity, imagined spontaneity, debated spontaneity, and pondered spontaneity—all within the formally structured and highly ritualized context of Song monastic life. They presumably spent precious little time actually living and acting "spontaneously."

Yet Dahui at least was engaged in the creation of a new approach to Buddhist self-cultivation. One of the ways to appreciate the significance of his novel approach is to consider its imitation by the Neo-Confucian Daoxue scholar Zhang Jiucheng (1092–1159) in his style of "investigating things" and "guarding the mind." In addition to using a type of quiet contemplation that obviously drew upon Buddhist meditation theories, Zhang's approach to the Confucian classics was remarkably similar to the Chan attitude toward the ancient sages. Here is Zhang's appreciation of the *Spring and Autumn Annals:*

> In the *Spring and Autumn* our master Confucius has fully revealed the Way of emperors and kings, the power of heaven and earth, the brilliance of the sun and the moon, and the movements of the seasons—how can this be perceived with the ordinary mind? If, in the space of a single word, you apprehend the forge and furnace of the sagely mind, then yin and yang will break open and clouds will send down their rain. This is all [contained within] our Master's *Spring and Autumn*—from "cultivating one's person to regulating the family, governing the state, and bringing peace to all under heaven," all is possible.[22]

Ari Borrell explains Zhang's understanding to be that, by reading the *Annals,* the student would "personally receive the transmission of the Master's 'method of the mind' *(xinfa)* and, 'Having gotten the mind [of Confucius], then [our own daily activities such as] eating and drinking, sleeping and resting, answering and responding will all be the actions of our Master [Confucius].'"[23] Although Zhang's presentation might be too straightforward for Dahui's liking, it would be possible to substitute Bodhidharma or Mazu for Confucius for a perfectly acceptable interpretation of Chan practice.

There is no doubt that Zhang Jiucheng's approach paralleled Dahui's. Nor should we overlook the political ramifications of the two men's positions—both were strong advocates of the "hawk" position that the Song dynasty should fight to retake the north, and there is a consistency in the dynamism of their styles of religious introspection and their political views. However, for our purposes it is more important to confirm the general parallel (observed for the first time at least a half-century ago) between the polarities in Chan practice and Neo-Confucian theory. If Dahui's dynamic "viewing the phrase" Chan resembled the "examination and knowing" of Daoxue, then how did the more quietistic "silent illumination" of the Caodong lineage resemble the "nourishing and cultivating" of the Cheng-Zhu faction of Neo-Confucianism?[24] We will return to the parallels between Chan and Neo-Confucian theory shortly, but first we should look at the other major configuration of Song-dynasty Chan practice.

"Silent Illumination" and the Teachings of Twelfth-Century Caodong Chan

It is useful to take Dahui's criticisms as the starting point for consideration of another important style of Song-dynasty Chan practice—important both for its presence in Chinese Buddhism and for its position within the Japanese Sōtō school founded by Dōgen (1200–53). This is the Caodong approach, commonly known as "silent illumination," which Dahui excoriates. While Dahui's criticisms certainly are not unimpeachable, we may consider them and their contemporary context as a prelude to understanding the larger significance of Caodong practice in its own right.

The most prominent members of the Caodong lineage in the Song dynasty were Zhenxie Qingliao and Hongzhi Zhengjue (1091–1157). As already noted (see p. 125), Dahui's earliest denunciations of "silent illumination" Chan, in 1134, may have been inspired by his proximity to a monastery run by Qingliao. Hongzhi had written his *Inscription on Silent*

Illumination (Mozhao ming) a few years before this, though (the preface is dated 1131), and scholars have long wondered whether he was the target of Dahui's criticisms. Very few other Caodong texts actually use the term *mozhao,* "silent illumination," so there could hardly have been a more likely target. However, there is good evidence that, although the two men met only once, Dahui and Hongzhi respected each other greatly as fellow Buddhists. Dahui praised Hongzhi several times during his period of the active denunciation of "silent illumination" practice, and after the other man's death Dahui praised Hongzhi's virtues in poetic form. During his life Hongzhi recommended Dahui for installation as abbot at one of the empire's most prestigious monasteries, and when about to die he asked that Dahui be in charge of his funeral.[25] So, how was it that Dahui could so vociferously oppose a signature doctrine of Hongzhi's while maintaining such cordial relations with him?[26]

During Dahui's life Caodong Chan, once on the brink of disappearance, was enjoying a revival. With the death of the last lineal successor to the founders of the school in 1037, the extinction of Caodong Chan would seem to have been assured. However, that last Caodong monk (named Dayang Jingxuan [942–1027]) asked a colleague in the Linji tradition to maintain his Caodong transmission in trust and pass it on to a suitable student. The student so chosen was Touzi Yiqing (1032–83), who was not even born when his supposed "master" died.[27] Yiqing's student Furong Daokai (1043–1118) seems to have been an innovative and productive individual, and his second-generation students Zhenxie Qingliao and Hongzhi Zhengjue were the most active and high-profile members of the Caodong revival. During the lifetimes of these two men, however, there were at least fifty-four active teachers in their grand-master Daokai's lineage. Both Qingliao and Hongzhi supposedly had thousands of followers, and they had fourteen and twenty-eight recognized Dharma heirs, respectively.

The Caodong resurgence straddled the loss of the north to the Jurchen Jin dynasty in 1126 and the ensuing decrease in government support for Chan Buddhism. This decrease in support was manifested by a drop in the numbers of official name plaques granted monasteries, restrictions on the ordination of monks, and so forth. Chan teachers thus felt increasingly compelled to aim their messages at literati, who were beginning to practice Chan meditation in significant numbers. As we have already seen, much of Dahui's message was molded through his emphasis on the literati audience, and the upsurge in Caodong activity no doubt intensified his competitive fire.

Although the Caodong teachers Daokai, Qingliao, and Hongzhi each had slightly different approaches to meditation practice, one crucial element determined Dahui's positive or negative response: effort.[28] If the style of practice could be characterized as simply waiting around for enlightenment to happen, or even disregarding the importance of the actual experience of enlightenment, then Dahui's attack was blistering. However, if he perceived a demand for constant and energetic application of effort, he was able to approve styles of meditation practice profoundly different from his own.

For example, Furong Daokai wrote:

If you can awaken to and understand [where] your own self [was] at the time of the empty eon, then it will be like hundreds or thousands of suns and moons whose radiance is inexhaustible, or like countless sentient beings all at once attaining liberation. But if you still don't understand, it is absolutely necessary that you retreat and come to a halt. You yourself must completely cease; you yourself should be completely at rest; you must be like a censer in an old shrine; the [instance of] one thought [of yours] should last for ten thousand years; and you should be like a man who doesn't take even a single breath. If you are able to be like this constantly for months and years, then, if you don't obtain the fruits of the Way, I am speaking nonsense and have been deceiving you all, and I will surely be born trapped in hell. I urge you all not to mistakenly apply your bodies and minds in trying to analyze the distance of the road ahead. Do not rely on an intermittent approach. It is necessary that you yourself put your strength into it; no one else can do it for you.[29]

In these passages Daokai counsels his students to make effort in a way that Dahui might have appreciated. However, the effort recommended here is to maintain oneself continuously in a state of total rest—not plunge on energetically, exhausting all one's resources until one achieved a sudden breakthrough, as Dahui would have it.

Qingliao's pronouncements on meditation practice, though, actually reject the notion of conscious effort:

Without taking a step you should constantly sit in your room and just forget about the teachings. Be like dried wood, or a stone, or a wall, or a piece of tile, or a pebble. Cut off "knowing" and "understanding" and be naturally vacuous and completely bright. You should not make the least bit of conscious effort here.

•

You should be like a baby who doesn't distinguish between north and south or know the difference between the six senses. You should rest your head at once and naturally be vacuous and bright and self-illuminating.

■

> In the middle of activity be constantly still, when in darkness increase bright-
> ness. Don't fall into dualistic extremes.[30]

Since Qingliao talks only of "rest[ing] your head at once" and being "constantly still" in the middle of activity—apparently without any counter-
vailing injunctions to be active within stillness, to strive without making
conscious effort—it is understandable that he aroused Dahui's ire.

Hongzhi's *Inscription on Silent Illumination* contains a similar attempt
to achieve balance between meditative serenity and energetic endeavor:

> Transcendent wisdom exists in the silence [of meditation];
> striving for achievement is forgotten in illumination.
> Where does transcendent wisdom exist?
> Alertly we destroy murkiness.
> The path of Silent Illumination
> is the basis for leaving the world of delusion.[31]

For Hongzhi the striving may be forgotten once illumination occurs, but
that implies that striving was necessary to bring on the experience. His
description of alertly destroying the murkiness of ignorance also implies
directed effort.

The *Inscription on Silent Illumination* also states:

> All the myriad things in the universe
> emit radiance and speak the Dharma.
> They all attest to each other,
> and correspond in dialogue.

> Corresponding in dialogue and attesting,
> they respond to each other perfectly.
> But if in illumination silence is lost,
> then aggressiveness will appear.

> Attesting and corresponding in dialogue,
> perfectly they respond to each other.
> But if in silence illumination is lost,
> then you will become turbid and leave behind the Dharma.

> But when silence and illumination both are operating and complete,
> the lotus flower opens and the dreamer awakens.
> The hundred rivers flow into the sea,
> and the thousand peaks face the great mountain.

> Like geese preferring milk,
> like bees seeking out flowers.

When Silent Illumination is perfected and obtained,
the teaching of our tradition is set in motion.[32]

Here Hongzhi emphasizes the balance between silence and illumination, in a manner that clearly resonates with the essence/function
(ti/yong) polarity of fourth-century and later Chinese Buddhism, as well
as with the writings of Shenhui in the eighth century. The former distinction, as found in the writings of various figures, is used to analyze
states or realities considered to be essentially unitary—such as nirvāṇa
or enlightenment—but which seem to have different characteristics according to the perspective used. Hence the enlightened mind may be
said to be essentially quiescent even as it exercises the functions of knowing. Similarly, Shenhui argues that the realms of meditation and wisdom cannot be considered as separate, so that the function of serene
meditation is wisdom and the essence of nominally active wisdom is
serene meditation.[33]

But where Shenhui argues a philosophical position that concentration
and wisdom must be identical to occur at all, Hongzhi is interested in the
balance between silence (concentration) and illumination (wisdom) that
is achieved by the meditator. And, as Morten Schlütter aptly observes, it
almost seems as if Hongzhi "is describing enlightenment as an event in
time when he says, 'the lotus flower opens and the dreamer awakens.'"[34]
Nevertheless, "enlightenment as a breakthrough event is downplayed,"
and the very concept was considered a hindrance. Hongzhi does not stress
the heroic effort considered necessary by Dahui, and he seems to consider silent illumination as the inherently enlightened quality of mind and
enlightenment as a natural and joyful state that is already fully present to
the practitioner. Elsewhere, he writes that "there is no need to trouble
about practice and enlightenment."[35]

Nevertheless, there *is* something to be done. Hongzhi writes,

Completely and silently be at ease. In true thusness separate yourself from all
causes and conditions. Brightly luminous without defilements, you directly
penetrate and are liberated. You have from the beginning been in this place;
it is not something that is new to you today. From the time before the vast
eon when you dwelled in your old [original] home, everything is completely
clear, unobscured, numinous, and singularly bright. *But although this is the case,
it is necessary that you act on it.* When you act on it in this way you must not
give rise to the smallest strand of hair and not conceal a speck of dust. Cold
and like dried wood, [you should practice] the great rest with broad and penetrating comprehension. If your rest and cessation is not complete and you

wish to go to the realm [of the Buddha] and to leave birth and death, then there is no such place. Just as you are you must break through, understanding without the defilement of discursive thinking, and be pure without any worries.[36]

Even from this brief consideration it is possible to detect both sensitivity and balance in Hongzhi's admonitions, paralleling those of the *Treatise on the Essentials of Cultivating the Mind* attributed to Hongren (see p. 38 above). That is, both sources subtly harmonize the need to exert oneself fully with recognition that the goallessness of *nirvāṇa* obviates the validity of striving.

Let me add one last observation about the relationship between Dahui and the Caodong teachers. Dahui reacts to Caodong growth with a very competitive spirit, but he was acting not so much on his own behalf as for the sake of Buddhism itself, as he understood it, and as reproduced in his own lineage. No doubt his anger at what he perceived as misguided teachings was sincere—but he acted protectively, on behalf of his lineage in ways characteristic of Chinese consociations in general. In the first chapter (see p. 9) I wondered whether Chan functioned to oppress Chinese religious practitioners in general, or to suppress certain groups of these practitioners. This is precisely the point: Dahui was in effect working to dominate the rhetorical community of Song-dynasty Chan, to ensure that his own approach was recognized as valid and all others rejected as invalid. The enlightenment of Dahui's students implied that the students of certain other types of teachers had to be unenlightened. This was true in a proximate sense of the Caodong teachers, but even more so in the broader context: the relative success of Dahui's approach to Buddhism implied the relative emasculation of Tiantai, Huayan, Pure Land, and other approaches.

Pairing Buddhist and Neo-Confucian Patterns

Over the course of these essays we have touched on a number of duels/polarities (see in particular the discussion beginning on p. 40), and now is the time to consider them in an integrated fashion. To begin with, it is possible to construct a neat set of parallels between patterns of practice that appear in proto- and early/classical Chan, the Caodong and Linji styles of Song-dynasty practice, and the two major trends in Song-dynasty Neo-Confucianism. These parallels play out as follows:

Proto-Chan:	entrance of principle	entrance of practice
Early/classical Chan:	maintaining the mind	encounter dialogue
Song-dynasty Chan:	silent illumination	viewing the phrase
Neo-Confucianism:	quiet sitting	investigating things

As discussed in chapter 2, the "entrance of principle" and "entrance of practice" attributed to Bodhidharma are not well-enough explained for us to understand exactly what they meant in concrete practical terms, but the relationship between the two is reasonably clear: the first represents the fundamental attitude of unshakable confidence in the existence of the Buddha-nature within one, and the second is a progression suggesting how one's every action and activity may be adapted so as to accord with that inward realization.[37]

The early Chan injunction to "maintain [awareness of] the mind," which is explained in the *Treatise on the Essentials of Cultivating the Mind* attributed to Hongren, is an elaboration of the Buddha-nature concept found in Bodhidharma's "entrance of principle." Just as that text enjoins one to have "profound faith," that is, unswerving conviction, in the existence of the True Nature within one, even though it may be covered over with illusory thoughts and desires, so is "maintaining the mind" the practice of cherishing just that same True Nature or Buddha-nature. The same text also contains two very different styles of meditation practice, one embodying the spiritual perspective just mentioned and the other focused on the activity of the deluded mind.

In both these cases, as well as in the "silent illumination" and "quiet sitting" of Song-dynasty Caodong Chan and Neo-Confucianism, there is the fundamental assumption that the true mind is an inherently brilliant source of illumination—that if one can simply remove the restraints placed upon it by normal patterns of discriminatory thought, then it will reveal itself as the preexistent state of perfect buddhahood. In Chinese Mahāyāna Buddhist terminology, the true mind within is in a state of originary or fundamental enlightenment, and the removal of illusions to reveal this inherent brilliance is known as temporal enlightenment. The general, almost universal, tendency in early Chan is to emphasize the importance of the Buddha-nature over the illusions that obscure it, and implicitly to favor originary enlightenment over the specific achievement of temporal enlightenment. There is thus a profound continuity between the entrance of principle, the early Chan understanding of Buddha-nature, and the Caodong approach to "silent illumination." For convenience, I will refer to this as the "immanentist" position, because of the emphasis on the immanent quality of the innermost mind.

There is a fundamental distinction between the immanentist posture just described and the "exemplification" style—the term I will use to speak of the entrance of practice—the encounter dialogue of classical Chan, the "viewing the phrase" approach of Song-dynasty Linji Chan, and the Neo-Confucian approach to "investigating things." Previous writers have tended to analyze these two approaches in terms of a static/dynamic polarity, with the immanentist position described as predominately static and the exemplification style seen as quintessentially dynamic. This style of analysis should be avoided, though, because it is so inherently value-laden. Indeed, such dyadic oppositions are often polemical in spite of their apparent inclusiveness—since that very act of inclusion conceals a hegemonic trope of supercession and domination. In potential contrast to modern valuations, of course, ancient and medieval Chinese writers would almost certainly have preferred to associate themselves with the more fundamental "essence" rather than the seemingly derivative "function."[38]

Just as the sudden/gradual typology has a polemical cast for traditional (and many modern) Chan Buddhists, so does the static/dynamic rubric seem to have a polemical cast for modern writers; for a combination of reasons, the authors who use this simple typology always seem to give pride of place to the dynamic, belittling the static. Actually, I would argue that, rather than static/dynamic, the early Chinese Buddhist polarity of essence/function (discussed initially on p. 43 and mentioned with regard to Hongzhi's thought on p. 137) is a more powerful analytical tool.

In fact, we may specify several ways in which we can differentiate the exemplification mode from the immanentist one. First, instead of the inward focus of the immanentist position, there is an outward focus on action, activity, dialogue, and interaction. This outward focus manifests itself in different ways, but it is generally, perhaps universally, accompanied by an emphasis on the actual process leading to and achievement of (temporal) enlightenment itself. One needs to actually experience enlightenment and, just as important, one needs to demonstrate the validity of that experience to a qualified teacher. Both action and interaction are necessary.

Second, the two styles have a fundamentally different stance regarding the significance of human culture and the identity of the practitioner. That is, whereas the immanentist posture requires nothing other than the practitioner's own mind and individual being, the exemplification style depends on the practitioner's role as a participant in a certain type of human tradition. In the Chan school, of course, this is a genealogical context, in which the practitioner achieves enlightenment through contemplation of the enlightened activities of his lineage predecessors, then verifies that experience in a genealogical encounter where he moves from child/outsider to adult/successor. In the Neo-Confucian case the tradition is the Chinese civil tradition, as exemplified in Confucian classics and patriarchs, the canonical source material by which contemporary situations both private and public are to be understood. It seems likely that this understanding of the Chinese Confucian tradition also occurred in a profoundly genealogical style, as manifested by Zhang Jiucheng and other advocates of the active style of the "investigation of things."

A certain caution is necessary here. There is a natural tendency to fill out tables of correspondences as far as one can, and in this case one might consider adding a fifth line, reading "sudden" and "gradual." The goal, of course, is not to line up the greatest number of pairs and argue that they are all parallel, but rather to use the parallels that seem valid or even merely suggestive as tools to achieve better and more nuanced understandings. Recognizing where the parallels cease to make sense is thus also a useful result of this procedure.[39]

The sudden/gradual distinction is a polemical one that by itself has only limited use as an analytical tool.[40] In the first place, each of the Song-dynasty Chan positions can legitimately be described as subitist and the other criticized as gradualist. Naturally, the terms by which such descriptions are made derive from sectarian considerations, but the result is that there is no clear-cut way in which the columns would line up. The immanentist position may be considered subitist because it admits of no stages and posits an "all-at-once" style of realization. (This position is elaborated most brilliantly in the writings of the Japanese Zen master Dōgen.) From this perspective the process-oriented style of the exemplification approach makes it appear gradualistic, and indeed many Linji and Rinzai Zen practitioners have been described as passing through a number of enlightenment experiences. From the exemplification perspective, on the other hand, the immanentist style seems to ignore the actual experience of enlightenment almost entirely, and certainly to downplay the sudden quality of its onset. And all those hours that Caodong monks spend in meditation, with so little talk about individual achievements, certainly made their Linji counterparts suspect some of them just were not getting any . . . spiritual attainments, that is.

In the second place, as a polemical slogan from the eighth century, the claim of "suddenness" made by different Chan teachers had long since lost its rhetorical novelty in the Song dynasty. The issue was still relevant in the lives of individual practitioners, as indicated for example in the ubiquitous invocation of the term in Dahui Zonggao's writings;[41] as an interpretive mode, however, it obscures instead of adds to our understanding.

The inapplicability of the sudden/gradual polarity should not restrain us from attempting other correlations. It is instructive, actually, to consider how the parallels stated above might bear on the concentration/insight polarity of traditional Buddhist meditation theory. Neither fits very well, but that should not be surprising, given the historical distances involved. One could make a case that the immanentist position resembles *vipaśyanā*, since both depend on the mind's innate capacity to understand. But *vipaśyanā* requires an object, and it would only be in its Mahāyāna understanding that it could be applied to the mind itself (at least in the sense of a primordial or transcendent entity). Such a position is found, of course, in the writings of Tiantai Zhiyi, who expatiated at great length on exactly this topic. And Chan texts from the early period onward clearly recognize the subtle problems with the notion of the mind "counter-illuminating" its own origin. Still, to illuminate something *with* the mind (even the mind itself) is different from the immanentist position that there is an innately illuminating mind to be revealed within all human beings.[42]

To then compare the exemplification approach to *śamatha* or concentration would take us even farther afield. Here the goal is not uninterrupted quiet, but total involvement in spontaneous activity. Even more, the exemplification style of practice requires a partner, in the form of a qualified teacher, while *śamatha* is effectively a solitary pursuit.[43] There is a strong resemblance between the Chinese notion of gradualism and *śamatha*, in the sense that both suggest progressive improvement. In addition, both represent an ancient dimension in Buddhism according to which liberation is explained in terms of an ascetic suppression or pacification of desire. However, even though subitism may have an underlying affinity with *vipaśyanā* (in the sense that both require an unconditioned moment of *prajñā*, wisdom), the parallel is by no means complete. What should be most instructive, in fact, is the very lack of congruence between the immanentist/exemplification, sudden/gradual, and *śamatha/vipaśyanā* pairs.

Intersubjectivity in Song-Dynasty Tiantai Practice

Instead of reaching back to the basic themes of Indian Buddhist meditation theory to understand the theoretical ramifications of Song-dynasty

Chan, it is better to consider a parallel that is closer in both time and space: the Home-mountain/Off-mountain *(shanjia/shanwai)* distinction in Song Tiantai thought.[44] Song-dynasty Tiantai was riven with controversy between a group centered on Mount Tiantai itself (hence the "home-mountain" label) and another group associated with other locations. For our purposes, one way to gauge the impact of Chan thought on Song-dynasty religious culture in general is to consider the extent to which the polarities we have been discussing apply to Song-dynasty Tiantai.

The best guide here is the work of Brook Ziporyn, who has analyzed the theme of "intersubjectivity" within Tiantai thought from Zhiyi to Zhili (960–1028). Intersubjectivity in this case refers to the recognition that spiritual endeavor takes place, not as solely individual action in a cosmos where other living beings are basically irrelevant, but in a context where the functional interrelationship of different consciousnesses is recognized from the outset. In terms of Buddhist soteriological theory, it is philosophically significant for Zhili that there are both ignorant sentient beings and enlightened buddhas and bodhisattvas in the world. Neither ignorant beings nor enlightened sages function in isolation of each other: sentient beings depend on the enlightened for assistance in achieving salvation, and the enlightened dedicate themselves to the act of salvation. With regard to the latter, as Ziporyn puts it, "[B]odhisattvas experience the world in a way that always references other experiencing beings and that constitutively takes into account those other experiences."[45] The same is true of the sentient beings. As Zhili states,

> The dharmas of Buddhas and sentient beings are what are called "other," but each inherently includes both all Buddhas and all sentient beings. If the sentient beings and Buddhas inherent in oneself become manifest, they are identical to the sentient beings and Buddhas that are inherent in any Buddha who stands as an other to oneself, and in this instance play the role of "the one who transforms" [in taking on various forms so as to guide and enlighten all beings]. The sentient beings and Buddhas inherent in sentient beings in that case play the role of "the ones who are transformed." Since all this takes place in one moment of experience, how can self and other be considered only different?[46]

Ziporyn explains that

> every sentient being and every Buddha equally has the entire system of "Buddhas taking on various forms to enlighten all sentient beings" replete and inherent in himself or herself. Both the guide and the guided are replete in each other, i.e., in both the guide and the guided. Thus every moment of experi-

ence is interpretable as the stimulus/response experience, and every encounter allows both agents to play both roles.[47]

For Zhili (and, in his understanding, also Zhiyi) the experience of life takes place within a network of intersubjectivity, in which the individual consciousnesses remain distinct but interact with each other in a multivalent variety of relationships. Since sentient beings and buddhas are ultimately interpenetrating, they exist within each other and function in mutual relationship.

Based on the Tiantai doctrine of the three truths, in which phenomena may be viewed from the perspective of the ultimately true, the provisional, and the middle, any action may be perceived in terms of the salvific activity of a buddha or bodhisattva, the ignorant striving of an ordinary sentient being, or something that involves both (or neither) of these aspects. Ziporyn explains that any event may thus be understood in at least four ways:

> All acts, if contemplated as identical to the threefold truth, reveal themselves to be stimuli that bring about Buddha-effects, and the effects are themselves identical to the stimuli that incited them. Every possible action, then, is simultaneously (1) an instance of deluded karma, (2) a stimulus bringing about Buddha-responses, and (3) a salvific, transformative Buddha-response brought about by this stimulus. Since an expedient transformation of a Buddha is (given the nonduality of provisional and ultimate) also the ultimate truth, any token may also be said to be (4) the ultimate being of the Buddha in himself. All four of these view points are contained in one and the same moment of experience, read simultaneously in four different interpretative contexts.[48]

In other words, in the Home-mountain thought typified by Zhili there is an intersubjective relationship between sentient beings and buddhas, or rather between each sentient being and each buddha. The interaction between each pair of unenlightened/enlightened individuals can thus be understood from different perspectives, with neither subjectivity reducible to the other.

In contrast, the Off-mountain faction consistently reduces the relationship between buddhas and sentient beings to a process of emanation from the true mind. Yuanqing (d. 997), the earliest representative of the Off-mountain position, states clearly that "Buddha means the true contemplation, sentient beings means delusion, and the mind is the mind in these two states, not separate from them. But the mind is the root of both Buddha [enlightenment] and sentient beings [delusion]."[49] Mind is thus the underlying source for all reality, and presumably the primary focus of attention in Off-mountain meditation efforts.

The historical relationship between Tiantai doctrine and Chan still needs further elucidation, but even this brief summary should be enough to suggest that the two dominant styles of Song-dynasty Chan practice were echoed to some degree in contemporaneous Tiantai thought. Although the quality of intersubjectivity detectable in Home-mountain Tiantai thought is different in kind from the interaction of Chan masters and students in encounter dialogue, or in the genealogical contemplation of the "critical phrases" of the *gong'an*, the parallels are suggestive. Similarly, the Off-mountain emphasis on the mind as the fundamental source for both ordinary and enlightened sentient beings can easily be correlated with the Caodong emphasis on the "silent illumination" of the mind within. The relationship between the two schools, which were so often at each other's throats in sectarian competition, deserves further analysis.

Chan and the Chinese Social Order

At this point I would like to add a few comments about the role of Chan Buddhism within the Chinese social order of the Tang through the Song dynasties. Instead of drawing our discussion to a close, in this and the next section I hope to show how it can be extended in future inquiries.

As a sublime combination of Indian and Chinese elements, Chan took a form (or forms) defined by the Chinese society within which it evolved. As such, it developed in ways that are unimaginable for Buddhism in India. But, without indulging in a thorough comparative investigation of the two cultures, how are we to understand these differences? One way to gain a quick foothold on this issue is to consider how funerary practice differs between India and China, under the theory that such customs reveal some of the most fundamental structures of any society. This will allow us to ask the question, Given the differences between those basic structures, how would we expect Buddhist spiritual cultivation to be conceived within Chinese rather than Indian society?[50]

Traditional Indian funerary ritual is designed to assist the deceased in separating from his or her worldly family. Following cleansing of the body, there is an offering of rice balls, and the body is cremated. With the cremation of the physical body, the deceased person acquires a subtle body which is for the next ten days by daily offerings. The family circumambulates the funeral pyre and bathes in a river before returning home, all the while avoiding looking back at the pyre and any open show of grief. At the family home a feast is prepared, and the death is celebrated. Lamentation may occur spontaneously, but it is ritually proscribed. On one of the following two days, the skull of the deceased is shattered and placed along with the bones in an earthware jar, which is then either thrown in a holy river or buried in consecrated ground. On the tenth day, the eldest son offers a ball of rice at the cremation ground so that the deceased can shed the subtle body and become a *preta,* or "ghost." For a year offerings are made on each new moon to sustain the *preta* body, after which time another ceremony assists the deceased in discarding the *preta* body and joining the world of the ancestors. In this ceremony four pots are used, one for the deceased and others for his father, grandfather, and great-grandfather. By pouring from one pot to the others while reciting appropriate incantations, the deceased becomes the first of the ancestors and, from this point on, the great-grandfather is omitted from ritual remembrance. If all goes well, the deceased will eventually move from the world of the ancestors to oneness with Brahman (the unconditioned substrate of the universe), but this is an individual accomplishment that cannot be influenced by funerary and memorial services.

Thus, the overall direction of the various observations prescribed in the classical Indian model is to assist the deceased to separate from the conditioned world and the ties of family, in order to make it possible for him or her to make the final step to liberation. Of course, things do not always work out that well, and it may be that, rather than achieving oneness with Brahman, the deceased *(a)* becomes a *deva,* or "god," *(b)* is reborn as a human on earth, or *(c)* is reborn as an animal or in one of the other unfortunate modes of existence. Hence the status of ancestor is temporary, and the familial bond is inevitably broken. Although being an ancestor is valued as a respite from the travails of mortal existence, it is still in essence a state of bondage, part of the realm of duality that is ultimately meant to be transcended.

In traditional Chinese culture (and the following account is simplified and limited, as was the preceding one), the entire goal of death ritual is exactly opposite to that described for India: the aim is to maintain an ongoing series of relationships between deceased ancestors and the living. Following ritual cleansing, the body may be placed in a temporary coffin and tomb for some time, until the proper moment arrives for the official funeral and burial proper. If economically possible, the tomb is a vault in which servants are buried in effigy and models of food, drink, and various useful objects are also included. Models of such objects, as well as money, are frequently made out of paper for inclusion in the grave, or they are sent to the deceased in the other world by ritual burning. (Modern funerals send the deceased off with paper televisions, paper cars, and huge wads of special funerary cash with which to bribe the underworld officials!) On the day of death the family, and especially the deceased's children, are encouraged to make open expressions of grief. The deceased's children do not eat until the burial (assuming it happens as usual, three days after death), and all the mourners eat a restricted diet, avoid soft beds, and drop their usual activities to prepare for the funeral. During this period meals are regularly offered to the deceased, and mourners address him or her directly. If the deceased was a male or married female, after the burial a tablet with the deceased's name on it is included in the family altar, and he or she is included in regular ancestral worship according to the place held within the lineage hierarchy. Ritual offerings for the deceased are made at various points over a two-year period, and the deceased's closest inferior relations (i.e., sons and daughters) restrict their activities through the third anniversary of the death. As long as the deceased remains in the memory of the living, he or she is kept informed about family events, such as weddings, births, and deaths. There is a bureaucratic or hierarchical sense to this, in that the deceased's status and place within the family, more than personality or individual achievements, determines the way in which he or she is treated. With the passing of generations, the deceased's tablet is moved further and further to the side on the lineage or family ancestral altar, and after seven generations (well beyond any living person's memory) he or she enters the realm of undifferentiated ancestors.

The preceding descriptions are highly generalized, of course, and in both cultures we may easily detect disparate vectors of practice and belief. One of the most exciting reevaluations of Indian Buddhism now nearing publication suggests that, rather than being only a lofty ideology of transcendence, it developed in part as a mortuary religion, providing a means for the subjugation of ghosts and spirits associated with death.[51] For the present purposes, though, the very idealized image of Indian funerary practices presented above will be sufficient. The goal here is not a comprehensive balanced comparison of the two cultures, which would be a challenging enterprise, to say the least. Rather, the task at hand is to use certain features of the Indian case to help in the analysis of the Chinese situation. We should remember that the interaction between Indian and Chinese cultures, such as it was, occurred only on Chinese soil. If we have isolated a limited set of features of Indian culture known to the medieval Chinese, so much the better.

In addition to the efforts suggested above to keep the deceased involved with the living, Chinese practices included several rituals intended to maintain separation between living and dead. Funerary offerings were used to provide the deceased with the accoutrements necessary for life in the next world, but at the same time measures were taken to restrict them to their tombs. Part of the motivation for ancestral offerings was to prevent the deceased from being let loose upon the world, where they might cause various sorts of difficulties. The famous trio of alternatives available to any deceased person in Chinese culture—to become either god, ghost, or ancestor—was of course partially dependent on the character of the deceased him- or herself and the heroic or tragic quality of his or her death, but it was even more strongly dependent on the actions of the living: If one's descendants provided the appropriate offerings, one became an ancestor, taking one's specified place within the celestial order. If people outside one's lineage made offerings, and if they did so in sufficient numbers because of the intercessions made by the deceased on behalf of non-kin, one became recognized as a god. If neither descendants nor others made the requisite offerings, one was forced to become a ghost and search for sustenance at large, often with unpleasant consequences for self and others. There is, as often noted, a bureaucratic quality to these proceedings, in that postmortem roles and religious charisma as a whole were determined more by status position within the hierarchy than by individual accomplishment.

My contention is that Chan provided a format for Buddhist practice that matched the pattern implied by Chinese funerary customs. The starting point for this analysis is John Jorgensen's observation of the structural similarities between Chan lineage assertions of the eighth century and funerary practice, in which the organization of halls venerating Chan patriarchs was seen to resemble that of conventional ancestral halls.[52] From a broader perspective, the proliferation of Chan lineages mimics that of conventional family genealogies, creating a parallel realm of filiation between living and dead. Indeed, where conventional genealogies are devoted individually to separate family groups, Chan "transmission of the lamp" texts create an entire universe of fictive relationships. Thus each individual practitioner is securely placed within a generational succession, and all of those succession relationships are concatenated into a massive network of interlocking identities. Where conventional family genealogies were in dialogue both with each other and with contemporary social practice, "transmission of the lamp" texts provide the Chan lineage system with its own global context for the idealization of religious identity.[53]

The overall impact of the genealogical pattern of Chinese Chan was thus to include each participating individual within an ongoing network of social relationships, to create a cosmologically natural social group that transcended ordinary society. Certainly, success in Chan spiritual practice has a definite real-world payoff: recognition as an enlightened master and formal inclusion within the lineage of Buddhas and Patriarchs. The cascades of sublineages that are documented in Chan "transmission of the lamp" texts represent the guidebooks for how participation within this "old boy" network occurred. The Chan school thus existed on one level as a set of inclusionary relationships.

On another level, the Chan genealogical network must have functioned as a means of exclusion. As Nancy Jay and others have noted, ritual provides a means for effecting both in-group solidarity and exclusion of the other. Even more to the point, the conjunction of patriarchal lineage and sacrificial practice in agrarian societies serves to support hierarchies of power that exclude women. Although the parallels are not exact, we may note that the Chan genealogical pattern effectively excluded—or, more to the point, worked to exclude—many types of religious practitioners from access to power within the Chinese Buddhist institution as a whole. Devotees of other styles of self-cultivation were marginalized or lumped together under the competing Tiantai banner. Even the Pure Land tradition was forced to adopt a lineage system to justify its existence,[54] and other rubrics for the understanding of Buddhist history were effaced by the genealogical model. And, of course, women were nowhere to be seen in Song-dynasty Chan—at least not without being reconfigured as surrogate males.[55] In other words, Chan provided Chinese Buddhists with a way of ordering their sacred heritage in a fashion that resembled other basic features of Chinese society.

All this is relatively straightforward. The next step is to explore the specific expectations and prohibitions that were built into this cosmology. Here I am using the term *cosmology* in the sense described by Mary Douglas, as the way in which people of a given culture take their understanding of the world as naturally true.[56] The Chinese cosmology, as is well known, places great emphasis on the continuity of family from deceased ancestors to living representatives. Jay has shown that there is a peculiar force to the combination of patrilineal succession and sacrifice, the result of which is "birth done better" than the defiled process of our actual maternal origins.[57] This is an analysis that certainly applies to Chinese society in general—Jay, who died before her research was published, was unable to consider the Chinese case—but the question here is whether or not it applies to Chinese Chan. Does Chan somehow represent "enlightenment done better," or "religious authority done better"? What natural lineaments of human culture did Chan evolve to subvert, or to sublimate and transform? We may have established some of the building blocks necessary for the construction of an argument discussing these issues, but that is all. Much remains to be done.

Finally, if Chinese Chan differs from Indian Buddhism in such fundamental ways, would it also be the case that the Chan "enlightenment experience" differed from the Indian one? Of course, we should be careful not to assume that Chan texts describe anything that matches our modern concept of "experience," or that we could divine how it actually "felt" for medieval Chinese Buddhists to become enlightened. Nevertheless, even without assuming that we could access the actual experiences of real individuals,[58] it would be useful to compare the descriptions of *bodhi* in Indian philosophical texts with those of enlightenment experiences in Chan texts. Where the former describe the ultimate goal in terms of wisdom and transcendence, I suspect that Chinese texts tend to a greater emphasis on realizations of the interdependence of all things. Or one might examine whether the rhetoric of *śūnyatā* is used differently in Indian and Chinese texts, with the former being used to obliterate worldly distinctions, and the latter being used in effect to reify them. (The "originary enlightenment" theories of medieval Japanese Buddhism seem to fit this latter case.) Obviously, the incredible genre differences between the sources available from South and East Asian cultures make any such comparisons difficult, but these are the sorts of theoretical issues that we are only now becoming able to address.

Erasing the Paradigm

At this point the reader may be expecting a grand conclusion, including a concise delineation of the Song-dynasty Chan climax paradigm. Rather than fulfill such expectations, however, I endeavor to transform them. In these last few paragraphs let me suggest how the analyses presented in this book may best be developed and exploited in the future.

The basic project undertaken here has been to catalyze different ways of thinking about Chinese Chan Buddhism. In carrying out this project, I have generated various explanatory schemes and strategies, and the use of "climax paradigm" rhetoric was merely one such scheme. The use of such terminology is ultimately metaphorical, heuristic, and I would not like it to be mistaken for historical fact or even historical interpretation. If we can understand the ideas, we should forget the words.[59]

The rhetoric of climax paradigm is limited in several ways. First, since my own field of research has been early Chan, this book constitutes my attempt to carry forward themes from that period to their natural conclusions in later periods. As such, the parameters of discussion have been defined by the continuities and discontinuities from early Chan through the Song dynasty. The basic strategy has thus been prospective, to use the themes and motifs of one period to explore those of later periods. To write history in this prospective fashion is useful, especially in the way it allows us to critique the many misconceptions apparent in the work of earlier authors, but it is not without its flaws. Technically speaking, this prospective style of analysis probably violates one of Fischer's "historians' fallacies."[60] In other words, in judging Song-dynasty Chan by the yardstick of earlier periods, we have programmed in a methodological inability to see it for itself.

Second, if the Song dynasty represents a period of far greater activity and vitality than the Tang or Five Dynasties periods, then the limitations of coverage here do not allow for a reasonable assessment of Song-dynasty Chan. At this point in the discussion I am painfully aware of how many aspects of Song-dynasty Chan Buddhism have been left untreated. From the "lettered Chan" of the Northern Song; to patterns of imperial, provincial, and local patronage; to the institutional realities (and fictions) of the monastic system; to the ongoing dialogues between representatives of different lineages, polemical or otherwise; to the elaborations of doctrinal and practice interpretive approaches; to variations of region and social status—to give fair treatment to all the subjects that deserve consideration would take at least one or two sizeable volumes.

And it is not only that our appraisal of Song-dynasty Chan is undergoing change: an important recent contribution by Ned Davis has suggested ways in which the dominant sinological treatment of society and the supernatural during this period needs fundamental revision. That is, instead of dealing with premodern Chinese society in terms of two basic groups, the Confucians and everyone else, we need to look more closely at how actual people actually behaved in dealing with issues involving the supernatural. Davis prefers a tripartite social division, which, in the case of Daoism, he would represent as (1) priests operating at court and other bureaucratic levels, (2) an expanding group of ritual masters, and (3) spirit-mediums working at the village level.[61] Evidence regarding Chan during the Song may be restricted largely to the first two levels, which might be defined as, first, formally ordained Buddhist monks and, second, communities of aspirants and practitioners. However, there is evidence from southwest China that Chan rhetoric had been absorbed into a complex

FIGURE 4. Bodhidharma worshiped as local deity,
Hall of the Three Teachings, Jianchuan, Yunnan Province.
Photograph by the author, 1996.

mélange of ritual practice, from at least the twelfth century on; we may
hope that future work will show the extent and timing of the penetration
by such Chan themes of the third social level of village practitioners. It is
unlikely that Chan practice itself could be maintained at the village level,
since substantial resources are required to support monastic training centers. This does not mean, though, that Chan religious motifs cannot move
beyond monastic walls. As one example of just such movement, see figure
4, which shows the image of Bodhidharma worshiped in a local village

FIGURE 5. Images of Śākyamuni, Confucius, and Laozi, with Bodhidharma to proper right, Hall of the Three Teachings, Jianchuan, Yunnan Province. Photograph by the author, 1996.

context in a Bai ethnic community in contemporary Yunnan. The hall in question is dedicated to the three religions and thus has images of Śākyamuni, Confucius, and Laozi (figure 5). In addition, the local deity Daheitian (Mahākāla) sits on the proper left side of the main altar, just as Bodhidharma, identified here by local residents as *zushī,* "the patriarch," sits on the proper right. In addition to providing better depth of vision on religious practice at different social levels, Davis's work is important for revealing the continuities between pre-Tang and Tang-dynasty practice and Song-dynasty manifestations. Only through analyses like his can we answer the question of whether what seems to appear for the first time in Song-dynasty documents actually indicates a "Tang-Song transition," as specialists in popular religion and culture so often affirm, or simply constitutes an explosion of evidence of long-term continuities from the medieval period. Given these indications that more sophisticated analysis will be possible in the future, the preliminary interpretation offered here is something like the finger pointing at the moon, and it should not be mistaken for a final assessment of all the fundamental themes and exquisite intricacies of Song-dynasty Chan.

Third, if there was something approximating a climax paradigm to Song-dynasty Chan, this could only be known by looking at how Chan evolves in later periods and in other contexts. To change metaphors, my claim is that Song-dynasty Chan represents the primary lens through which subsequent developments in Chan were understood, whether those developments took place in China, Korea, Japan, or even the modern, non-Asian world. Therefore, in order to appreciate the true dimensions of the "Song-dynasty climax paradigm" we would have to evaluate the dynamics of evolution and transmission that govern Chan in later times and other places. To the extent that the study of Chan/Sŏn/Zen/Thien as a whole has been based on the mistaken romanticism and simplistic thinking manifested so clearly in writing about Chinese Chan, we will have to rework our most cherished theories about these later times and other places as well. What were the constraints—and possibilities— placed on the tradition as it developed in post-Song China, or in Korea, Japan, and Vietnam? If participants in the tradition in those cultures looked through the lens of Song-dynasty Chan, what exactly did they see? In answering this question we will have to consider how the participants in those cultures saw themselves, their own pasts, and the role of Buddhism in their lives. The avenues of inquiry are virtually endless—such exciting possibilities for future research, so many different ways of seeing through Zen.

Notes

Chapter 1: Looking at Lineage

1. There is a convenient chart of the Chán patriarchs as given in different sources up to 801 in Philip B. Yampolsky, *The Platform Sutra of the Sixth Patriarch: The Text of the Tun-huang Manuscript with Translation, Introduction, and Notes,* 8–9.

2. See Robert H. Sharf, "The Zen of Japanese Nationalism."

3. Gregory Schopen has pointed out that manifestations of filial piety do not always represent East Asian influence; see his "Filial Piety and the Monk in the Practice of Indian Buddhism: A Question of 'Sinicization' Viewed from the Other Side."

4. The rhetoric of this first rule echoes Hú Shì's statement that 99 percent of Chán lore was false, suggesting that "it's not true, and therefore we may disregard it." The crucial importance of Chán legendary material is obviously not because it is false, but because it is culturally generated, which renders it "false" from a naïve historicist perspective.

5. This is a fundamental Mahāyāna Buddhist concept that will come up repeatedly. For an excellent overview, see Paul Williams, *Mahāyāna Buddhism: The Doctrinal Foundations,* 60–63.

6. The Chinese for this is *yìnkě* 印可, literally meaning "[to give one's] seal of approval" and deriving from the basic Sanskrit form *mudrā.* The Chinese compound occurs with the meaning "approval" in the translations of the *Abhidharmakośa* and *Vimalakīrti Sūtra,* and with intimations of the Chán nuance in the *Record of the Masters and Disciples of the Laṅkāvatāra,* an early-eighth-century Chán text.

7. Robert H. Sharf has recently argued against the use of "experience" as a natural category of human religion, in "Buddhist Modernism and the Rhetoric of Meditative Experience" and "Experience." Sharf's contribution is especially useful in the observation that the contemporary category of experience derives from a distinctly modern intellectual background that should not be applied indis-

criminately to premodern sources, and in the analysis of the philosophical un-tenability of ostensive definitions of different states of realization. However, it is simply not the case that Chinese Buddhists (or Indian Buddhists, I suspect) had no similar categories for the transformative personal experiences Sharf discusses. Regarding the conspicuous reticence Chán texts display in the description of en-lightenment experiences, at least two factors were involved. First, Vinaya regula-tions established a certain code of silence (see p. 114 and n. 14 to chap. 5). Second, the East Asian tradition demonstrates a disinclination to autobiography, on which see Pei-yi Wu, *The Confucian's Progress: Autobiographical Writings in Tra-ditional China*. Also, Gimello's observation that Buddhist meditation is not so much a set of practices leading to mystical experience, but a style of meditative analysis and psychosomatic enhancement of beliefs through meditative experi-ence, is potentially applicable to Chinese Chán as well. Although Gimello's analy-sis can be refined further, it applies whether one takes the meditative states re-ferred to as existing ostensively or not. See R. M. Gimello, "Mysticism and Meditation." In the future I hope to address the claims made for the irrational-ity of Zen and the Zen "enlightenment experience" more closely, but this is a sub-ject beyond the scope of the present book.

8. Some of the preceding analysis is given with greater elaboration in John R. McRae, "Encounter Dialogue and the Transformation of the Spiritual Path in Chi-nese Ch'an."

9. See Nancy B. Jay, *Throughout Your Generations Forever: Sacrifice, Religion, and Paternity*. I am grateful to Andrew Junker for introducing me to Jay's work and its relevance to Chinese religion. See Junker's Master's thesis, "Clergy, Clan, and Country: Tang Dynasty Monastic Obeisance and Sacrificial Religion."

10. The quotation is from David Hackett Fischer, *Historians' Fallacies: Toward a Logic of Historical Thought*, 151. For an earlier discussion of the "string of pearls" fallacy, see John R. McRae, *The Northern School and the Formation of Early Ch'an Buddhism*, 7–8 and 252–53.

11. Of course, the Dūnhuáng caves and manuscripts found there include much more than this, providing insights into a wide range of subjects in Chinese and Central Asian religion and culture, social and economic history, painting and sculp-ture. For a lively account of the discovery and exploitation of the Dūnhuáng finds, see Peter Hopkirk, *Foreign Devils on the Silk Road: The Search for the Lost Cities and Treasures of Chinese Central Asia;* for information about the texts themselves, see the web site of the International Dunhuang Project (www.idp.org).

12. Here and elsewhere I use *evolution* to refer to a generalized process of change over time, without any Darwinian or teleological connotations.

13. This concept might be compared to Ortner's "key scenarios." See Sherry B. Ortner, "On Key Symbols"; *High Religion: A Cultural and Political History of Sherpa Buddhism*, 60 ff.; and "Patterns of History: Cultural Schemas in the Found-ings of Sherpa Religious Institutions," 60 ff. I am grateful to Robert Company for this observation.

14. See Bernard Faure, "Bodhidharma as Textual and Religious Paradigm," esp. 193–95.

15. See Eric Hobsbawm and Terence Ranger, eds., *The Invention of Tradition*.

16. For a detailed narration of the history of Chinese Chán, see Heinrich Dumoulin, S. J., *Zen Buddhism: A History*, 2 vols., especially the revised version of vol. 1. Although Dumoulin's work is a useful resource, I criticize its simplistic and romanticized image of Chán beginning on p. 152 in this volume.

17. None of the appended comments can be dated or even associated with known historical figures, and some of the text's accretions may derive from as late as the mid-eighth century or so. For a discussion of the identity and contents of this text (whose attribution to Bodhidharma cannot be accepted simplistically) and a translation of its beginning sections, see McRae, *Northern School,* 101–17. For a recent translation of the entire work, see Jeffrey L. Broughton, *The Bodhidharma Anthology: The Earliest Records of Zen;* cf. my review in the *Journal of Chinese Religions.*

18. One of the many important topics to be explored further is the relationship between Chinese Chán meditation practices and the earlier Buddhist and indigenous Chinese meditation traditions. I have devoted some attention to the former topic in John Robert McRae, "The Northern School of Chinese Ch'an Buddhism" (Ph.D. diss.), 23–30; the reader would do better to consult the brilliant recent contribution by Nobuyoshi Yamabe 山辺能宜, "*The Sūtra on the Ocean-Like Samādhi of the Visualization of the Buddha:* The Interfusion of the Chinese and Indian Cultures in Central Asia as Reflected in a Fifth Century Apocryphal Sūtra" (Ph.D. diss.). On the relationship between Chán practice, Chinese Buddhist meditation, and indigenous Chinese practices, see Harold D. Roth, *Original Tao: Inward Training and the Foundations of Taoist Mysticism.* Roth suggests that there was a pre-Hàn form of "mystical" meditation that very closely resembles the later Chán Buddhist emphasis on non-discrimination. However, he ignores the likelihood that *shén* 神 or *shénmíng* 神明, which he translates as "numen" or "numinous" and defines as a category of abstract energy or understanding, simply refers to the spirits that inhabit the body and universe in early Chinese thought. Rather than a precursor to abstract nondualism, the *Inward Training* may also be read more as adumbrating Daoist styles of meditative practice in which the goal was to visualize the spirits within the body and keep them there. On this, see Isabelle Robinet, *Taoist Meditation: The Mao-Shan Tradition of Great Purity.*

19. I use the term *school* because it is usefully vague. It is important to remember that Chinese Buddhist schools had virtually no institutional dimension; hence my strict avoidance of *sect* or even *denomination* (although I do use *sectarian*). See the discussion of this issue beginning on p. 177.

20. I am indebted to Jeffrey Broughton for the term *metropolitan Chán.*

21. The term *encounter dialogue* was first used in my translation of YANAGIDA Seizan 柳田聖山, "The Development of the 'Recorded Sayings' Texts of the Chinese Ch'an School." It renders the Japanese *kien mondō* 機縁問答, which would correspond to Chinese *jīyuán wèndá*—except that the form occurs only rarely in Chán texts and should be understood as a modern descriptive.

22. In another context it would be interesting to compare the medieval and modern idealizations of Chán and Zen masters. Here I use *romantic* in a non-

technical sense, without broader historical implications. For a different use of the term, see Dale S. Wright, *Philosophical Meditations on Zen Buddhism*, ix–x, 13, 16–17, and *passim*. Incidentally, Wright's incisive instructions on the activity of reading texts should themselves be required reading for every student.

Chapter 2: Beginnings

1. What follows is an abbreviated (and unavoidably selective) recitation of the highlights of the Bodhidharma legend, as found in the *Jǐngdé chuándēng lù* 景德傳燈錄 (Record of the transmission of the lamp [compiled during the] Jǐngdé [Era]), T 51.217a9–20b25. The interview with Emperor Wǔ occurs at 219a26 ff., and Huìkě cuts his arm off at 219b17. Some of the information about Bodhidharma is included in the entry for Huìkě, beginning at 220b26.

2. The wonderful ink painting by Young-hee Ramsey used as the frontispiece for this book depicts this legendary event.

3. The ability to liberate oneself by means of a simulated corpse is well known from Chinese sources from long before the emergence of Chan. See the explanation in Robert F. Campany, *To Live As Long as Heaven and Earth: A Translation and Study of Ge Hong's* Traditions of Divine Transcendents, 52–60.

4. See Bernard Faure, *The Rhetoric of Immediacy: A Cultural Critique of Chan/Zen Buddhism* (25 and 27), citing Jacques Derrida, *Of Grammatology*. In Faure's "Bodhidharma as Textual and Religious Paradigm" (197), there is a similar reference to Lévi-Strauss's concept of the character who serves as the "virtual focus" of a myth, who functions as the obscure source around which biographical details proliferate but whose shadow alone is real. (Here Faure refers to Claude Lévi-Strauss, *The Raw and the Cooked*, 5.) In "Bodhidharma as Textual and Religious Paradigm," Faure derides the quest for biographical accuracy as a sort of "mortuary washing" (188), in which the bones of various specimens are cleansed of detail and strung together to create a useful fiction, a patched-up skeleton, the desiccated remains of a being that never existed. I do not believe that participation in this enterprise is inevitable: the reason I use "It's not true, and therefore it's more important" as the first rule of Zen studies is in effect to differentiate between the analysis appropriate to scholarly inquiry and the mortuary washing of the hagiographical process.

5. Bruce Lincoln, in *Theorizing Myth: Narrative, Ideology, and Scholarship*, points out that, in contrast to the conventional treatment of myth as "a logical structure that essentially writes itself" (149), myth ultimately derives from a narrative process in which multiple people had authorial agency. Also see his reference to "impersonal processes" (18).

6. For a detailed consideration of Bodhidharma's biography, teachings, and students, see my *Northern School*, 15–29. The mid-seventh-century work alluded to here is Dàoxuān's 道宣 *Continued Transmissions of Eminent Monks (Xù gāosēng zhuàn* 續高僧傳), which was completed in 645. At this point I am not including the additions to this text, made up until Dàoxuān's death in 667.

7. The following enumeration is based largely on the detailed study of the evolution of Bodhidharma's hagiographical sources in SEKIGUCHI Shindai 関口真大, *Daruma no kenkyū* 達磨の研究.

8. There is no clear and specific antecedent to this myth involving Huìkě, but an association may have been drawn with the example of the future Śākyamuni as "Snowy Mountain Youth" in the *Nirvāṇa Sūtra,* who throws his body off a cliff in order to hear the second half of a verse (*gāthā*). See T 374, 449b7–51b5, and the discussion in Hubert Durt, "Du lambeau de chair au démembrement: Le renoncement au corps dans le bouddhisme ancien," esp. 8. On such ritual undertakings of self-mortification, see John Kieschnick, *The Eminent Monk: Buddhist Ideals in Medieval Chinese Hagiography,* 35–50 (the anecdote involving Huìkě is mentioned on 41). Kieschnick introduces Victor Turner's notion of "root-paradigm," which he defines as "a set pattern of special behavior with particular symbolic associations." (See Victor Turner, *Dramas, Fields, and Metaphors: Symbolic Action in Human Society,* 60–97.) Although I would prefer to think in terms of multiple root-paradigms, the self-sacrifice of fingers and arms is potentially applicable to the Chinese case. He writes, "Self-mutilation before relics of the Buddha was not only a sacrifice; it was an appropriation. By burning himself, the adept drew on the power of the Buddha's body, purifying his own body and transforming himself into a holy, living relic" (44). The legend surrounding Huìkě no doubt developed out of similar forces, based on the attempts of the proto- and early Chán community to arrogate similar power to their chosen patriarch. For a related discussion (involving only self-sacrifice by immolation), see James A. Benn, "Where Text Meets Flesh: Burning the Body as an Apocryphal Practice in Chinese Buddhism."

9. See Bernard Faure, "The Daruma-shū, Dōgen, and Sōtō Zen." Although *śarīra* may be generated spontaneously, the primary mode of their creation is through cremation.

10. I suspect that further research would push the appearance of this reference back into the twelfth century.

11. The reference is to the *Yìjīn jīng* 易筋經, or *Tendon-Changing Scripture,* sometimes referred to in English as the *Muscle Relaxing Scripture.* The earliest woodblock printing of this text dates from 1642. Less critical writers on the history of Chinese martial arts accept the validity of its two prefaces, which claim to be from the Táng and Sòng. However, ZHŌU Jiànnán 周劍南 has shown conclusively that both are later forgeries. See his "Xíngyì quán zhī yánjiū" 刑意拳之研究 (A study of Xingyi boxing), 88–89, and "Wǔshù-zhōng Shàolín-pài zhī yánjiū" 武術中少林派之研究 (A study of the Shaolin school of the martial arts), esp. 156–57.

12. See the *New Encyclopædia Britannica,* 15th ed., s.v. "Bodhidharma." The information given here also occurs in the entry for "Bodhidharma" in *Britannica Online.*

13. For a complete translation, see Broughton, *The Bodhidharma Anthology.*

14. T 2060, 50.551c7–12; translation from McRae, *Northern School,* 103.

15. See YANAGIDA Seizan, "Hokushūzen no shisō" 北宗禅の思想 (The

thought of Northern-school Chán), 71–72, as explained in McRae, *Northern School*, 111.

16. See Zhìyǎn's 智儼 essay on the *Flower Garland Sūtra* (華嚴經內章門等雜孔目章), T 1870, 45.559a28–b3.

17. See Dàoxuān, *Xù gāosēng zhuàn*, T 2060, 50.596c9.

18. Paul Swanson, "Wall-gazing, *Vipaśyanā*, and Mixed Binomes." A CBETA (Chinese Buddhist Electronic Text Association; cbeta.org) search on the character *bì* 壁 has revealed only a single use as a transliteration character (T 85.1205b7), and this is from a Dūnhuáng manuscript of an anthology of scriptural sayings. This might have been a scribal or typographic error, but the term that is being transliterated in this case is *pratyekabuddha* (given as 壁支迦佛, more commonly using an initial 辟), in which a reversal of the *t* and *k* sounds by metatheses would allow for the use of *bì* 壁, which in Early Middle Chinese was pronounced pɛjk. For this reconstruction, see Edwin G. Pulleyblank, *Lexicon of Reconstructed Pronunciation in Early Middle Chinese, Late Middle Chinese, and Early Mandarin*, 34.

19. Zhìyǐ, *Great Calming and Contemplation (Mohe zhiguan)*, T 1911, 46.58a18–19. I do not know of any previous association of Zhìyǐ's *bìdìng* 壁定 with Bodhidharma's *bìguān*.

20. Zhànrán 湛然. *Zhǐguān fǔxíng zhuàn hóngjué* 止觀輔行傳弘決, T 1912, 46.305c21–27 and below.

21. Sēngchóu was a very important personage who was the figurehead of a national meditation center system that formed an important precedent for such temple systems as the Kāiyuánsì 開元寺 in China and Kokubunji 国分寺 in Japan. See McRae, "The Northern School" [Ph.D. diss.], pp. 31–50.

22. The Chinese character in question, *xíng* 行, is used in a variety of meanings within Buddhist texts, including *saṃskāra*, "conditioning force"; the Chinese word means "process" or, in a more general sense, "activity." I have retained the rendering "practice" to maintain the overlap with the word's meaning as "self-cultivation."

23. For a convenient explanation of "Dàoxìn's" teachings, but one that does not take into account the issue of retrospective composition, see David W. Chappell, "The Teachings of the Fourth Ch'an Patriarch Tao-hsin (580–651)."

24. See McRae, *Northern School*, 121–22. The quotation does not occur in either Vasubandhu's *Treatise on the Sūtra on the Ten Stages* (*Shídì jīng lùn* 十地經論, T 1522, 26.123a1–203b2), in which there is only one reference to the "orb of the sun," *rìlún* 日輪, at 26.126a23, a straightforward metaphor for the Buddha's wisdom, nor in any of the versions of the scripture on which this *Treatise* might have drawn (T 278.22, 279.26, or 285). It is not clear where quotation stops and explanation begins, so the punctuation is arbitrary.

25. See McRae, *Northern School*, 130–31.

26. Although, of course, this is an assertion as ancient as the beginning line of Patañjali's *Yogasūtra: yogaś citta-vṛtti-nirodhaḥ*, "spiritual discipline is the cessation of the fluctuations of mind."

27. Although the name chosen for the "Chán school" (*chánzōng* 禪宗) clearly derives from the title used for meditation masters in China (*chánshī* 禪師), the

nuances of the character *chán* in the medieval Chinese understanding are still unclear. Two intriguing issues are Tiāntái Zhìyí's transition from the use of *chán* and *chán bōluómì* 禪波羅蜜 (*dhyāna pāramitā*, "perfection of concentration") to *zhǐguān* 止觀 (*śamatha-vipaśyanā*, "concentration and insight") and the translator Xuánzàng's 玄奘 near-total avoidance of the word *chán*. The former issue has been commented on frequently, but the latter has not yet been explored, as far as I know. On related issues, see T. Griffith Foulk, "The Ch'an School and Its Place in the Buddhist Monastic Tradition."

28. Recent scholarship suggests that Mahāyāna Buddhism was never as significant in India and Central Asia as it became in East Asia. In order to reflect this situation, as well as to avoid the obvious pejorative connotation of "Hīnayāna," I use "Mainstream Buddhism" to refer to the non-Mahāyāna schools and traditions of South, Southeast, and Central Asia.

29. For a sophisticated analysis of Mainstream Buddhist meditation theory, see R. M. Gimello, "Mysticism and Meditation."

30. It would be intriguing to ponder why this is the case—why indeed should understanding imply liberation? This is, I believe, a most fundamental assumption of the Buddhist tradition, so basic that it is simply never addressed. Presumably, in the background of this fundamental Buddhist attitude lie the Vedic concepts of the ritual efficacy of knowledge, the power of naming, and the combined meaning of √*vid* as "knowing" and "doing." However, this topic must be left for another occasion.

31. This treatise (*Wù bù qiān lùn* 物不遷論) is one of a set of essays known collectively as the *Book of Zhao* (*Zhào lùn* 肇論); see T 1858, 45.151a10–14. The scriptural quotation does not occur in the present text of the *Fàngguāng jīng* 放光經 or *Light-Emitting Sūtra*, T 221, 8.1a–146c29.

32. See TĀNG Yòngtóng 湯用彤, *Hàn Wèi liǎng Jìn Nánběicháo Fójiào shǐ* 漢魏兩晉南北朝佛教史, 334. Also see E. Zürcher, *Buddhist Conquest*, 88, 89, and 92. The subject of *tǐ/yòng* is discussed again on pp. 137 and 140; also see this terminology attributed to Mǎzǔ 馬祖 on p. 79 and invoked in the *Wǔ fāngbiàn* 五方便 (*Five Skillful Means*) on p. 91.

Chapter 3: Metropolitan Chan

1. Although the English word *empress* is gender-specific, in Chinese she was represented during her rule as a full "child of heaven."

2. On Empress Wǔ's religious and political identity, see the two excellent volumes by Antonino Forte: *Political Propaganda and Ideology in China at the End of the Seventh Century: Inquiry into the Nature, Authors, and Function of the Tunhuang Document S. 6502, Followed by an Annotated Translation;* and *Mingtang and Buddhist Utopias in the History of the Astronomical Clock: The Tower, Statue, and Armillary Sphere Constructed by Empress Wu.* For the use of Daoist motifs in the support of her reign, see Stephen R. Bokenkamp, "Medieval Feminist Critique of the Chinese World Order: The Case of Wu Zhao." (Be aware that this publication did

not undergo the ordinary authorial review of proofs and is marred by typographical and editorial errors.)

3. From *Annals of the Transmission of the Dharma Treasure (Chúan fǎbǎo jì* 傳法寶紀) in McRae, *Northern School,* 51 and 266, with minor changes.

4. From *Record of the Men and Teachings of the Laṅkāvatāra (Léngqié rénfǎ zhì* 楞伽人法誌), as quoted in the *Record of the Teachers and Disciples of the Laṅkāvatāra (Léngqié shīzī jì* 楞伽師資記) in McRae, *Northern School,* 8–9.

5. From the epitaph by Zhāng Yuè 張說 in McRae, *Northern School,* 52.

6. In 701 Empress Wǔ's power was unquestioned, but her demise was only a matter of time. On Shénxiù as a member of the imperial family and a well-known defender of Buddhism, see McRae, *Northern School,* 46–50. Of course, Shénxiù was not the only Buddhist monk favored by Empress Wǔ (one other notable example is Fǎzàng 法藏, a specialist in the *Flower Garland* tradition).

7. I am using the phrase "production of history" in emulation of David William Cohen, *The Combing of History,* xiii–xxv, esp. xv–xvi.

8. The two "Northern school" texts are the *Annals of the Transmission of the Dharma Treasure,* mentioned in n. 3 above, and the *Record of the Teachers and Disciples of the Laṅkāvatāra,* mentioned in n. 4 above. Actually, the latter text traces the beginnings of the Chán lineage to Guṇabhadra rather than Bodhidharma (see p. 26), an aberration ignored by the later Chán tradition.

9. The Chinese terms used here are *fāngbiàn* 方便, from Sanskrit *upāya; zhèng chán'yì* 證禪義, a Chinese concoction (see T 50.724c12 for this term in reference to Shenxiu); *guānxīn* 觀心; and *kànxīn* 看心. Luis O. Gómez, in "Purifying Gold: The Metaphor of Effort and Intuition in Buddhist Thought and Practice," points out that the exegetic strategies of Shénxiù's *Guānxīn lùn* 觀心論 (Treatise on the contemplation of mind) are dissimilar from those of the Northern school's *Wǔ fāngbiàn* (151–52, n. 106); specification of the precise differences remains an important task. He also observes that the metaphoric expressions found in the *Guānxīn lùn* should not be described as "extended metaphor"—presumably because they represent an *extensive* use of metaphor but not necessarily *extended* (i.e., complex, multidimensional) metaphor. However, he misapprehends my earlier suggestion that the strategy of "contemplative analysis" (which he correctly suggests rendering as "contemplative interpretation") is characteristic of the Northern school, taking it to imply that it was the exclusive property of that school, which is expressively contrary to the passage he cites from my "The Ox-Head School of Chinese Ch'an Buddhism: From Early Ch'an to the Golden Age," 231–32.

10. These are from Shenxiu's *Guānxīn lùn,* as cited in McRae, *Northern School,* 199–200. The metaphor introduced under "casting and painting of images" reminds one of Daoist interior alchemy.

11. Ibid., 200–201.

12. From a memorial to the throne, cited in McRae, *Northern School,* 53.

13. For information on these two figures and their teachings of "enlightenment in this body," see Paul Groner, "Shortening the Path: Early Tendai Interpretations of the Realization of Buddhahood with This Very Body" (*Sokushin Jōbutsu*). Also see Jacqueline Stone, *Original Enlightenment and the Transformation of Medieval Japanese Buddhism,* 31–33, and Ryūichi Abé, *The Weaving of Mantra: Kūkai and*

the Construction of Esoteric Buddhist Discourse, esp. 300–302. A translation of Kūkai's 空海 text on the subject may be found in Yoshito S. Hakeda, *Kūkai: Major Works Translated,* 225–34. None of these sources, however, provides significant discussion of Kūkai's potential indebtedness to Chinese Chán.

14. The generic title governing this material is *Wǔ fāngbiàn* 五方便. See McRae, *Northern School,* 172–74. Phrases in italics represent ritualized, almost choral, responses. In the last paragraph, it is not entirely clear how "locus of non-being" (*wúchù* 無處) is to be understood. The term is used in slightly later Chán texts (i.e., from the late eighth and early ninth centuries) in a manner that invites further analysis; at this point the meaning might simply be "absence of place." The "four tempters" are of course the four Māras; see NAKAMURA Hajime 中村元, *Bukkyōgo daijiten* 仏教語大辞典 (Encyclopedia of Buddhist terms), 532a.

15. This is from Shénhuì's *Definition of the Truth;* see McRae, *Zen Evangelist.*

16. John Jorgensen has pointed out how Shénhuì's argument against the "Northern school" worked according to the patterns of Chinese ancestral worship, but he does not notice that Shénhuì's lineage hall is modeled on one established by Pǔjì 普寂. See Jorgensen's "The 'Imperial' Lineage of Ch'an Buddhism: The Role of Confucian Ritual and Ancestor Worship in Ch'an's Search for Legitimation in the Mid-T'ang Dynasty."

17. See McRae, "Shenhui's Vocation on the Ordination Platform and Our Visualization of Medieval Chinese Ch'an Buddhism."

18. This is excerpted from the beginning of Shénhuì's *Platform Sermon,* forthcoming in McRae, *Zen Evangelist.*

19. This commentator is HU Shih [Hú Shì] 胡適 (1891–1962), whose interpretation of Chán is discussed in John R. McRae, "Religion as Revolution in Chinese Historiography: HU Shih (1891–1962) on Shen-hui (684–758)."

20. These distinctions have been introduced earlier, beginning on pp. 32 and 37.

21. These citations are all from McRae, "Ox-Head School," 201–3. In the last quotation, "school" renders *zōng* 宗, which originally meant "male primogenitor" and hence came to mean "patriarchal principle" (this is Yanagida's rendering) and eventually "school."

22. One of the most common translation errors of modern times is the failure to recognize that *dào* 道, lit. "path," was also used in Chinese Buddhist texts to render *bodhi, dharma, yāna, gati,* and the implied abstract features meaning "-hood" or "-ship" (as in "buddhahood," "arhatship"), and so forth. The most common example is the explanation of the name for martial arts practice facilities, *dōjō,* as "place of the way," when in fact the term *dàochǎng* 道場 is a Chinese translation of *bodhimaṇḍa,* the Buddha's "place of enlightenment" under the *bodhi* tree.

23. See McRae, "Ox-Head School," 214–15. The term "counter-illumination" in the last paragraph refers to the enlightened mind's ability to reflect back upon and thus illuminate itself, after the fashion of the setting sun that shines back from across the horizon. Incidentally, the explanation of the "pacification of the mind" at the beginning of this passage might be the source for the story about Bodhidharma's pacification of Huìkě's mind. As already noted (see p. 26), this story

first appears in written texts only in 952. The Bodhidharma/Huìkě dialog is also a fictional (but thus important because of, not in spite of, its fictionality) scripting of how Chán training and enlightenment might occur.

24. See Paul Swanson, *Foundations of T'ien-t'ai Philosophy: The Flowering of the Two Truths Theory in Chinese Buddhism*, 150–56.

25. The technical term for this style of philosophical elevation is *aufhebung* (abolition, abrogation, annulment) in German, or *zhǐyáng* 止揚. The Indian philosopher referred to here is Bhāvaviveka, who suggests that one first assumes distinctions drawn from ordinary life, then denies those same distinctions, then reappropriates them in a transformed way. See Malcolm David Eckel, *To See the Buddha: A Philosopher's Quest for the Meaning of Emptiness*, 29–42.

26. I have published a simplified version of the following material as "The Story of Early Ch'an." The passages from the *Platform Sūtra* here and just below are drawn from the translation by Philip Yampolsky, *The Platform Sutra of the Sixth Patriarch*, 129–32, with changes.

27. One of the problems is that the term *kyōdai* 鏡台, "mirror-stand," corresponding to the Chinese *jìngtái* 鏡臺, occurs as a bound form meaning simply "mirror" in modern Japanese.

28. See McRae, *Northern School*, 235. The English "suchlike" renders the word *rú* 如, as in the Chinese translation of Tathāgata, *rúlái* 如來, when used as a modifier.

29. If this reconstruction of Shénxiù's usage is correct (even approximately), it implies that the *Platform Sūtra* verse's presentation has garbled his ideas somewhat. Although this would not be surprising, it makes any integrated interpretation of the verses tenuous. In spite of the speculative interpretation I have given in the text, the *bodhi* tree and the mirror may be two entirely separate metaphors only awkwardly conjoined in the verse.

30. See n. 9 above.

31. On the importance of the *Platform Sūtra* in the spiritual career of the Korean Sŏn master Chinul, though, see Robert E. Buswell Jr., *The Korean Approach to Zen: The Collected Works of Chinul*, 23 and 34.

32. It is in Shénhuì's writings that the Chán patriarchs are first listed with ordinal numbers indicating their generation.

33. Shénhuì certainly would have recounted the anecdote involving the mind-verses if he had known of it. The other arguments stated here are presented at greater length in McRae, *Zen Evangelist*.

34. The phrasing used here invokes that of Hobsbawm and Ranger, *The Invention of Tradition*, 199.

35. The image of Huineng as a "seeming dullard and diligent sweeper" is mentioned in Michel Strickmann, "Saintly Fools and Chinese Masters (Holy Fools)," 52. Although Strickmann's subject matter here is drawn largely from much later sources, the topos of a student performing manual labor, specifically "sweeping and sprinkling" the floor, for his master goes back at least to Gé Hóng's 葛洪 *Shénxiān zhuàn* 神仙傳. In addition to Gé Hóng's comments about himself, see the example of Chén Ānshì 陳安世, which plays on this imagery, in Campany, *To Live As Long as Heaven and Earth*, 14 and 137–39.

36. This interpretation is worked out in greater detail in McRae, "The Legend of Hui-neng and the Mandate of Heaven." On the ideological uses of the Huìnéng legend, compare Bruce Lincoln's definition of myth as "ideology in narrative form" in *Theorizing Myth,* 147.

37. See McRae, *Northern School,* 344, n. 340, based on T 18.945a22–24.

38. Unfortunately, the Chinese esoteric Buddhist tradition is not well studied—I would say, in fact, that it is *the* least well-studied tradition of East Asian religion. The most important recent exception is Charles D. Orzech's *Politics and Transcendent Wisdom: The Scripture for Humane Kings in the Creation of Chinese Buddhism.* For a critique of Orzech's work, see my review in *Journal of Chinese Religions.*

39. See ONO Genmyō 小野玄妙, *Bussho kaisetsu daijiten* 佛書解説大辞典, separate volume, 170a–74a.

40. Lewis Lancaster made this observation, in personal communications of May 1993 and July 2001. He noticed the phenomenon while preparing, in collaboration with Sung-bae Park, *The Korean Buddhist Canon: A Descriptive Catalogue.* On the change in Táng policy, see Ono, *Bussho kaisetsu daijiten,* separate volume, 180b.

41. For the date of the conquest of Khotan, see Prods Oktor Skjærvø, "Khotan, An Early Center of Buddhism in Chinese Turkestan," 290, as well as the sources mentioned at 290, n. 4.

42. On the Sòng-dynasty translation bureau, see HUÁNG Qǐjiāng 黃啓江 [Huang Chi-chiang], Běi-Sòng di yìjīng rùnwénguān yǔ Fójiào 北宋的譯經潤文官與佛教.

Chapter 4: The Riddle of Encounter Dialogue

1. This is from *Jīnlíng Qīngliáng yuàn Wényì chánshī yǔlù* 金陵清涼院文益禪師語錄, T 1991, 477777.591a24–25. This question became a popular subject in Chán dialogue, with hundreds of exchanges occurring in the literature. See, for example, the *Record of Linji* (鎮州臨濟慧照禪師語錄, T 1985, 47.504a15–18; Ruth Fuller Sasaki, trans., *The Recorded Sayings of Ch'an Master Lin-chi Hui-chao of Chen Prefecture,* 46–47; or Burton Watson, trans., *The Zen Teachings of Master Lin-chi: A Translation of the* Lin-chi lu, 100). Also see YANAGIDA Seizan, "The Life of Lin-chi I-hsüan."

2. This brief exchange is most commonly cited from the *Gateless Barrier* (*Wúmén guān* 無門關 [Wúmén's barrier]), T 2005, 48.292c22–93a14. Of its frequent discussions in Dàhuì's recorded sayings (大慧普覺禪師語錄), Robert E. Buswell Jr. recommends the treatment at T 1998A, 47.921c7–19 in his "The 'Shortcut' Approach of K'an-hua Meditation: The Evolution of a Practical Subitism in Chinese Ch'an Buddhism," 369, n. 95.

3. This is most commonly cited from the *Emerald Cliff Record* 佛果圜悟禪師碧巖錄, T 2003, 48.152c19 ff.

4. The information given here is from Robert H. Sharf, "On the Buddha-Nature of Insentient Things (or: How to Think about a Ch'an Kung-an)."

5. See IRIYA Yoshitaka 入矢義高, supervising editor, and KOGA Hidehiko 古賀 英彦, compiler, *Zengo jiten* 禅学研究, 3 and 433a.

6. On the origins of the English term *encounter dialogue*, see n. 21 to chapter 1.

7. This is only the most elementary form of literary analysis that might be used in the study of Chán encounter dialogue transcriptions. Although encounter dialogue emerged in a highly literate society, it still seems likely that some aspects of the perspective explained by Walter Ong with regard to orality in nonliterate societies might be relevant; previous work on "Zen language" has been marred by (1) a lack of technical understanding of Chinese Chán expressions themselves and (2) overly simplistic notions of orality and narrative realism. See Walter J. Ong, *Orality and Literacy: The Technologizing of the Word*. In addition, given the generation of Chán encounter dialogue in the social and literary context of medieval Chinese culture, it will obviously be necessary to devote more sophisticated attention to Chinese styles of literary interpretation. For example, we should consider the potential relevance of the narratological and historiographical issues discussed in David Schaberg, *A Patterned Past: Form and Thought in Early Chinese Historiography*, 163–221 and 256–300.

8. This translation is drawn from Peter N. Gregory, *Tsung-mi and the Sinification of Buddhism*, 237, with minor changes.

9. See *Transmission of the Lamp*, T 51.240c19–28. The note "this is Great Master Mazu" at the beginning of this passage is in the original. Jan Nattier has pointed out that, although to feel as though one had drunk ghee (clarified butter) no doubt refers to an exalted spiritual experience, a lactose-intolerant Chinese person might actually have a very different reaction!

10. YANAGIDA Seizan, *Sodōshū* 祖堂集 (Anthology of the patriarchal hall), 72a14–b3.

11. *Vimalakīrti Sūtra*, T 14.539c18–27.

12. There is a more distant parallel in the story of Cūḷa Panthaka in the Pāli canon, who is instructed by the Buddha to keep rubbing a dirty piece of cloth while reciting "removal of dirt, removal of dirt," until he realized that his anxious efforts at self-cultivation constituted an impediment to his own progress. See Eckel, *To See the Buddha*, 87. (The use of a dirty rag as a metaphor for purity is well known in East Asian texts, primarily from the *Nirvāṇa Sūtra*.)

13. See Marshall McLuhan, *Understanding Media: The Extensions of Man*, 22–32.

14. Throughout this book I have avoided describing earlier figures as influencing later ones, which would imply a misplacement of the human agency involved. On this subject see Michael Baxandall, *Patterns of Intention: On the Historical Explanation of Pictures*, 1–11 and esp. his "Excursus against 'Influence'," 41–73.

15. Personal communication, May 1993.

16. I cannot explore these deeper connections here. The best work on the *Zhuāngzi* is by Angus Graham; see A. C. Graham, *Chuang-tzu: The Inner Chapters*, and *Disputers of Tao: Philosophical Argument in Ancient China*. Chinese philosophical discourse reaches something of a pinnacle in lively dialogue in the *Shìshuō xīnyǔ* 世説新語, on which see Richard B. Mather, trans., *A New Account of Tales of the World*.

17. The following exposition in the text is summarized from McRae, "The Antecedents of Encounter Dialogue in Chinese Ch'an Buddhism."

18. See McRae, *Northern School*, 36.

19. Ibid., 264, 56–59, and 64–65; and see Bernard Faure, *The Will to Orthodoxy: A Critical Genealogy of Northern Chan Buddhism*, 100–105 and 78–81.

20. See McRae, *Northern School*, 91–95. The Chinese is *zhǐshì wènyì* 指事問義; *zhǐshì* is also used in traditional Chinese dictionaries to indicate characters whose meanings can be quickly inferred from their shapes, such as those meaning "up," "down," "one," and "two," and so forth. See OGAWA Tamaki 小川環樹 et al., *Kadokawa shinjigen*, 413a.

21. See McRae, *Northern School*, 92–93. Although the question "Is this a mind that exists?" resembles one posed near the beginning of the *Perfection of Wisdom in Eight Thousand Lines*, for example, no Indian antecedent for this genre of questions has been identified. Kumārajīva's Chinese translation reads, "Does this mind of no-mind exist?" (T 227, 8.537b15). The reference here is not to any thought or state of mind, but to *bodhicitta*, the inspiration to achieve buddhahood on behalf of all sentient beings. (A misleading rendering of the Sanskrit may be found in Edward Conze, *The Perfection of Wisdom in Eight Thousand Lines*, 84.)

22. See Sekiguchi, *Daruma no kenkyū*, 335–43, and the comments in McRae, *Northern School*, 93 and 302, n. 239.

23. See McRae, *Northern School*, 95, 294, n. 161, and 302, n. 243.

24. Ibid., 95–96 and 302, n. 244.

25. Ibid., 96 and 302, n. 245.

26. Ibid., 96 and 302, n. 246.

27. The best example of this is Xiángmó Zàng 降魔藏 (d.u.); see McRae, *Northern School*, 63.

28. And of course their somewhat later successors were quite reluctant to explain their activities openly. Perhaps they were profoundly incapable of doing so, for reasons we have not yet thought to explore.

29. See McRae, *Northern School*, 184–85.

30. Ibid., 174 (from *Five Skillful Means*, section 1, A). On the English term *suchlike*, see chap. 3, n. 28.

31. Ibid., 175 (same, section 1, D). Jan Nattier wonders (private communication) whether the reference to the "universally 'same' *dharmakāya* of the Tathāgata" here is playing on one of the Chinese renderings of *samyaksambuddha*.

32. Ibid., 178 (same, section 1, J).

33. Ibid., 179 (same, section 1, M).

34. Ibid., 180 (same, section 2, A). On the use of italics here, see chap. 3, n. 14.

35. I have already discussed the relevance of some of the phraseology here for our understanding of Northern school doctrine and the construction of the *Platform Sūtra;* see the conclusion to McRae, *Northern School*, 238. Other aspects of this material that deserve mention include its bearing on the indebtedness of early Chan to previous formulations within the Chinese Buddhist meditation tradition. The formulations of Tiāntái Zhìyǐ (538–97) were particularly important as background for the emergence of Chan. I have already mentioned (see p. 33) Shén-

xiù's twenty-five-year residence at Jade Spring Temple (Yùquánsì 玉泉寺), which was previously Zhìyǐ's place of residence. David Eckel has pointed out (private communication, May 5, 2002) that the pattern suggested here demonstrates a widely shared attitude toward words and their incorporation in Buddhist pedagogical approaches. Specifically, he notes a parallel between this pattern and the Tibetan style of learning first by hearing, then memorization, then active debate. Tibetan debate style is very active, effectively inscribing the subject matter into the students' minds through physical gestures and bodily movements.

36. See T. Griffith Foulk, "Myth, Ritual, and Monastic Practice in Sung Ch'an Buddhism," esp. 159–60 and 179–81.

37. These titles are abbreviations; for full details see McRae, "Shenhui and the Teaching of Sudden Enlightenment." I no longer maintain the thesis argued in this essay, that these texts preceded Shenhui's writings.

38. See John P. Keenan, *How Master Mou Removes Our Doubts: A Reader-Response Study and Translation of the* Mou-tzu Li-huo lun.

39. Translation from KUBO Tsugunari and YUYAMA Akira, trans., *The Lotus Sutra, BDK English Tripiṭaka* 13-I, 197–98, with slight changes in line breaks.

40. The phrase "back room" used here is derived from Erving Goffman, *The Presentation of Self in Everyday Life,* 106–40, esp. 109–13. I have addressed these issues in a paper given at the annual meeting of the Association for Asian Studies in November 1988, entitled "Up Front, Out Back, and in the Field: Three Models of Buddhist Endeavor in East Asia."

41. David Eckel (private communication, May 5, 2002) has pointed out that the similarity of the Indian Buddhist conception of the *mārga* to a board game is no accident, since board games were invented in ancient India and represented an important metaphor by which the world was understood; see A. L. Basham, *The Wonder That Was India: A Survey of the Culture of the Indian Sub-Continent before the Coming of the Muslims,* 208. For a much later but specifically Buddhist board game, see Mark Tatz and Jody Kent, *Rebirth: The Tibetan Game of Liberation.*

42. The game of *liùbó* 六博 is not well understood, but one theory is that each player placed six pieces on the board and advanced them against the opponent's forces on the basis of throwing six sticks; see Ogawa et al., *Kadokawa shinjigen,* 97a.

43. For an earlier but more extended treatment of these ideas, see McRae, "Encounter Dialogue and the Transformation of the Spiritual Path."

44. Stephen Bokenkamp points out (private communication, March 2002) that this is largely the rule for all Chinese texts, whether rhymed or transcribing speech, in which the capital dialect is taken as the standard.

45. See Christian Wittern, *Das Yulu des Chan-Buddhismus: die Entwicklung vom 8.–11. Jahrhundert am Beispiel des 28. Kapitels des* Jingde Chuandenglu *(1004).*

Chapter 5: Zen and the Art of Fund-Raising

1. See YAMADA Shōji, "The Myth of Zen in the Art of Archery."

2. The term *Oshō* 和尚 refers to any senior Buddhist monk, or more specifically one qualified to perform ordinations. In Zen contexts the title occurs most often

in daily ritual recitations of the lineage of Buddhas and Patriarchs; no East Asian priest would ever take the title for himself. Incidentally, I am told that "Osho's" books are actually being read sometimes in Japanese Zen training temples today; they are certainly prominently available in Japanese translation in Tōkyō bookstores.

3. I am using this English term to cover the period from the end of the Hàn to the unification of China under the Suí. This usage is designed to avoid the northern bias of the standard Chinese terminology.

4. The critique of previous scholarship on Chan presented here is similar to that by Foulk in "Myth, Ritual, and Monastic Practice"; see esp. 147–49 and 191–93.

5. See Dumoulin, *Zen Buddhism*, 170–71.

6. Ibid., 211. Dumoulin's suggestion that Chinese Buddhist monasteries contributed "little of economic benefit to Chinese society" no doubt derives in part from the anti-Buddhist bias that pervades Jacques Gernet, *Chinese Society: An Economic History from the Fifth to the Tenth Centuries*. (This is a richly annotated update of a 1956 publication, which Dumoulin certainly read.)

7. Dumoulin, *Zen Buddhism*, 212–13. On the nonexistence of any such independent "Zen monasteries," see the discussion beginning on p. 168.

8. Ibid.

9. Ibid., 243–44.

10. On Hú Shì (Hu Shih), see McRae, "Religion as Revolution in Chinese Historiography." Hú's theory was also adopted in works on Chinese Buddhism by Arthur F. Wright and Kenneth K. S. Ch'en (see discussion on p. 175), but in this case that theory has influenced Dumoulin's very understanding of the Chán school itself. On Suzuki, see Sharf, "Zen of Japanese Nationalism."

11. The ingot in question bears markings from the rebel side, who either had a similar (albeit undocumented) effort or had simply captured the fruits of the government's program. On ordinations and ordination certificates, see Stanley Weinstein, *Buddhism under the T'ang*, 59–61 and 65; and Gernet, *Chinese Society*, 54–57.

12. The term involved is *fǔ* 府. Mario Poceski has suggested (private communication, November 2000) that there is some textual ambiguity regarding this citation, but I am unaware of the specifics.

13. The geographical pattern referred to here is described in the research of Suzuki Tetsuo 鈴木哲雄, *Tō-Godai no Zenshū—Konan Kōsei hen,* and *Tō-Godai Zenshūshi,* although the inference regarding government policy is mine. Mario Poceski suggests that, in addition to the expansion through Jiāngxī mentioned here, the Hóngzhōu school demonstrated a remarkable capacity to draw followers and dispatch teachers throughout virtually all of China. If his interpretation of the evidence is correct, this is an interesting parallel with the East Mountain teaching of Dàoxìn and Hóngrěn, albeit involving greater numbers of individuals. See Mario Poceski, "The Hongzhou School of Chan Buddhism during the Mid-Tang Period."

14. For a monk or nun to make false claims to laypeople of the attainment of *dhyāna* states or the achievement of stream-enterer status (the first of four levels of sagehood in Mainstream Buddhism) was one of the most serious categories

(pārājika) of offenses; see Peter Harvey, *An Introduction to Buddhism: Teachings, History, and Practices,* 225.

15. One of my current research interests is the intersection between two of the most massive phenomena of East Asian cultural history: the sinification of non-Hàn peoples from the first millennium B.C.E. onward and the introduction and evolution of Buddhism from the first century B.C.E. onward. Scholars have worked on one or the other of these two issues (see, for example, C. P. FitzGerald, *The Southern Expansion of the Chinese People;* and Kenneth K. S. Ch'en, *The Chinese Transformation of Buddhism*), but to date no one has systematically considered the interrelationship between them. A common pattern has been to invoke the rhetoric of sinification without applying any significant analysis of its historical realities. This statement applies to Peter Gregory's excellent study of Zōngmì and Táng-dynasty Buddhism, *Tsung-mi and the Sinification of Buddhism,* which, in spite of the title, never addresses the conceptual issues or broader processes involved. Robert Sharf, *Coming to Terms with Chinese Buddhism* (esp. 77–132), provides some very provocative comments regarding the "process that logically precedes the intentional adaptation and domestication of Buddhism by Chinese apologists" (98), which he refers to as the "hermeneutics of sinification" (132), but he does not consider the actual historical dynamics involved. I believe that we can achieve significant new insights about Chinese religion by considering how participants in East Asian Buddhism were also active contributors to the dynamics of sinification. The terminological distinction between *sinicization* and *sinification* adopted here is arbitrary, but it is designed to follow that used in Michel Strickmann, "The Tao among the Yao: Taoism and the Sinification of South China." (Both Gregory and Sharf use "sinification" to refer to what is labeled "sinicization" here.)

16. An excellent example of this is the hagiography of Luán Bā 欒巴 in Gé Hóng's *Shénxiān zhuàn;* see Campany, *To Live as Long as Heaven and Earth,* 252–54.

17. The most widely used study of this phenomenon is Rolf A. Stein, "Religious Taoism and Popular Religion from the Second to the Seventh Centuries." Other relevant secondary sources are listed in Campany, *To Live as Long as Heaven and Earth,* 252–53, n. 439.

18. Weinstein, *Buddhism under the T'ang,* 147.

19. See Jan Nattier, *Once Upon a Future Time: Studies in a Buddhist Prophecy of Decline,* 130–31 and 227.

20. This impression is speculative; the very brief preface to the text does not provide a good explanation of its origins.

21. Although I will not argue the point here, the government's appetite for officially recognizing "transmission of the lamp" texts probably fit within the hegemonic desire of its ministers to rule all aspects of the society within their purview.

22. These are the *Record of the Transmission of the Lamp [Compiled during the] Jingde [Period]* (*Jǐngdé chuándēng lù* 景德傳燈錄, 1004); *Extensive Record of the Lamp [Compiled during the] Tiansheng [Period]* (*Tiānshèng guǎngdēng lù* 天聖廣燈錄 1036); *Supplementary Record of the Lamp [Compiled during the] Jianzhong Jing-*

guo [Period] (*Jiànzhōng jìngguó xùdēng lù* 建中靖國續燈錄, 1101); *Outline of Linked Lamps* (*Liándēng huìyāo* 聯燈會要, 1183); *Record of the Universal Lamp [Compiled during the] Jiatai [Period]* (*Jiātài pǔdēng lù* 嘉泰普燈錄, 1204); and *Collated Essentials of the Five Lamp* [Records] (*Wǔdēng huìyuán* 五燈會元, 1252). The extent to which successive dynasties used Chán as the Mín 閩 regime had during the Five Dynasties period, in an attempt to standardize Buddhist practice, remains to be seen.

23. The two-stage structure of Sòng-dynasty Chán genealogies resembles that of domestic family genealogies during the same period, which also tend to begin with monolineal successions followed by a cascade of subdivisions. See Johanna M. Meskill, "The Chinese Genealogy as a Research Source," esp. 143–47; and Patricia Ebrey, "The Early Stages in the Development of Descent Group Organization." I am grateful to Lynn Struve for making this observation and providing these references (personal communication, May 2002).

24. See Holmes Welch, *The Practice of Chinese Buddhism, 1900–1950;* T. Griffith Foulk, "Myth, Ritual, and Monastic Practice in Sung Ch'an Buddhism"; and YIFA, *The Origins of Buddhist Monastic Codes in China.* For a discussion of Sòng government policies towards Buddhism and their effect on the Chán school, see Morten Schlütter, "Vinaya Monasteries, Public Abbacies, and State Control of Buddhism under the Sung Dynasty (960–1279)."

25. Welch, *Practice of Chinese Buddhism,* 41.

Chapter 6: Climax Paradigm

1. The definition of *climax* in Roger J. Lincoln, Geoff Boxshall, and Paul Clark, *A Dictionary of Ecology, Evolution, and Systematics* is "a more or less stable biotic community which is in equilibrium with existing environmental conditions and which represents the terminal stage of an ecological succession; sometimes used as a synonym of formation *q.v.*" (61b).

2. It may also be the case that Chinese Buddhism as a whole also achieved something of a climax paradigm as well, perhaps only after that of Chán and the other major Chinese Buddhist schools. However, we have not considered the entirety of Chinese Buddhism in this book, so we cannot make unduly broad claims about it here. To understand Chinese Buddhism during the Sòng, we would obviously have to consider the Pure Land and Tiāntái schools, not to mention the worship of Guānyīn (Avalokiteśvara) Bodhisattva and other vectors of religiosity not ordinarily covered under the heading of "school." Chán is but one important species within the ecological inventory.

3. See Arthur F. Wright, *Buddhism in Chinese History;* Kenneth K. S. Ch'en, *Buddhism in China: A Historical Survey;* Jacques Gernet, *Chinese Society: An Economic History from the Fifth to the Tenth Centuries;* and Wm. Theodore de Bary, *East Asian Civilizations: A Dialogue in Five Stages.* For an extended discussion of these issues, see McRae, "Religion as Revolution in Chinese Historiography."

4. I am using the word *community* to represent what may be a heterogeneous

combination of features; like *school*, however, it represents an appropriate level of precision (or vagueness) for the present purposes. (On the terms *school, sect,* and *sectarian,* see chap. 1, n. 19.)

5. As this book goes to press I understand that Foulk has at least one manuscript accepted for publication, which I have not yet seen.

6. MIZUNO Kōgen 水野弘元, in "Zenshū seiritsu izen no Shina no zenjō shisōshi josetsu" 禅宗成立以前のシナの禅定思想史序説 [Introductory explanation of meditation theory in China prior to the formation of the Chán school], esp. 17–18, has tabulated the percentage of monks listed as meditation specialists (*chán-shī* 禅師) in the *Gāosēng zhuàn* 高僧傳 of 518 C.E., at 16+%; the *Xù gāosēng zhuàn* 續高僧傳 of 667 C.E., at 45+%; and the *Sòng gāosēng zhuàn* 宋高僧傳 of 978 C.E., at 36+%, adjustable to around 65–70% due to the suffusion of meditation specialists in other categories.

7. The following account is based closely on the work of Miriam Lindsey Levering, "Ch'an Enlightenment for Laymen: Ta-hui and the New Religious Culture of the Sung."

8. On this important figure, see Urs App, *Master Yunmen: From the Record of the Chan Teacher "Gate of the Clouds."*

9. See Levering, 24–25, with minor changes. The line about the *xūn* 薰 wind in the palace quotes an exchange of poetry at the court of Emperor Wénzōng 文宗 (r. 821–41) of the Táng; see the *Jiù Táng shū* 舊唐書 169–4312a. (The "East Mountain" mentioned here is not that at Huángméi.) The description of Dàhuì's training under Yuánwù is seamlessly consistent with Dàhuì's later teachings, but for the present purposes I ignore any possibility of retrospective projection.

10. For analysis of the methodological issues involved in extracting historical data from normative sources, see Jan Nattier, *A Few Good Men: The Bodhisattva Path According to* The Inquiry of Ugra *(Ugraparipṛcchā),* chap. 3, "The Ugra as a Historical Source: Methodological Considerations."

11. See Morten Schlütter, "Silent Illumination, Kung-an Introspection, and the Competition for Lay Patronage in Sung Dynasty Ch'an."

12. The translation is from Levering, "Ch'an Enlightenment for Laymen," 38, with minor changes.

13. Translation by Miriam Levering, "Miao-tao and Her Teacher Ta-hui," 201, from T 47.865c24–28, with transcription changes.

14. Quoted in Buswell, "'Short-cut' Approach," 349, based on the *Dàhuì yǔlù* 大慧普覺禪師語錄 26, T 1998A, 47.921c2–6.

15. On the emergence and definition of *kànhuà Chán*, see Buswell, "'Short-cut' Approach," 344–56; Ding-hwa Evelyn Hsieh, "Yüan-wu K'o-ch'in's (1063–1135) Teaching of Ch'an Kung-an Practice: A Transition from Literary Study of Ch'an Kung-an and the Practical K'an-hua Ch'an"; and Ding-hwa Evelyn Hsieh, "A Study of the Evolution of K'an-hua Ch'an in Sung China: Yüan-wu K'o-ch'in (1063–1135) and the Function of Kung-an in Ch'an Pedagogy and Praxis."

16. There is occasional confusion about these terms, which are important to the discussion that follows. The characters for *huàtou* 話頭 mean literally "topic-head," but the second character is used purely as a grammatical suffix meaning "a

(prominent) bit of [the preceding character]." A parallel example is *shítou* 石頭, "a piece of stone," that is, "a rock." In modern colloquial Chinese, including that of Buddhist monks, a *gōng'àn* simply means story, and in vernacular Chinese literature it refers to a genre of mystery stories. The compound originally referred to the desk on which a magistrate would place a case for legal consideration, so that by metonymy the word means "legal precedent."

17. *Emerald Cliff Record*, T 48.194c7–95a13. The translation is adapted from Katsuki Sekida, *Two Zen Classics: Mumonkan and Hekiganroku*, 319–20. The interlineal glosses are as found in the original.

18. See the secondary sources introduced in chap. 2, n. 8.

19. There are two source texts of the *Bìyán lù* 碧巖錄 (Emerald cliff record), which may derive from the two separate occasions on which Yuánwù lectured on the cases in question. Given the marked variation between the two source texts, it seems best to characterize Yuánwù's interpretation as a style of response rather than a set of interpretations. See the critical edition in ITŌ Yūten 伊藤猷典, *Hekiganshū teihon* 碧巖集定本.

20. See Buswell, "'Short-cut' Approach," 321–77.

21. The term *consociation* is adopted from the research of Avron Boretz (personal communication, May 2002), which is based primarily on ethnographic research on contemporary Taiwanese religious praxis. When dealing with the outside world, the consociation adopts a pose of unanimity behind its leader/figurehead; within the organization, however, there is intense and uninterrupted competition by individuals for status within the group. Depending on the context, either the entire Chán lineage (in cases of national religious dialogue, for example) or the various sublineages of Chán (in cases of individual monastic appointments, for example) might be considered separate consociative groups. I look forward to exploring this anthropological analogy between medieval Chán and contemporary Chinese religion in the future.

22. Translated by Ari Borrell, in his "*Ko-wu* or *Kung-an?* Practice, Realization, and Teaching in the Thought of Chang Chiu-ch'eng," 88, with minor changes (i.e., the omission of Chinese terms); from ZHĀNG Jiǔchéng 張九成, *Héngpú jí* 橫浦集, 14.7a (391b).

23. Ibid., 89; from the same source, 14.4a–b (390a).

24. I am drawing the terminology here from Borrell, who in turn cites an observation made by KUSUMOTO Masatsugu 楠本正継 (1896–1963), in "Sō-Min ryō shisō no kattō" 宋一明両思想の葛藤 (The dilemma of Sòng and Míng thought), especially 177. I have not seen this article (and my interpolation of Japanese characters and interpretation of the title may be in error), but it is the earliest such observation of which I am aware.

25. Schlütter, "Silent Illumination," 109.

26. Morten Schlütter resolves this dilemma in a two-pronged analysis, first, of the state of competition between the Línjǐ and Cáodòng lineages at this point in time and, second, of the different emphases placed by various Cáodòng masters on meditation practice. The following summary is based on Schlütter's masterful analysis, which draws in part on the contributions of ISHII Shūdō.

27. Although Schlütter suggests that this arrangement was "unique in Ch'an history" ("Silent Illumination," 127), something like this must have happened in the evolution of the Oxhead school—unless that faction's lineage scheme was completely fabricated around its sixth generation.

28. For Dàhuì's emphasis on effort, see Buswell, "'Short-cut' Approach," 354–55.

29. Translated by Schlütter, in "Silent Illumination," 124–25; from *Xù gǔzūnsú yǔyāo* 續古尊宿語要, *Xù zàng jīng* 續藏經 118.453d11–16.

30. The three passages here are translated in Schlütter, "Silent Illumination," 121–22 and 124; they are from *Zhēnxiē Qīngliǎo chánshī yǔlù* 真歇青了禪師語錄, X 124.314a18–b2, 323c13–14, and 311b3, respectively.

31. Translation by Schlütter, in "Silent Illumination," 117, with minor reformatting, from *Hóngzhì chánshī guǎnglù* (宏智禪師廣錄), T 2001, 48.100a26–b1.

32. Ibid., 118, with minor reformatting, from *Hóngzhì chánshī guǎnglù*, T 48.100b5–11.

33. On the *tǐ/yòng* distinction, see the discussion on p. 70. Shénhuì states his understanding of the relationship between meditation and wisdom in the *Platform Sermon:* "This is the combined cultivation of concentration and wisdom, [the two of] which cannot be separated. Concentration does not differ from wisdom, and wisdom does not differ from concentration, just as a lamp and its light cannot be separated. . . . When we consider concentration, it is the essence of wisdom; when we consider wisdom, it is the function of concentration." See McRae, *Zen Evangelist.*

34. Schlütter, "Silent Illumination," 119.

35. Ibid., 123; from *Hóngzhì chánshī guǎnglù*, T 48.1c2–3.

36. Ibid., 123–24; from *Hóngzhì chánshī guǎnglù*, T 48.74b25–c2 (emphasis in original). This passage is cited in ISHII Shūdō 石井修道, *Sōdai zenshūshi no kenkyū* 宋代禅宗史の研究 [Studies in the history of Sòng-dynasty Chán], 345, and translated in Taigen Dan Leighton, *Cultivating the Empty Field: The Silent Illumination of Zen Master Hongzhi,* 10.

37. The word *practice* here should be understood as "process" or "activity"; see chap. 2, n. 22.

38. I am grateful to Robert Campany for this observation (personal communication, May 2, 2002).

39. One recent study that flagrantly violates this good-sense rule is a monumental foray into neurophysiology and introspection: James H. Austin, M.D., *Zen and the Brain: Toward an Understanding of Meditation and Consciousness.* In Tables 1 and 2 (pp. 10 and 31), for example, Austin carries out the uncritical generation of parallels to a ludicrous extreme, applying highly value-laden generalizations to the Sōtō and Rinzai traditions. The highly sectarian nature of Austin's understanding of Zen severely prejudices his massive edifice of neurophysiological hypothesis, which extends far beyond the realm of experimental evidence. For a perceptive comment on a significant epistemological contradiction in Austin's enterprise, see Arthur J. Deikman's review in the *Times Literary Supplement,* 30. (At the time of the review Deikman was professor of psychiatry at the University of California, San Francisco.) Hopefully, some middle way between Sharf's and Austin's approaches will be possible in the future (see chap. 1, n. 7).

40. As Robert Buswell has pointed out (private communication, May 10, 2002), "Chán materials from both the Táng and Sòng provide a much more sophisticated analysis of these terms than simply sudden and gradual: note the multiple combinations of 'sudden' and 'gradual,' 'cultivation' and 'enlightenment' employed in the works of Zōngmì 宗密, Yánshòu 延壽, and Chinul 智訥 in Korea to analyze different Chán schools."

41. See Buswell, "'Short-cut' Approach," and Dàhuì's use of short-cut rhetoric itself.

42. We should not mistake these positions as entirely East Asian, let alone unique to Chán. For example, Peter Harvey, in *The Selfless Mind: Personality, Consciousness and Nirvāṇa in Early Buddhism,* points out that the notion of an innately illuminating mind within all sentient beings is also found in Pāli canonical and postcanonical sources, as well as the texts of several Mainstream schools (155–79, esp. 157–60 and 174–75).

43. This statement refers to the appreciation of these positions within the Chán tradition. In Indian Mainstream Buddhism it may even be the case that an experienced meditation instructor is more important for the practice of *śamatha* rather than *vipaśyanā.*

44. For a convenient summary of these two positions, see Chi-wah Chan, "Chih-li (960–1028) and the Crisis of T'ien-t'ai Buddhism in the Early Sung," 413–18.

45. Brook Ziporyn, "What Is the Buddha Looking At? The Importance of Intersubjectivity in the T'ien-t'ai Tradition as Understood by Chih-li," 443 (original passage in italics). The subject matter of this article is given more detailed attention in Brook Ziporyn, *Evil and/or/as The Good: Omnicentrism, Intersubjectivity, and Value Paradox in Tiantai Buddhist Thought,* 199–239.

46. Translation from Ziporyn, "What Is the Buddha Looking At?" 459, with minor punctuation changes; from *Shí bù'èr mén zhǐyāo chāo* 十不二門指要鈔, T 1928, 46.718a10–12. (The same passage is also introduced in Ziporyn, *Evil and/or/as The Good,* 218.)

47. Ziporyn, "What Is the Buddha Looking At?" 459.

48. Ibid., 454. Also see the very similar passage in Ziporyn, *Evil and/or/as The Good,* 212–13.

49. Translation from Ziporyn, "What Is the Buddha Looking At?" 460, from *Fǎhuá shìmiào bù'èr mén shìzhū zhǐ* 法華十妙不二門示珠指, X 100.111a15–17.

50. In posing this question, I am indebted to Peter D. Hershock, *Liberating Intimacy: Enlightenment and Social Virtuosity in Ch'an Buddhism,* 31–39. He, in turn, has drawn his Indian material from Dakshinaranjan Shastri, *Origin and Development of the Rituals of Ancestor Worship in India,* 290–98, and his Chinese material from Patricia Ebrey, *Confucianism and Family Rituals in Imperial China,* 16–23. Although I have some doubts about the success of Hershock's project as a whole, his use of the analogy of funerary practice to initiate a comparative analysis of Indian and Chinese religious practice was very insightful. See McRae, review of Hershock, as well as Hershock, rejoinder to McRae, and my surrejoinder.

51. This refers to the forthcoming book by Robert DeCaroli, *Haunting the Buddha.*

52. See John Jorgensen, "The 'Imperial' Lineage of Ch'an Buddhism."

53. On conventional family genealogies, see Ebrey, *Confucianism and Family Rituals*. With additional study of Sòng-dynasty recorded sayings literature, we may recognize intralineage efforts at identity creation that parallel those of individual family genealogies.

54. See Daniel A. Getz Jr., "T'ien-t'ai Pure Land Societies and the Creation of the Pure Land Patriarchate."

55. In order to generate discussion, my statement of these propositions here is intentionally stark and contentious. I do not have the space to consider them fully here, and I look forward to their future elaboration and/or modification by other scholars.

56. Mary Douglas, *Natural Symbols: Explorations in Cosmology.*

57. See Jay, *Throughout Your Generations Forever.*

58. See chap. 1, n. 7, and n. 39 to this chapter for two very different approaches to individual religious experience.

59. Of course, as an author, I am deeply interested in the extent to which my ideas—and phrasings—are adopted by readers and colleagues. Here it is best to let the Chinese nuns of Fóguāng Shān have the last word: At the end of my seminar there in 1992 they gave me a thank-you card that included the touching sentiment, "Professor McRae, what you teach is not true—and therefore it's more important!"

60. Fischer, *Historians' Fallacies,* xx–xxii.

61. See Edward L. Davis, *Society and the Supernatural in Song China,* esp. 7–8.

Character Glossary

Ān Lùshān (Roxanna): 安祿山
Annals of the Transmission of the Dharma Treasure: Chúan fǎbǎo jì 傳法寶紀
Anthology of the Patriarchal Hall: Zǔtáng jí 祖堂集
Bái 白族
Bǎizhàng Huáihǎi: 百丈懷海
bìdìng: 壁定
bìguān: 壁觀
body: see "essence"
Book of Zhao: Zhào lùn 肇論
bú lì wénzi, jiàowài biézhuàn: 不立文字、教外別傳
Cáodòng (Japanese: Sōtō) school: 曹洞宗
Cáoqī (Cáoxī): 曹溪
Cáoshān Běnjì: 曹山本寂
Chén Ānshì: 陳安世
Chinul: 智訥
Chōngyuǎn: 崇元
Chùjì: 處寂 (= Reverend Táng 唐和尚)
Dàhēitiān: 大黑天
Dàhuì Zōnggǎo: 大慧宗杲
Dàoxìn: 道信
Dàoxuān: 道宣
Definition of the Truth (Definition of the Truth [Regarding] Bodhidharma's Southern School): Pútídámó nánzōng dìng shìfèi lùn 菩提達摩南宗定是非論
Dōgen: 道元

Dòngshān Liángjiè: 洞山良价

Dūnhuáng: 敦煌

East Mountain teaching: *dōngshān fǎmén* 東山法門

Eastern Peak: 東岳 (= Mount Tài 泰山)

Emerald Cliff Record: Bìyán lù 碧巖錄

Emperor Gāozōng: 高宗

Emperor Wénzōng: 文宗

Emperor Wǔ of the Liáng: 梁武帝

Empress Wǔ: 則天武后 (Wǔ Zhào 武曌; Wǔ Zétiān 武則天)

essence (body)/function: *tǐ/yòng* 體用

fāngbian: 方便, "skillful means, expedient means"

Fǎqīn: 法欽

Fǎrú: 法入

Fǎyǎn: 法眼

Fǎyún: 法雲

Fǎzàng: 法藏

Five Dynasties: Wǔdài 五代

Five Houses: *wǔ jiā* 五家

Five Skillful Means: Wǔ fāngbiàn 五方便

four practices: *sì xíng* 四行

Fújiàn: 福建

function: 用 *yòng*

furyū monji: see *bú lì wénzi*

Gateless Barrier (Wumen's Barrier): Wúmén guān 無門關

Gé Hóng: 葛洪

go: 碁

gōng'àn: 公案 (Japanese: *kōan*) "precedent"

guān: 觀, *vipaśyanā*, "insight"

Hakuin Ekaku: 白隱慧鶴

Hán Zǐcāng: 韓子蒼

Hóngrěn: 弘忍

Hóngzhì Zhēngjué: 宏智正覺

Hóngzhōu: 洪州

Hóngzhōu school: 洪州宗

Hu Shih [Hú Shì]: 胡適

Huángméi: 黃梅 (= Qízhōu 蘄州), Hubei

Húběi: 湖北

Huìkě: 慧可

Huìnéng: 慧能

Huìzhēn: 惠真

Húnán: 湖南

Jade Spring Temple: Yùquánsì 玉泉寺

Jiāngxī: 江西

Jiǎorán: 皎然

jiàowài biézhuàn: 教外別傳

Jīn dynasty: 金朝

Jìngshān (Temple): 徑山

Jǐngxián: 景賢

Jīngzhōu: 荊州

kànhuà Chán: 看話禪

kien mondō: 機緣問答 (Chinese: *jīyuán wèndá*)

kōan: see *gōng'àn*

Kūkai: 空海

kyōge betsuden: see *jiàowài biézhuàn*

Lǎo'ān: 老安

Layman Páng: 龐居士

Light-Emitting [Perfection of Wisdom] Sūtra: Fàngguāng jīng 放光經

Lín'ān: 臨安

Línjǐ [Rinzai] school: 臨濟宗

Línjǐ Yìxuán: 臨幾義玄

Liǔ Zōngyuán: 柳宗元

Luòyáng: 洛陽

Mǎzǔ Dàoyī 馬祖道一

Miàodào: 妙道

Mín: 閩

mòfǎ: 末法

Mount Aśoka Temple: 阿育王山寺

Mount Sōng: 嵩山

Mount Tiāntái: 天台山

Móuzi: 牟子

mòzhào: 默照

Musang: 無相 (Chinese: Wúxiāng; = Rev. Kim 金和尚 [Chinese: Jīn héshàng])

Nánquán Pǔyuàn: 南泉普願

Nányáng Huìzhōng: 南陽慧忠

Nányuè Huáiràng: 南岳懷讓

Néngrénsì: see Śākyamuni Temple

Nirvāṇa Sūtra: 涅槃經

nonthought: *wúniàn* 無念

Northern Zhōu: 北周

Platform Sermon (Platform Sermon by the Reverend of Nanyang on Directly Comprehending the Nature According to the Chan Doctrine of the Sudden Teaching and Emancipation): Nányáng héshàng dùnjiào jiětuō chánmén zhī liǎoxìng tányǔ 南陽和尚頓教解説禪門直了性壇語

Platform Sūtra of the Sixth Patriarch: Liùzǔ tán jīng 六祖壇經

Pǔjì: 普寂

Qīngliǎo: see Zhēnxiē Qīngliǎo

Qīngyuan Xíngsī 青原行思

Qízhōu: see Huángméi

Record of the Men and Teachings of the Laṅkāvatāra: Léngqié rénfǎ zhì 楞伽人法誌

Record of the Teachers and Disciples of the Laṅkāvatāra: Léngqié shīzī jì 楞伽師資記

Record of the Transmission of the Lamp (Compiled during the) Jingde (Period): Jǐngdé chuándēng lù 景德傳燈錄

Reverend Jīn (Korean: Kim): see Musang

Reverend Táng: see Chùjì

rìlún: 日輪

Rinzai: see Línjǐ

Rúhǎi: 如海

Saichō: 最澄

Śākyamuni Temple: 能仁寺

Sēngcàn: 僧璨

Sēngchóu: 僧稠

Sēngzhào: 僧肇

Shāndōng: 山東

shānjiā: 山家

shānwài: 山外

Shaolin Temple: Shàolínsì 少林寺

Sháozhōu: 韶州

Shénhuì: 神會

Shènxiù: 神秀

shífāng cōnglín: 十方叢林

Shítou Xīqiān: 石頭希遷

shǒuxīn: 守心

Shuāngfēng: 雙峰

Sìchuān: 四川

Sōtō school (Japan): see Cáodòng

Śubhākarasiṃha: Shànwúwèi 善無畏

Sūtra of the Contemplation of the Buddha Amitāyus: Guān Wúliàngshòu Fó jīng
    觀無量壽佛經

Suzuki, D[aisetsu] T[eitarō]: 鈴木拙貞太郎

Suzuki Tetsuo: 鈴木哲雄

Tāng Yòngtóng: 湯用彤

Tánlín: 曇林

Tendon-Changing Scripture: Yìjīn jīng 易筋經

tǐ: "essence, body"

Tiānníngsì: 天寧寺

Tiāntái [Tendai] school: 天台宗

Tiāntái Zhìyǐ: 天台智顗

*Transmissions of Eminent Monks (Compiled During the) Song (Dynasty): Sòng
    gāosēng zhuàn* 宋高僧傳

Transmissions of Treasure Grove (Temple): Bǎolín zhuàn 寶林傳

Treatise on the Contemplation of Mind: Guānxīn lùn 觀心論

Treatise on the Essentials of Cultivating the Mind: Xiūxīn yāo lùn 修心要論

Treatise on the Immutability of Things: Wù bù qiān lùn 物不遷論

Treatise on the Sūtra on the Ten Stages: Shídì jīng lùn 十地經論

Treatise on the Transcendence of Cognition: Juéguān lùn 絕觀論

Treatise on the Two Entrances and Four Practices: Èrrù sìxíng lùn 二人四行論

two entrances: *èrrù* 二人

Ui Hakuju: 宇井伯汴

wall contemplation: *bìguān* 壁觀

wéiqí: 圍棋

Wúxiāng: see Musang

Wǔ Zétiān: see Empress Wǔ

Wǔzǔ Fǎyǎn: 五祖法演

xiānchéng gōng'àn: 現成公案 (Japanese: genjō kōan)

Xiángmó Zàng: 降魔藏

xīnfǎ: 心法

xíng: 行

Xuánlǎng: 玄朗

Xuánsù: 玄素

Xuánzàng: 玄奘

Xuědòu Zhòngxiǎn: 雪竇重顯

Xuěfēng Yìcún: 雪峰義存

xūn: 薰

YAMADA Shōji: 小田奬治

YANAGIDA Seizan: 柳田聖山

Yìfú: 義福

yìnkě: 印可

Yīxíng: 一行

yòng: 用, "function"

Yǒngjiā Xuánjué: 永嘉玄覺

Yuánqīng: 源清

Yuánwù Kèqín: 圜悟克勤

Yúnmén Wényǎn: 雲門文偃

Yúnnán: 雲南

Yùquánsì: see Jade Spring Temple

Zhāng Jiǔchéng: 張九成

Zhāng Shāngyīng: 張商英

Zhànrán: 湛然

Zhào lùn: 肇論

Zhēnxiē Qīngliǎo: 真歇青了

zhǐ: 止, *śamatha,* "concentration"

zhǐguān: 止觀, *śamatha-vipaśyanā,* "concentration-insight"

Zhīlǐ: 知禮

zhǐshì wènyì: 指事問義

Zhuāngzi: 莊子

zōng: 宗

Zōngmì: 宗密

zǔshī: 祖祎, "patriarch"

Bibliography

PRIMARY SOURCES

Emerald Cliff Record (Fóguǒ Yuán wù Bìyán lù 佛果圜悟禪師碧巖錄): T 2003, 48.139a1–225c14.

Five Skillful Means (Wǔ fāngbiàn 五方便): McRae, *Northern School,* 171–96 (English; for textual information, see 327–30, n. 161). One ms. is printed at T 2834, 85.1273b9–78a7.

Great Calming and Contemplation (Móhē zhǐguān 摩訶止觀): T 1911, 46.1a1–140c19.

Light-Emitting Sūtra (Fàngguāng bōre jing 放光般若經): T 221, 8.1a1–146c29.

Perfection of Wisdom in Eight Thousand Lines (Xiǎopin bōrě bōluómì jīng 小品般若波羅蜜經): T 227, 8.536c15–586c7.

Record of the Transmission of the Lamp [Compiled in] the Jingde [Period] (Jǐngdé chuándēng lù 景德傳燈錄): T 2076, 51.196b9–467a28.

Taishō shinshū daizōkyō 大正新修大藏經. Takakusu Junjirō 高楠順次郎 and Watanabe Kaikyoku 渡辺海旭, eds. Tōkyō: Nihon Tōkyō Daizōkyō Kankōkai, 1924–32.

Tendon-Changing Scripture (Yìjīn jīng 易筋經): *Yìjīn jīng* editorial group 易筋經編寫小組. *Yìjīn jīng* 易筋經, 2d ed. Beijing: Renmin tiyu chubanshe 人民体育出版社, 1977.

Treatise on the Essentials of Cultivating the Mind (Xiūxīn yāo lùn 修心要論): McRae, *Northern School,* 121–32 (English) and 1–16 (from the back; Chinese).

Treatise on the Immutability of Things (Wù bù qiān lùn 物不遷論): T 1858, 45.151a8–c29.

Treatise on the Two Entrances and Four Practices (Èrrù sìxíng lùn 二入四行論): Yanagida, *Daruma no goroku.*

Xù zàng jīng 續藏經. Taibei: Xinwenfeng chubanshe 新文豐出版社, n.d. Originally published as: *Dai Nihon zoku Zōkyō: Dai isshu, Indo, Shina senjutsut* 大日本續藏經.第壹輯,印度.支那選述. Maeda Eun 前田慧雲, ed. Kyōto: Zōkyō shoin 藏經書院, 1905–1912.

SECONDARY SOURCES

Abé, Ryuichi. *The Weaving of Mantra: Kūkai and the Construction of Esoteric Buddhist Discourse.* New York: Columbia University Press, 1999.

App, Urs. *Master Yunmen: From the Record of the Chan Teacher "Gate of the Clouds."* New York, Tōkyō, and London: Kodansha International, 1994.

Austin, James H., M.D. *Zen and the Brain: Toward an Understanding of Meditation and Consciousness.* Cambridge, MA, and London: MIT Press, 1998.

Basham, A. L. *The Wonder That Was India: A Survey of the Culture of the Indian Sub-Continent before the Coming of the Muslims.* London: Sidgwick and Jackson, 1954.

Baxandall, Michael. *Patterns of Intention: On the Historical Explanation of Pictures.* New Haven, CT, and London: Yale University Press, 1985.

Benn, James A. "Where Text Meets Flesh: Burning the Body as an Apocryphal Practice in Chinese Buddhism." *History of Religions* 37, no. 4 (May 1998): 295–322.

Bokenkamp, Stephen R. "Medieval Feminist Critique of the Chinese World Order: The Case of Wu Zhao." *Religions* 28 (1998): 383–92.

Borrell, Ari. "*Ko-wu* or *Kung-an*? Practice, Realization, and Teaching in the Thought of Chang Chiu-ch'eng." In Gregory and Getz, *Buddhism in the Sung,* 62–108.

Broughton, Jeffrey L. *The Bodhidharma Anthology: The Earliest Records of Zen.* Berkeley and Los Angeles: University of California Press, 1999.

Buswell, Robert E., Jr. *The Korean Approach to Zen: The Collected Works of Chinul.* Honolulu: University of Hawai'i Press, 1983.

———. "The 'Short-cut' Approach of *K'an-hua* Meditation: The Evolution of a Practical Subitism in Chinese Ch'an Buddhism." In Gregory, *Sudden and Gradual,* 321–77.

Campany, Robert F. *To Live as Long as Heaven and Earth: A Translation and Study of Ge Hong's* Traditions of Divine Transcendents. Berkeley and Los Angeles: University of California Press, 2001.

CBETA. Electronic texts of the *Taishō* canon, published by the Chinese Buddhist Electronic Texts Association. (www.cbeta.org).

Chan, Chi-wah. "Chih-li (960–1028) and the Crisis of T'ien-t'ai Buddhism in the Early Sung." In Gregory and Getz, *Buddhism in the Sung,* 409–41.

Chappell, David W. "The Teachings of the Fourth Ch'an Patriarch Tao-hsin (580–651)." In Whalen Lai and Lewis R. Lancaster, eds., *Early Ch'an in China and Tibet.* Berkeley: Asian Humanities Press, 1983, 89–129.

Ch'en, Kenneth K. S. *Buddhism in China: A Historical Survey.* Princeton, NJ: Princeton University Press, 1964.

———. *The Chinese Transformation of Buddhism.* Princeton, NJ: Princeton University Press, 1973.

Cohen, David William. *The Combing of History.* Chicago and London: University of Chicago Press, 1994.

Davis, Edward L. *Society and the Supernatural in Song China.* Honolulu: University of Hawai'i Press, 2001.

de Bary, Wm. Theodore. *East Asian Civilizations: A Dialogue in Five Stages.* Cambridge, MA: Harvard University Press, 1988.

DeCaroli, Robert. *Haunting the Buddha: Popular Religion and the Formation of Indian Buddhism.* New York: Oxford University Press, forthcoming (2004).

DeFrancis, John, ed. *ABC Chinese Dictionary.* Hong Kong: Chinese University of Hong Kong; Honolulu: University of Hawai'i Press, 1996.

Deikman, Arthur J. Review of James H. Austin, M.D., *Zen and the Brain.* In *Times Literary Supplement,* August 6, 1999, 30.

Derrida, Jacques. *Of Grammatology.* Trans. Gayatri C. Spivak. Baltimore, MD: Johns Hopkins University Press, 1974.

Douglas, Mary. *Natural Symbols: Explorations in Cosmology.* New York: Vintage Books, 1973.

Dumoulin, Heinrich, S. J. *Zen Buddhism: A History.* 2 vols. Trans. James W. Heisig and Paul Knitter. New York: Macmillan, 1988–89; rev. ed., vol. 1, 1994.

Durt, Hubert. "Du lambeau de chair au démembrement: Le renoncement au corps dans le bouddhisme ancien." *Bulletin de l'École Française d'Extrême-Orient* 87 (2000): 7–22.

Ebrey, Patricia. *Confucianism and Family Rituals in Imperial China.* Princeton, NJ: Princeton University Press, 1991.

———. "The Early Stages in the Development of Descent Group Organization." In Patricia Buckley Ebrey and James L. Watson, eds., *Kinship Organization in Late Imperial China, 1000–1940.* Berkeley and Los Angeles: University of California Press, 1986, 16–61.

Eckel, Malcolm David. *To See the Buddha: A Philosopher's Quest for the Meaning of Emptiness.* Princeton, NJ: Princeton University Press, 1992.

Faure, Bernard. "Bodhidharma as Textual and Religious Paradigm." *History of Religions* 25, no. 3 (1986): 187–98.

———. "The Daruma-shū, Dōgen, and Sōtō Zen." *Monumenta Nipponica* 42, no. 1 (spring 1987): 25–55.

———. *The Rhetoric of Immediacy: A Cultural Critique of Chan/Zen Buddhism.* Princeton, NJ: Princeton University Press, 1991.

———. *The Will to Orthodoxy: A Critical Genealogy of Northern Chan Buddhism.* Stanford, CA: Stanford University Press, 1997.

Fischer, David Hackett. *Historians' Fallacies: Toward a Logic of Historical Thought.* New York: Harper & Row, 1970.

FitzGerald, C. P. *The Southern Expansion of the Chinese People.* New York: Praeger, 1972.

Forte, Antonino. *Mingtang and Buddhist Utopias in the History of the Astronomical Clock: The Tower, Statue, and Armillary Sphere Constructed by Empress Wu.* Roma: Istituto italiano per il Medio ed Estremo Oriente; Paris: Ecole française d'Extrême-Orient, 1988.

———. *Political Propaganda and Ideology in China at the End of the Seventh Century: Inquiry into the Nature, Authors and Function of the Tunhuang Document S. 6502, Followed by an Annotated Translation.* Napoli: Istituto universitario orientale, Seminario di studi asiatici, 1976.

Foulk, T. Griffith. "The Ch'an School and Its Place in the Buddhist Monastic Tradition." Ph.D. diss. University of Michigan, 1987.

——. "Myth, Ritual, and Monastic Practice in Sung Ch'an Buddhism." In Patricia Buckley Ebrey and Peter N. Gregory, eds., *Religion and Society in T'ang and Sung China.* Honolulu: University of Hawai'i Press, 1993, 147–208.

Gernet, Jacques. *Chinese Society: An Economic History from the Fifth to the Tenth Centuries.* Trans. Franciscus Verellen. New York: Columbia University Press, 1995.

Getz, Daniel A., Jr. "T'ien-t'ai Pure Land Societies and the Creation of the Pure Land Patriarchate." In Gregory and Getz, *Buddhism in the Sung,* 477–523.

Gimello, Robert M. "Mysticism and Meditation." In Steven T. Katz, ed., *Mysticism and Philosophical Analysis.* London: Oxford University Press, 1978, 170–99.

Goffman, Erving. *The Presentation of Self in Everyday Life.* Garden City, NY: Doubleday, 1959.

Gómez, Luis O. "Purifying Gold: The Metaphor of Effort and Intuition in Buddhist Thought and Practice." In Gregory, ed., *Sudden and Gradual,* 67–165.

Graham, A. C. *Chuang-tzu: The Inner Chapters.* London: Unwin Paperbacks, 1986.

——. *Disputers of Tao: Philosophical Argument in Ancient China.* La Salle, IL: Open Court, 1989.

Gregory, Peter N., ed. *Sudden and Gradual: Approaches to Enlightenment in Chinese Thought.* Kuroda Institute, Studies in East Asian Buddhism, no. 5. Honolulu: University of Hawai'i Press, 1987.

——. *Tsung-mi and the Sinification of Buddhism.* Princeton, NJ: Princeton University Press, 1991.

Gregory, Peter N., and Daniel A. Getz, Jr., eds. *Buddhism in the Sung.* Honolulu: University of Hawai'i Press, 1999.

Groner, Paul. "Shortening the Path: Early Tendai Interpretations of the Realization of Buddhahood with This Very Body *(Sokushin Jōbutsu).*" In Robert E. Buswell Jr. and Robert M. Gimello, eds., *Paths to Liberation: The Marga and Its Transformations in Buddhist Thought.* Honolulu: University of Hawai'i Press, 1992, 439–73.

Hakeda, Yoshito S. *Kūkai: Major Works Translated, with an Account of His Life and a Study of His Thought.* New York: Columbia University Press, 1972.

Harvey, Peter. *An Introduction to Buddhism: Teachings, History, and Practices.* Cambridge, U.K.: Cambridge University Press, 1990.

——. *The Selfless Mind: Personality, Consciousness and Nirvāṇa in Early Buddhism.* Surrey, U.K.: Curzon Press, 1995.

Herrigel, Eugen. *Zen and the Art of Archery.* Trans. Richard F. C. Hull, with an introduction by D. T. Suzuki. New York: Pantheon Books, 1953.

Hershock, Peter D. *Liberating Intimacy: Enlightenment and Social Virtuosity in Ch'an Buddhism.* Albany: State University of New York Press, 1996.

——. Rejoinder to McRae, review of *Liberating Intimacy. Journal of Asian Studies* 57, no. 1 (February 1998): 161–67.

Hobsbawm, Eric, and Terence Ranger, eds. *The Invention of Tradition.* Cambridge and New York: Cambridge University Press, 1992.

Hopkirk, Peter. *Foreign Devils on the Silk Road: The Search for the Lost Cities and Treasures of Chinese Central Asia*. Amherst: University of Massachusetts Press, 1980.

Hsieh, Ding-hwa Evelyn. "A Study of the Evolution of K'an-hua Ch'an in Sung China: Yüan-wu K'o-ch'in (1063–1135) and the Function of Kung-an in Ch'an Pedagogy and Praxis." Ph.D. diss. University of California, Los Angeles, 1993.

——. "Yüan-wu K'o-ch'in's (1063–1135) Teaching of Ch'an Kung-an Practice: A Transition from Literary Study of Ch'an Kung-an and the Practical K'an-hua Ch'an." *Journal of the International Association of Buddhist Studies* 17, no. 1 (1994): 66–95.

HUANG Qijiang 黃啓江 [Huang Chi-chiang]. "Bei-Song di yijing runwenguan yu Fojiao" 北宋的譯經潤文官與佛教. In *Bei-Song Fojiaoshi lun'gao* 北宋佛教史論稿. Taipei: Taiwan shangwu yinshuguan 臺灣商務印書館, 1997, 68–92.

IRIYA Yoshitaka 入矢義高, supervising editor, and KOGA Hidehiko 古賀英彦, compiler. *Zengo jiten* 禪語辭典 (Dictionary of Chan terms). Kyōto: Shibunkaku shuppan 思文閣出版, 1991.

ISHII Shūdō 石井修道. *Sōdai zenshūshi no kenkyū* 宋代禪宗史の研究 (Studies in the history of Song-dynasty Chan). Tōkyō: Daitō shuppansha 大東出版者, 1987.

ITŌ Yūten 伊藤猷典. *Hekiganshū teihon* 碧巖集定本 (Authoritative text of the *Emerald Cliff Record*). Tōkyō: Risōsha 理想社, 1963.

Jay, Nancy B. *Throughout Your Generations Forever: Sacrifice, Religion, and Paternity*. Chicago: University of Chicago Press, 1992.

Jorgensen, John. "The 'Imperial' Lineage of Ch'an Buddhism: The Role of Confucian Ritual and Ancestor Worship in Ch'an's Search for Legitimation in the Mid-T'ang Dynasty." *Papers on Far Eastern History* 35 (March 1987): 89–133.

Junker, Andrew. "Clergy, Clan, and Country: Tang Dynasty Monastic Obeisance and Sacrificial Religion." M.A. thesis. Department of Religious Studies, Indiana University, 2000.

Keenan, John P. *How Master Mou Removes Our Doubts: A Reader-Response Study and Translation of the* Mou-tzu Li-huo lun. Albany: State University of New York Press, 1994.

Kieschnick, John. *The Eminent Monk: Buddhist Ideals in Medieval Chinese Hagiography*. Kuroda Institute, Studies in East Asian Buddhism, no. 10. Honolulu: University of Hawai'i Press, 1997.

KUBO Tsugunari and YUYAMA Akira, trans. *The Lotus Sutra, BDK English Tripiṭaka* 13–I. Berkeley, CA: Numata Center for Buddhist Translation and Research, 1993.

KUSUMOTO Masatsugu 楠本正繼. "Sō-Min ryō shisō no kattō" 宋—明兩思想の葛藤 (The dilemma of Song and Ming thought). In *Kusumoto Masatsugu sensei chūkoku tetsugaku kenkyū* 楠本正繼先生中国哲学研究. Tōkyō: Kokushikan Daigaku fuzoku toshokan 国士舘大学付属図書館, 1975, 167–92.

Lancaster, Lewis R., with Sung-bae Park. *The Korean Buddhist Canon: A Descriptive Catalogue*. Berkeley and Los Angeles: University of California Press, 1979.

Leighton, Taigen Dan, with Yi Wu, trans., *Cultivating the Empty Field: The Silent Illumination of Zen Master Hongzhi*. Boston, MA: Tuttle, 2000.

Levering, Miriam Lindsey. "Ch'an Enlightenment for Laymen: Ta-hui and the New Religious Culture of the Sung." Ph.D. diss. Harvard University, 1978.

———. "Miao-tao and Her Teacher Ta-hui." In Gregory and Getz, eds., *Buddhism in the Sung*, 188–219.

Lévi-Strauss, Claude. *The Raw and the Cooked*. New York: Harper & Row, 1969.

Lincoln, Bruce. *Theorizing Myth: Narrative, Ideology, and Scholarship*. Chicago: University of Chicago Press, 1999.

Lincoln, Roger J.; Geoff Boxshall; and Paul Clark. *A Dictionary of Ecology, Evolution, and Systematics*. Cambridge and New York: Cambridge University Press, 1998.

Mather, Richard B., trans. *A New Account of Tales of the World*. By Liu I-ch'ing, with commentary by Liu Chün. Minneapolis: University of Minnesota Press, 1976.

McLuhan, Marshall. *Understanding Media: The Extensions of Man*. New York: McGraw-Hill, 1964.

McRae, John R. [John Robert McRae]. "The Antecedents of Encounter Dialogue in Chinese Ch'an Buddhism." In Steven Heine and Dale S. Wright, eds., *The Kōan: Texts and Contexts in Zen Buddhism*. New York: Oxford University Press, 2000, 46–74.

———. "Encounter Dialogue and the Transformation of the Spiritual Path in Chinese Ch'an." In Robert E. Buswell Jr. and Robert M. Gimello, eds., *Paths to Liberation: The Marga and Its Transformations in Buddhist Thought*. Honolulu: University of Hawai'i Press, 1992, 339–69.

———. "The Legend of Hui-neng and the Mandate of Heaven." In *Fo Kuang Shan Report of International Conference on Ch'an Buddhism*. Kaohsiung, Taiwan: Fo Kuang Publisher, 1990, 69–82.

———. *The Northern School and the Formation of Early Ch'an Buddhism*. Kuroda Institute, Studies in East Asian Buddhism, no. 3. Honolulu: University of Hawai'i Press, 1986.

———. "The Northern School of Chinese Ch'an Buddhism." Ph.D. diss. Yale University, 1983.

———. "The Ox-head School of Chinese Buddhism: From Early Ch'an to the Golden Age." In Robert M. Gimello and Peter N. Gregory, eds., *Studies in Ch'an and Hua-yen*. Kuroda Institute, Studies in East Asian Buddhism, no. 1. Honolulu: University of Hawai'i Press, 1983, 169–253.

———. "Religion as Revolution in Chinese Historiography: Hu Shih (1891–1962) on Shen-hui (684–758)." *Cahiers d'Extrême-Asie*, 12 (2001): 59–102.

———. Review of Broughton, *The Bodhidharma Anthology*. In *Journal of Chinese Religions* 28 (2000): 193–99.

———. Review of Hershock, *Liberating Intimacy*. In *Journal of Asian Studies* 56, no. 2 (May 1997): 474–76; surrejoinder in *Journal of Asian Studies* 57, no. 1 (February 1998): 167–68.

———. Review of Orzech, *Politics and Transcendent Wisdom*. In *Journal of Chinese Religions* 27 (1999): 113–21.

———. "Shenhui and the Teaching of Sudden Enlightenment in Early Chan Buddhism." In Gregory, *Sudden and Gradual*, 227–78.

——. "Shenhui's Vocation on the Ordination Platform and Our Visualization of Medieval Chinese Ch'an Buddhism." *Annual Report of the Institute for Zen Studies, Hanazono University* 24 (December 1998): 43–66.

——. "Shenshi chuancheng—chenshu Chanzong di ling yizhong fangshi" 審視傳承一陳述禪宗的另一種方式 (Looking at lineage: A different method of describing the Chan school). Trans. KUAN Tse-fu [Guan Zefu] 關則富. *Chung-Hwa Buddhist Journal* 13 (2000): 281–98.

——. "The Story of Early Ch'an." In Kenneth Kraft, ed., *Zen: Tradition and Transition.* New York: Grove Press, 1988, 125–39.

——. "Up Front, Out Back, and in the Field: Three Models of Buddhist Endeavor in East Asia." Oral presentation, Association for Asian Studies, November 1988. Unpublished.

——. "Yanagida Seizan's Landmark Works on Chinese Ch'an." *Cahiers d'Extême-Asie* 7 (1993–1994): 51–103.

——. *Zen Evangelist: Shenhui (684–758), Sudden Enlightenment, and the Southern School of Chinese Chan Buddhism.* Honolulu: University of Hawai'i Press, forthcoming (2004).

McRae, John R., trans. "The Development of the 'Recorded Sayings' Texts of the Chinese Ch'an School." See under YANAGIDA Seizan.

Meskill, Johanna M. "The Chinese Genealogy as a Research Source." In Maurice Freeman, ed., *Family and Kinship in Chinese Society.* Stanford, CA: Stanford University Press, 1970, esp. 143–47.

MIZUNO Kōgen 水野弘元. "Zenshū seiritsu izen no Shina no zenjō shisōshi josetsu" 禅宗成立以前のシナの禅定思想史序説 (Introductory explanation of meditation theory in China prior to the formation of the Chan school). *Komazawa Daigaku Bukkyō Gakubu kenkyū kiyō* 駒沢大学仏教学部研究紀要 15 (March 1957): 15–54.

NAKAMURA Hajime 中村元. *Bukkyōgo daijiten* 仏教語大辞典 (Encyclopedia of Buddhist terms). Tōkyō: Tōkyō shoseki 東京書籍, 1981.

Nattier, Jan. *A Few Good Men: The Bodhisattva Path according to* The Inquiry of Ugra *(Ugrapariprcchā).* Honolulu: University of Hawai'i Press, 2003.

——. *Once Upon a Future Time: Studies in a Buddhist Prophecy of Decline.* Nanzan Studies in Asian Religions, no. 1. Berkeley: Asian Humanities Press, 1991.

OGAWA Tamaki 小川環樹 et al. *Kadokawa shinjigen, kaitei ban* 角川新字源、改定版 (Kadokawa new word source). Tōkyō: Kadokawa shoten 角川書店, 1994.

Ong, Walter J. *Orality and Literacy: The Technologizing of the Word.* New York: Methuen, 1982.

ONO Genmyō 小野玄妙. *Bussho kaisetsu daijiten* 佛書解説大辞典 (Encyclopedia of Buddhist texts). Tōkyō: Daitō shuppansha 大東出版者, 1932–36.

Ortner, Sherry B. *High Religion: A Cultural and Political History of Sherpa Buddhism.* Princeton, NJ: Princeton University Press, 1989.

——. "On Key Symbols." *American Anthropologist* 75 (1973): 1338–46.

——. "Patterns of History: Cultural Schemas in the Foundings of Sherpa Religious Institutions." In Emiko Ohnuki-Tierney, ed., *Culture Through Time: Anthropological Approaches.* Stanford, CA: Stanford University Press, 1990, 57–93.

Orzech, Charles D. *Politics and Transcendent Wisdom: The Scripture for Humane*

Kings in the Creation of Chinese Buddhism. University Park: Pennsylvania State University Press, 1998.

OZAKI Yūjirō 尾崎雄二郎 et al. *Kadokawa daijigen* 角川大字源 (Kadokawa large word source). Tōkyō: Kadokawa shoten 角川書店, 1992.

Poceski, Mario. "The Hongzhou School of Chan Buddhism during the Mid-Tang Period." Ph.D. diss. University of California, Los Angeles, 2000.

Pulleyblank, Edwin G. *Lexicon of Reconstructed Pronunciation in Early Middle Chinese, Late Middle Chinese, and Early Mandarin*. Vancouver, B.C.: UBC Press, 1991.

Robinet, Isabelle. *Taoist Meditation: The Mao-Shan Tradition of Great Purity*. Trans. Julian F. Pas and Norman J. Girardot. Albany: State University of New York Press, 1993.

Roth, Harold D. *Original Tao: Inward Training and the Foundations of Taoist Mysticism*. New York: Columbia University Press, 1999.

Sasaki, Ruth Fuller, trans. *The Recorded Sayings of Ch'an Master Lin-chi Hui-chao of Chen Prefecture*. Kyōto: The Institute for Zen Studies, 1975.

Schaberg, David. *A Patterned Past: Form and Thought in Early Chinese Historiography*. Cambridge, MA, and London: Harvard University Asia Center and Harvard University Press, 2001.

Schlütter, Morten. "Silent Illumination, Kung-an Introspection, and the Competition for Lay Patronage in Sung Dynasty Ch'an." In Gregory and Getz, *Buddhism in the Sung*, 109–47.

———. "Vinaya Monasteries, Public Abbacies, and State Control of Buddhism under the Sung Dynasty (960–1279)." In William Bodiford and Paul Groner, eds., *Going Forth: Vinaya and Monastic Power in East Asian Buddhism*. Honolulu: University of Hawai'i Press, forthcoming.

Schopen, Gregory. "Filial Piety and the Monk in the Practice of Indian Buddhism: A Question of 'Sinicization' Viewed from the Other Side." *T'oung Pao* 70 (1984): 110–26.

Sekida, Katsuki. *Two Zen Classics: Mumonkan and Hekiganroku*. Ed. A. V. Grimstone. New York and Tōkyō: Weatherhill, 1977.

SEKIGUCHI Shindai 関口真大. *Daruma no kenkyū* 達磨の研究 (A study of Bodhidharma). Tōkyō: Iwanami shoten 岩波書店, 1967.

Sharf, Robert H. "Buddhist Modernism and the Rhetoric of Meditative Experience." *Numen* 42 (1995): 228–83.

———. *Coming to Terms with Chinese Buddhism: A Reading of the Treasure Store Treatise*. Kuroda Institute, Studies in East Asian Buddhism, 14. Honolulu: University of Hawai'i Press, 2002.

———. "Experience." In Mark C. Taylor, ed., *Critical Terms for Religious Studies*. Chicago and London: University of Chicago Press, 1998, 94–116.

———. "On the Buddha-nature of Insentient Things (or: How to Think about a Ch'an Kung-an)." Unpublished paper, 1998.

———. "The Zen of Japanese Nationalism." In Donald S. Lopez Jr., ed., *Curators of the Buddha: The Study of Buddhism Under Colonialism*. Chicago: University of Chicago Press, 1995, 107–60.

Shastri, Dakshinaranjan. *Origin and Development of the Rituals of Ancestor Worship in India*. Calcutta: Bookland, 1963.

Skjærvø, Prods Oktor. "Khotan, An Early Center of Buddhism in Chinese Turkestan." In John R. McRae and Jan Nattier, eds., *Buddhism Across Boundaries: Chinese Buddhism and the Western Regions. Collection of Essays, 1993*. Taipei: Fo Guang Shan Foundation for Buddhist and Culture Education, 1999, 265–345.

Stein, Rolf A. "Religious Taoism and Popular Religion from the Second to the Seventh Centuries." In Holmes Welch and Anna Seidel, eds., *Facets of Taoism: Essays in Chinese Religion*. New Haven, CT: Yale University Press, 1979, 53–82.

Stone, Jacqueline. *Original Enlightenment and the Transformation of Medieval Japanese Buddhism*. Kuroda Institute, Studies in East Asian Buddhism, no. 12. Honolulu: University of Hawai'i Press, 1999.

Strickmann, Michel. "Saintly Fools and Chinese Masters (Holy Fools)." *Asia Major* 3rd ser., 7, no. 1 (1994): 35–57.

———. "The Tao among the Yao: Taoism and the Sinification of South China." In Sakai Tadao sensei Koki Shukuga Kinen no Kai 酒井忠夫先生古稀祝賀記念の会編, eds. *Rekishi ni okeru minshū to bunka, Sakai Tadao Sensei koki shukuga kinen ronbunshū* 歴史における民衆と文化：酒井忠夫先生古稀祝賀記念論集. Tōkyō: Kokusho kankōkai 国書刊行会, 1982, 23–30.

SUZUKI Tetsuo 鈴木哲雄. *Tō-Godai no Zenshū—Konan Kōsei hen* 唐五代の禅宗—湖南江西篇—(The Chan school in the Tang and Song: Hubei and Jiangxi edition). Tōkyō: Daitō shuppansha 大東出版者, 1984.

———. *Tō-Godai Zenshūshi* 唐五代の禅宗 (History of the Chan school in the Tang and Song). Tōkyō: Sankibō Busshorin 山喜房仏書林, 1985.

Swanson, Paul. *Foundations of T'ien-t'ai Philosophy: The Flowering of the Two Truths Theory in Chinese Buddhism*. Berkeley, CA: Asian Humanities Press, 1989.

———. "Wall-gazing, *Vipaśyanā,* and Mixed Binomes." Unpublished paper presented at the Japan Forum of The Edwin O. Reischauer Institute of Japanese Studies, October 2, 1997.

TANG Yongtong 湯用彤. *Han Wei liang Jin Nanbeichao Fojiao shi* 漢魏兩晉南北朝佛教史 (History of Buddhism in the Han, Wei, the two Jin, and the North-South Dynasties). Changsha 長沙 and Chongqing 重慶: Shangwu yinshuguan 商務印書館, 1928; reprint, Taipei 臺北: Guoshi yanjiushi 國史研究室, 1974.

Tatz, Mark, and Jody Kent. *Rebirth: The Tibetan Game of Liberation*. Garden City, NY: Anchor, 1977.

Turner, Victor. *Dramas, Fields, and Metaphors: Symbolic Action in Human Society*. Ithaca, NY: Cornell University Press, 1975.

Watson, Burton, trans. *The Zen Teachings of Master Lin-chi: A Translation of the Lin-chi lu*. Boston, MA, and London: Shambala, 1993.

Weinstein, Stanley. *Buddhism under the T'ang*. Cambridge: Cambridge University Press, 1987.

Welch, Holmes. *The Practice of Chinese Buddhism, 1900–1950*. Cambridge, MA: Harvard University Press, 1967.

Williams, Paul. *Mahāyāna Buddhism: The Doctrinal Foundations*. London: Routledge, 1989.

Wittern, Christian. *Das Yulu des Chan-Buddhismus: die Entwicklung vom 8.–11. Jahrhundert am Beispiel des 28. Kapitels des* Jingde Chuandenglu *(1004)*. Schweizer asiatische Studien, Monographien, Bd. 31. Bern and New York: P. Lang, 1998.

Wright, Arthur F. *Buddhism in Chinese History*. Stanford, CA: Stanford University Press, 1959; New York: Atheneum, 1965.

Wright, Dale S. *Philosophical Meditations on Zen Buddhism*. Cambridge: Cambridge University Press, 1998.

Wu, Pei-yi. *The Confucian's Progress: Autobiographical Writings in Traditional China*. Princeton, NJ: Princeton University Press, 1990.

Yamabe, Nobuyoshi 山辺能宜. "*The Sūtra on the Ocean-like Samādhi of the Visualization of the Buddha:* The Interfusion of the Chinese and Indian Cultures in Central Asia as Reflected in a Fifth-Century Apocryphal Sūtra." Ph.D. diss. Yale University, 1999.

YAMADA Shōji. "The Myth of Zen in the Art of Archery." *Japanese Journal of Religious Studies* 28, nos. 1–2 (2001): 1–30.

Yampolsky, Philip B. *The Platform Sutra of the Sixth Patriarch: The Text of the Tun-huang Manuscript with Translation, Introduction, and Notes*. New York and London: Columbia University Press, 1967.

YANAGIDA Seizan 柳田聖山. *Daruma no goroku—Ninyū shigyō ron* 達磨の語録—二入四行論. Zen no goroku 禅の語録, no. 1. Tōkyō: Chikuma shobō 筑摩書房 1969.

———. "The Development of the 'Recorded Sayings' Texts of the Chinese Ch'an School" (Zenshū goroku no keisei) 禅宗語録の形成. *Indogaku Bukkyōgaku kenkyū* 印度学仏教学研究 18, no. 1 (December 1969): 39–47. Reprinted in Lewis Lancaster and Whalen Lai, eds., *Early Ch'an in China and Tibet,* trans. John R. McRae. Berkeley Buddhist Studies, no. 5. Berkeley, CA: Lancaster-Miller Press, 1983, 185–205.

———. "Goroku no rekishi" 語録の歴史 (The history of recorded sayings). *Tōhō gakuhō Kyōto* 東方学報京都 57 (March 1985): 211–663.

———. "Hokushūzen no shisō" 北宗禅の思想 (The thought of Northern-school Chan). *Zenbunka Kenkyūjo kiyō* 禅文化研究所紀要 6 (1974): 67–104.

———. "The Life of Lin-chi I-hsüan." *Eastern Buddhist* n.s. 5, no. 2 (October 1972): 70–94.

———. "The *Li-tai fa-pao chi* and the Ch'an Doctrine of Sudden Awakening." In Whalen Lai and Lewis Lancaster, eds., *Early Ch'an in China and Tibet,* trans. Carl Bielefeldt. Berkeley Buddhist Studies Series, no. 5. Berkeley, CA: Asian Humanities Press, 1983, 13–49.

———. *Shoki Zenshū shisho no kenkyū* 初期禅宗史書の研究 (Studies in the historical works of the Early Chan school). Kyōto: Hōzōkan 法蔵館, 1967.

———. *Sodōshū* 祖堂集 (Anthology of the patriarchal hall). Kyōto: Chūbun shuppansha 中文出版者, 1972.

Yifa. *The Origins of Buddhist Monastic Codes in China: An Annotated Translation and Study of the* Chanyuan qinggui. Kuroda Institute, Classics in East Asian Buddhism. Honolulu: University of Hawai'i Press, 2002.

ZHOU Jiannan 周劍南. "Wushu-zhong Shaolin-pai zhi yanjiu" 武術中少林派之 研究 (A study of the Shaolin school of the martial arts). *Zhongguo wushu shi-liao jikan* 中國武術史料集刊 4 (1979): 125–57.

———. "Xingyi quan zhi yanjiu" 刑意拳之研究 (A study of Xingyi boxing). *Zhong-guo wushu shiliao jikan* 中國武術史料集刊 2 (1975): 88–107.

Ziporyn, Brook. *Evil and/or/as The Good: Omnicentrism, Intersubjectivity, and Value Paradox in Tiantai Buddhist Thought*. Cambridge, MA, and London: Harvard University Asia Center and Harvard University Press, 2000.

———. "What Is the Buddha Looking At? The Importance of Intersubjectivity in the T'ien-t'ai Tradition as Understood by Chih-li." In Gregory and Getz, *Buddhism in the Sung*, 442–76.

Zürcher, E. *The Buddhist Conquest of China: The Spread and Adaptation of Bud-dhism in Early Medieval China*. Leiden: E. J. Brill, 1959.

Index

Linji Yixuan, 3 (fig. 1),13 (fig. 2), 19, 78, 100, 115, 120, 129
liubo (Chinese game), 98
Liu Zongyuan, 57
Lotus Sūtra, 4; dragon king's daughter, 95
Luoyang, 16 (map 1), 22, 23, 26, 28, 34, 37, 46, 47, 54

Mādhyamika, 83
"maintain (awareness of) the mind" *(shou-xin),* 39, 139; in *Treatise on the Essentials of Cultivating the Mind,* 43
mārga ("spiritual path"), 97
Mather, Richard B., 166n16
Mazu Daoyi, 3 (fig. 1), 13 (fig. 2), 19, 78, 80, 81, 82, 83, 108, 110, 115, 120, 127, 133; Buddha-nature doctrine, 79; legendary image, 96; official residence in Hongzhou, 109
McLuhan, Marshall, 130, 166n13; on hot and cold media, 82; "the medium is the message," 2
meditation practice, Caodong school, 135
merit, religious, 22
Meskill, Johanna M., 171n23
"method of the mind" *(xinfa),* in Zhang Jiucheng's thought, 133
metropolitan Chan, 18, 35, 36, 45, 48
Miaodao, 125, 127
middle Chan, 13 (fig. 2), 18, 76, 93, 122; relationship to classical Chan, 19
Min (Southern Tang; Fujian Province), 20 (map 2), 112
mind, in Caodong Chan and Neo-Confucianism, 139
"mind-ground, purify the" (in *Five Skillful Means*), 52
"mind-verses" *(xinjie):* attributed to Huineng, 64; basis for both in Northern school writings, 67; echo in dialogue between Mazu and Huairang, 81; interpretation of, 63–65; in *Platform Sūtra,* 60, 61; as unknown to Shenhui, 63
mirror, as metaphor, 61, 62, 64; in *Platform Sūtra,* 65
Mizuno Kōgen, 172n6
mofa ("end period of the Dharma"), 112
monastic institution, Chan administrative predominance, 102–3, 117–18; legendary ascription to Baizhang, 104; operation in twentieth century, 115,

117; Song-dynasty operation, 115–17; "transmission of the lamp" texts and management of power/patronage, 114
"motionlessness," in *Five Skillful Means,* 89
Mount Aśoka Temple, 126
Mount Lu, 16 (map 1)
Mount Song,16 (map 1), 22, 37, 46, 54
Mount Tai (Eastern Peak), 16 (map 1), 54
Mount Tiantai, 16 (map 1), 117, 143
Mount Zhongnan, 16 (map 1)
Mouzi, 95
Musang (Wuxiang, Reverend Jin or Kim), 83

Nakamura Hajime, 163n14
"Nanquan Cuts the Cat in Two" (*Emerald Cliff Record* case), 128–30
Nanquan Puyuan, 19, 78, 108, 128–31
Nanyang Huizhong, 82
Nanyue Huairang, 3 (fig. 1), 80–83; biography, 82
Nattier, Jan, 112, 166n9, 167n31, 170n19, 172n10
Nengrensi (Śākyamuni Temple, Jingshan), 125, 126
Neo-Confucianism, xx, 106, 107, 132, 133, 138–41; Cheng-Zhu faction, 133; parallel with Caodong Chan, 139
Nirvāṇa Sūtra: account of Snowy Mountain Youth, 159n8; quoted by Shenhui, 55; quoted in early Chan "questions about things," 86
"no mind" *(wuxin),* in *Treatise on the Transcendence of Cognition,* 58
"non-activation of the mind," in *Five Skillful Means,* 89, 90
"nonthought" *(wunian),* in critique of Northern school meditation practice, 70; in *Treatise on the Transcendence of Cognition,* 58
Northern school, 3 (fig. 1), 12, 13 (fig. 2), 14, 18, 40, 48, 52, 54–58, 62, 66–68, 70, 82, 83, 85, 87–89, 91–93, 99, 107; as label created by Shenhui, 18, 48, 54–55, 57
Northern Zhou, 28
North/South Dynasties period, 103, 106
"not a single thing": in *Five Skillful Means,* 52, 53, 90; in Northern school style Dunhuang manuscript, 67; in Northern school writings, 67; in *Platform Sūtra* "mind-verse," 62

Compositor:	Integrated Composition Systems
Text:	10/13 Galliard
Display:	Galliard
Printer and binder:	Maple-Vail Manufacturing Group